Showers Brothers Furniture Company

QUARRY BOOKS

an imprint of INDIANA UNIVERSITY PRESS *Bloomington & Indianapolis*

SHOWERS
·BROTHERS·
FURNITURE COMPANY

THE SHARED FORTUNES OF
A FAMILY, A CITY, AND
A UNIVERSITY

CARROL KRAUSE

This book is a publication of

QUARRY BOOKS

an imprint of

Indiana University Press
601 North Morton Street
Bloomington, Indiana 47404-3797 USA

iupress.indiana.edu

Telephone orders   800-842-6796
Fax orders   812-855-7931

Manufactured in the United States of America

Library of Congress Cataloging-in-Publication Data

Krause, Carrol.
  Showers Brothers Furniture company : the shared
fortunes of a family, a city, and a university/ Carrol
Krause.
    p. cm. — (Quarry books)
  Includes bibliographical references and index.
  ISBN 978-0-253-00203-7 (pbk. : alk. paper) —
ISBN 978-0-253-00224-2 (e-book) 1. Showers
Brothers Furniture Factory (Bloomington,
Ind.)—History. 2. Furniture industry and trade—
Indiana—Bloomington—History. I. Title.
  HD9773.U5K73 2012
  338.7'645409772255—dc23

                                        2011045346

1 2 3 4 5 17 16 15 14 13 12

I lovingly dedicate this book to my husband, Frank,
and my son, Miles, whose patience, support,
and good humor are endless.

Contents

Introduction

JIM HOLLAND, a descendant of the Showers family of Bloomington, Indiana, carefully unrolled the old quilt and spread it flat across the tabletop. The quilt had been handed down by four successive generations of the family but had never been used. The Tumbling Block pattern featured more than three hundred multicolored squares only a few inches high, arranged diagonally across a white background. Above each block was the name of a person who had once been a citizen of Bloomington, neatly embroidered in a tiny chain stitch. The men, women, and children of many families were represented on the quilt: it was easy to spot the three Showers brothers and their wives; their in-laws the Smiths, the Hendrixes, the Hewsons, and the Sears; their friends and associates the McPheeters, the Grahams, and the Easts; and hundreds of others. In one corner the year 1884 was embroidered, and in the opposite corner a price: $57.00.

This may seem a meager price to pay for a quilt, but when adjusted for inflation the amount is equivalent to approximately $1,300 in today's monetary values. This was no ordinary bedspread. Over the years the family, to its lasting regret, has forgotten the story that once went with the quilt; but the quilt was obviously made for a fundraiser, each person named on it having purchased a block. It could not have been a church project, since the people on it belonged to different denominations. We turn to the records to discover what event in 1884 in Bloomington would have required a fundraiser. That summer Showers Bros. (as it was then called), the furniture factory owned by the Showers family, suffered a devastating fire. The family turned to its friends in the community for help with relocating and rebuilding its factory. The fact that the Showers family preserved the quilt for so many years suggests it was an important part of its fundraising effort. The Showers women appear to have made this quilt in order to lend their own efforts to the family fundraising. The Tumbling Block pattern is also sometimes called Building Block; this latter name would have been extremely appropriate for a Showers quilt, since the men and women of that family were outstanding for having promoted municipal construction, civic growth, and home ownership by their workers.

Curiously, the names of the Showers parents, C. C. and Elizabeth Showers, were included on the quilt top even though they had both died several years previously. The seven Showers children may have included the names of their deceased parents on the quilt in order to honor their lasting contribution to the family business, but we will never know for sure since all the family members who once knew the story of the quilt are long gone. The quilt epitomizes the problem of trying to tell the Showers story: although we have some of the obvious facts, such as the names on the quilt and the date, far more has been permanently forgotten and can never be recovered. The company records were inadvertently lost and very few family letters or papers were preserved. Myths have grown up while the facts have been obscured by the passage of time. This is partly due to familial modesty, the reluctance on the part of well-mannered people to promote their own accomplishments, but the result is that an enormous amount of vital information has been lost.

The myths about the Showers family that have sprung up over time are persistent because they appeal to our storytelling natures. The primary myth is a classic American rags-to-riches success fable: *There once was a wandering preacher who practiced woodworking on the side in order to feed his wife and seven children. His sons learned cabinetmaking in their father's modest two-room shop, and afterward founded what became the nation's largest furniture factory.* Another myth thrills us with a ghoulish claim: *The Showers company started by selling coffins during the Civil War.* Both of these myths contain kernels of truth that have been stretched out of proportion, as this book will show. There's no place in these legends for the fact that much of the preacher's furniture was made elsewhere by other manufacturers; or the fact that he was a bad businessman who borrowed money he could not repay; or the fact that he wasn't even a minister for the first ten years of his wanderings. No one remembers the once well-known fact that during the late 1800s, all furniture establishments sold coffins and often provided undertaking services.

Another fact that every Bloomington citizen of the late 1800s knew and took for granted was completely forgotten over the years and now re-emerges to surprise us: beginning in 1887 one of the partners at Showers Bros. was a young woman, a suffragist who married three times. It's easy—but very misleading—to think of Victorian-era women as being hobbled by the rigid dictates of society, physically hindered by corsets and ill health, and politically constrained owing to the lack of the vote. But the Showers women of the Victorian era had no interest in staying at home and being mere housewives. They were too busy getting things accomplished by working within their extensive network of women's organizations. Showers women worked tirelessly in philanthropic ventures, improving the city's library and cemetery; educating and lobbying to improve public sanitation, health, and hygiene; and founding Bloomington Hospital.

Leaving myths behind, the real story is how several generations of one extended family gradually built up their furniture enterprise to national prominence while ceaselessly promoting Bloomington's growth and quality of life. These efforts were aided by the resilient and intelligent women of that family. James and William Showers founded a prosperous and growing business while undergoing grievous personal losses that included the gruesome death of their father, the deaths of both their young wives, and the unexpected loss of their vivacious younger brother and partner. The brothers shouldered their burdens, worked long hours alongside their own laborers, and treated their workforce fairly and generously. They welcomed their intelligent and gifted sister-in-law as a member of their firm. The family company manufactured a substantial amount of the furniture sold through the catalog of Sears, Roebuck & Co. during the early twentieth century, and in the 1920s set national records for the production of affordable furniture.

Beginning with the preacher's furniture store and ending with the final sale of the furniture factory by the family's fourth generation, the family business endured for nearly a century. The management staunchly opposed organized labor but strove to make unions unnecessary by offering attractive incentives to employees. For decades, the company helped its workers save their money and purchase and insure their own homes, and provided a variety of entertainments for workers' leisure hours. During the First World War, Showers Brothers was one of the first companies in its community to hire women workers. In an era when many factory owners had no ethical scruples about exploiting their workforce to obtain as much labor as possible from it, the two

Showers brothers knew their workers by name, hired members of extended families, and treated them all with respect, having started out in life as ordinary workmen themselves.

The dark side of this story concerns the company's decline and failure after the brothers relinquished control of the company. Only twenty years after proclaiming itself "the largest furniture factory in the world," the company was repeatedly paralyzed by workers' strikes during the 1930s and '40s that maimed its production. The company had opened three new plants during the 1910s and '20s, two of them in other communities, but this only increased the burden of supervising its own production. The Great Depression arrived precisely when the company was most vulnerable and lacked the ability to innovate or invest in new machinery. The company was forced to sell off its subsidiary factories and by the end was reduced to operating with a fraction of its former workforce, its disheartened and aging employees laboring at decades-old machinery. The company's collapse was abject and complete.

But during their many decades of prosperity, members of the Showers family served as civic leaders who did much to advance the community. Their elegant homes on North Washington and North Walnut Streets impressed the public, as did their actions in modernizing and improving the city of Bloomington. Progressive in their outlook, driven by strong ethics, they strove to reward the city that had helped them to thrive. Showers family members served on the Bloomington city council and on the boards of banks and real estate associations; assisted the formation of the electric and water utilities; helped organize the telephone company; helped start up Bloomington Hospital; were deeply involved with the Bloomington Rotary Club, the Kappa Kappa Kappa philanthropic sorority, and Bloomington's Chamber of Commerce; actively boosted Indiana University's School of Medicine; worked for women's suffrage; improved public hygiene and sanitation; beautified the city; and were prominent in philanthropic and benevolent associations.

Although the Reverend C. C. Showers had seven children, all of whom married and had children of their own, the family was so well-endowed with daughters that the family surname vanished after the lives of his grandchildren. Today many of the fine old Showers mansions have been demolished or broken up into apartments. The rehabilitated former Showers furniture factory now serves as Bloomington's City Hall, and many in the community have no idea what function the building was originally designed for. Showers Plaza

Close-up of the 1884 Showers family quilt, showing the
blocks for C. C. and Elizabeth Showers.

and Showers-Miller Park are just names to most passers-by. No living person today remembers the company in its heyday; the few people who can recall the Showers factory still in operation are elderly and knew it only during its years of sad decline. This book about the Showers family and its accomplishments aims to correct that void in the public consciousness.

A Note on the Sources and Monetary Values

THE BUSINESS RECORDS of the Showers company have unfortunately been lost, and only a handful of the annual furniture catalogs survive, despite decades of publication. We no longer have the training materials that the company distributed to its salesmen, and we have virtually no remaining business correspondence. As for family papers, we possess only the handwritten memoir of James Showers, the spiritual daybook of his mother, Elizabeth, and a small handful of family photographs. There is also no comprehensive Bloomington history that sums up the major events or characters in the company's history. Owing to the lack of records, this work relies largely upon accounts published in newspapers of the period. This record is fragmentary during the early years, and we cannot consider any of it as fully accurate or complete, because of the political partiality of the newspaper publishers. Nevertheless, newspaper records are the single largest remaining source of information available about the Showers family and its company, so this book reflects countless hours spent at the microfilm machines at the public library, perusing the headlines of bygone times. Perhaps this history will be revised by future historians who can sift through even more newspaper records after locating the missing company records; but until that time arrives, this book summarizes what we do know.

Finally, many monetary values are stated in the course of the book: wages paid, the value of the company, the cost of new buildings, and so forth. Equivalent amounts are given in 2010 dollars, according to the most recent inflation calculator available at the time of this writing (2011).

Showers Family Information

CHARLES CHRISTOPHER SHOWERS, referred to during his lifetime as the Rev. C. C., was born on May 22, 1815, and married Elizabeth Hull (birthdate unknown, but probably born around 1817). They had seven children, listed here in order of birth:

Sarah Elizabeth Showers, born on February 27, 1837. Sarah married John Sears in 1855 in Orleans, Indiana, but moved to Monroe County around the same time as her parents did in 1856. She and her husband are buried with her parents in Bloomington's Rose Hill Cemetery. Sears men worked for the Showers company from the 1860s until the 1920s. Sarah and John's children were John, Charles, Lula, James, Mary, and Mattie.

Mary Eleanor ("Ellen") Showers was born on March 31, 1839, and married James Hendrix in 1859. Her husband worked with the Rev. C. C. at the first incarnation of the family furniture workshop in the 1860s. He also worked with his brothers-in-law James and William in the early Showers furniture factory during the 1870s. He had connections in Brazil, Clay County, and one of his and Ellen's two daughters taught school there. Their children were Laura and Nellie.

James David Showers was born on July 11, 1841, and married the sixteen-year-old Loretta (Lauretta) Fish in 1864. She miscarried a few months after their marriage and died the following year. He then married Isabella ("Belle") Allen on January 31, 1866. James and his brother William founded the enterprise that later became the Showers Brothers Company. James's children were Martha Elizabeth ("Mattie"), Charles T., and Maude A. Showers.

Anne Manerva ("Annie") Showers was born in 1845. She married Henry Hewson, who was first a shoemaker and subsequently worked as a traveling salesman for the Showers factory and in other capacities afterward. Their children were Bessie, Lola, and Edna.

William Norton Showers, born on May 28, 1846, married Eliza Jane ("Lida") Hanlon in 1866. She died in childbirth in February 1868, leaving an infant daughter, Jennie. William then married a second time to Hanna Lou Hendrix (the sister of his brother-in-law) in October 1869. The children of this second marriage were Nellie Showers and W. Edward Showers.

Martha ("Lola") Showers, born on March 7, 1852, married John Smith in 1874. John Smith ran a furniture store on the square, where he sold Showers furniture at a discounted price. His nephew Joseph married William's daughter Jennie Showers. Their daughter was Rossenya ("Roxie") E. Smith (or Smythe).

Charles Hull ("Hullie") Showers, born on October 13, 1860, married Ella ("Maud") Coatney on October 15, 1879. The children of Hull and Maud were Erle and Beryl. A third infant, Clide, was born 1886 but died the following year.

Acknowledgments

I WOULD LIKE to thank Randi Richardson, for without her genealogy of the Showers family I would have floundered, unsure where to begin first. Thanks are also due to Nancy Hiestand for her help with photographs and her great patience while reading early versions of the draft. The entire wonderful staff of the Monroe County History Center deserves warm praise and thanks, as does the staff of the Monroe County Public Library's Indiana Room, and particularly Christine Eykholt Friesel. Grateful thanks are due to Brad Cook of the Indiana University Archives; Ellen Sieber of the Mathers Museum; Elizabeth Bridgwaters and William Coulter. I also would like to give warm thanks to Showers family members Nancy Teter Smith, Jim Holland, James and Martha Helm, Boo Kiesler, Judy Brush, and Jim Shaw. Valuable groundwork was done in the 1980s by Showers researcher John Bendix, who painstakingly pulled together many different sources and debunked some of the myths; without his research this project would have been much more difficult. I also want to thank Eryn Brennan, whose thesis describing the physical structure of the Showers factory building was invaluable. Special thanks should go to the editors at Indiana University Press who helped me negotiate the project: Linda Oblack, Nancy Lightfoot, Angela Burton, and Maureen Epp. And a very special thanks to Nancy Hiller for recommending me at the very beginning.

Showers Brothers Furniture Company

Chapter

1

THE REVEREND AND
HIS FAMILY

IN THE LATE 1850S, the community of Bloomington, Indiana, did not appear to be a promising location for a future furniture empire. Located far from other industrialized regions of the United States, Bloomington called itself a city even though it had fewer than 2,700 inhabitants. The town was ten blocks long and five blocks wide, stretching from Jackson Street on the west to Dunn Street on the east, and extending from what is now Eighth Street on the north to Third Street on the south. The unpaved roads turned to deep, sticky mud after heavy rains despite repeated attempts to macadamize the streets. Pedestrians walked on boardwalks of wooden planks raised above the bare surface of the road. The brick courthouse that served as the county seat was surrounded by a square where storefronts were interspersed with small homes left over from the early settler years. The roadbeds had not yet been leveled, so the buggies and wagon teams that drove the length of the city labored up small inclines and down into hollows, lurching through several creek beds and muddy seeps along the way.

In the 1850s the nation was predominantly rural. The people who lived in Bloomington were considerably outnumbered by the much larger population in the surrounding county. Outside the city lay countless homesteads and farms, with houses that ranged from log cabins to stately brick homes. The soil was adequate for agricultural purposes but not as good as the rich, dark soils found further north in the state. Deep stands of hardwood forest stood undisturbed in many places. Monroe County had no mineral wealth except for small traces of coal and iron ore, and there was no river capable of carrying shipping. The town of Bloomington had come into existence for the simple reason that it lay at the geographic center of the county and was therefore a good location for the courthouse.

Although portions of the nation were already industrialized by that time, the Industrial Revolution had been slow to penetrate the interior. Bloomington had its own small industry: a wool mill, sawmills, grain mills, tanneries, a mitten works, a hattery, the Seward foundry, and similar manufactories, but none of them employed more than a handful of workers. The arrival of the railroad in 1853 marked a turning point for the community, linking the once-isolated town to the rest of the nation and opening up new possibilities of commerce, prosperity, and travel. Nearby towns of similar size with no rail service soon began to decline, leaving Bloomington as the county's eminent community. Even though early trains moved slowly (often less than ten miles per hour), creeping up hills and stopping dead in deep snow, the presence of the railroad meant that shoppers on Bloomington's courthouse square could obtain exotic consumer goods unknown ten years earlier, including quality cigars, imported fabrics, and barrels of oysters. The town's few manufacturers could send their finished goods via rail if they chose, and they could obtain replacement machinery from the East.

Many people within the city kept cows and chickens in outbuildings in their backyards. Swine roamed freely through the streets, rooting through garbage piles and scratching themselves against fences. There would be no city water or sewers for nearly another half century, and every home and business had a privy in the back. A well on the courthouse grounds provided water that was probably tainted to some degree and was occasionally vandalized by teen pranksters who tossed refuse or rotten eggs down the shaft, to the anger of their elders. Each year there were outbreaks of cholera, malaria, typhoid, smallpox, and scarlet fever. The dead were buried in the weed-infested city cemetery that lay almost a mile west of the square downtown. Each year during the late summer the rains would stop and a dry spell would ensue, but every few years there would be a serious and long-lasting drought that made the leaves droop on the trees and the earth split into a mosaic of cracks. Thrifty people constructed subterranean brick cisterns to store rainwater for their homes.

Bloomington was distinguished by a feature shared by few other communities of similar size: the state university, at that time an institution consisting of fewer than ten professors and approximately one hundred young men. There would be no women students until after the Civil War. College Avenue dead-ended about half a mile south of the courthouse at the small campus of Indiana University, at that time still commonly referred to as the State College. The university was not yet a magnetic force that would create what we think of today as a "college town": a dynamic and invigorating place, surrounded by restaurants, boutiques, bookstores, music, and nightlife. All this would come in the twentieth century. Instead, the university was more like a cloister where young men studied Latin, Greek, and rhetoric, and attended mandatory chapel on Sunday.

The presence of the university had a significant impact on housing in Bloomington. In the 1850s there were not enough houses to shelter the population and the students, a situation that would bedevil the town for decades to come. Because there were no dormitories, private individuals and boarding houses provided room and board to students who doubled and tripled up in spare bedrooms and unused parlors. Renting to students was a common way to make a little side income. The housing stock of the city was motley. A number of old log cabins were still in use, their exteriors disguised with clapboards or shingles; but they were considered uncomfortable and old-fashioned and were rapidly disappearing, either torn down or enveloped by bigger frame houses that were constructed directly around them. Those who had the means to do so built tall frame or brick houses that loomed over the small and flimsy two-room cottages nearby. But housing was expensive and there was never enough to meet the demand, which resulted in great hardship for the poor.

THE SHOWERS FAMILY COMES TO BLOOMINGTON

In 1856, the Showers family arrived in this little community. Up to this point Charles Christopher Showers, known as C. C., had led a nomadic existence with his wife, Elizabeth, relocating their ever-growing family at least fifteen times over the course of eighteen years across the greater Midwest. Beginning in 1838 in Coudersport, Pennsylvania, and zigzagging through Indiana, Ohio,

Illinois, Iowa, Tennessee, and Louisiana, jolting by wagon over rough dirt tracks and floating along rivers on flatboat and steamboat, the family's series of removes totaled approximately 3,500 miles. This would be an impressive sequence of moves today, but it was far more grueling and hazardous in the early to mid-1800s, when the only roads between communities were rough and unpaved. It's likely that C. C. and Elizabeth had family connections in several of the communities they moved to.

C. C. served for a time as a Methodist circuit rider who traveled on horseback to preach to people who lacked established churches in rural frontier areas, which may explain some of his family's apparently random wanderings. Although many people called him "Reverend," it is not clear if he was in fact ever formally ordained as a minister. One account states that he was "licensed to preach" beginning in 1847, almost a decade after he left Pennsylvania;[1] but his name is not included on the official lists of early Methodist ministers assigned to the state of Indiana. He may have been a supernumerary minister who assisted the main minister, and there is at least one record of him performing a marriage. But the money earned through itinerant preaching was not sufficient to feed a family, so C. C. was also an entrepreneur and businessman. It's not clear how much money he had; a poor man could not have afforded to relocate a large family as many times as he did, but a wealthy man would not have continued to uproot himself and his family in this manner. His income was probably somewhere between modest and moderate, never descending to abject poverty.

Elizabeth Hull had married C. C. in Coudersport, Pennsylvania, on May 16, 1836, at the age of nineteen, and followed him on his wanderings across the nation, a baby in her arms during each relocation. Each of their seven children was born in a different community. Her life must have been extremely difficult, living in a succession of pioneer villages with a growing number of children, but she raised seven children to adulthood without any deaths despite the frequent outbreaks of epidemics and lack of good medical treatment. Elizabeth suffered from chronic ill-health and appears haggard and worn in the single photograph of her that still exists, but she was a *survivor* in a way that modern people can barely imagine. She gave birth to seven babies in primitive conditions; she suffered the ravages of yellow fever for five weeks; and she probably endured smallpox and malaria. An ongoing affliction was severe asthma, which left her gasping for breath. Sweeping and dusting a house cannot have been easy for her, nor preparing meals each day on a wood- or coal-burning

Between 1837 and 1856 the Showers family lived in Coudersport, Pennsylvania; Fort Wayne, Indiana; Johnsville, Mansfield, and Cincinnati, Ohio; Evansville, Indiana; Peoria, Illinois; Rock Island and Cedar Rapids, Iowa; Memphis, Tennessee; Shreveport, Louisiana; and finally New Albany, Orleans, Owensburg, and Bloomington, Indiana. *Courtesy Miles Reiter.*

stove. Stoic and dutiful, Elizabeth was deeply pious and had complete faith that God would see her through her hardships, as the entries in her spiritual daybook show. The daybook, written in a small, clear script using irregular spelling and no punctuation marks, tells us much about Elizabeth. In it she recalls her childhood experiences of religion:

"at the age of thirteen I became powerfully convicted that I was a greate sinner in the sight of god and greatly needed salvation though I was of a disposition to conceal my feeling from any one seeking reliefe alone in the secret place of devotion giving vent there to my feelings in teares trying at the same time to give myself to the savior the sinners friend but oh how much I needed light and instruction."[2]

In this breathless manner she composed her spiritual thoughts. Her day-book gives us almost no information about her day-to-day life but contains powerful affirmations of her faith and her ongoing struggles to achieve "sanctification," which finally occurred on October 15, 1854, when she was thirty-seven years old. Beginning in October 1859 and continuing until the end of her life, Elizabeth commemorated each anniversary of her sanctification by spending the day apart from her family in a closed room, on her knees, reading the Bible and praying. Each year on January 1 she wrote an entry thanking God for allowing her to live to see one more year. Her daybook gives no account of family moves and never mentions that she was pregnant or had given birth; there is no indication that her country was teetering upon the brink of a great war that would tear it apart; nor is there any record of her sons and daughters marrying and moving out of the family home. Her sole topic was her spiritual relationship with God. Elizabeth had much in common with the saints and martyrs of the ancient church. Although she loved her husband and children, one gets the uneasy sense that Elizabeth may also have regarded them as impediments to a closer relationship with God.

It is not clear why C. C. and his family came to Bloomington: family connections, church opportunities, and business prospects are all equally possible reasons. Although he was a Methodist, C. C. left that church the year after his arrival in Bloomington to become a Baptist pastor, a move that filled Elizabeth with dismay.

Aprile the 13th 1857

This has been a week of ample temptation and trial the time having come that the tie that bound me so closely to the church of my early choice is to be severed oh how selfe would draw back but oh thy will be don my dearest Lord after living in the M.E. Church 27 years I to day tak my letter and join the Baptist Church that my husband is pastor of with a strang impression that I shall again live and die with the people I so much love though this is all in the future yet I would submit my all to the most gracious god oh help thy feeble child in this time of need one year and six mounthes I have tarried back had it not been that my dear husband was a Baptist minister and I seen that the lord ownd his labours I could not got the consent of my mind to make the

This unlabeled photo from a Showers family album is probably C. C. Showers sometime in the 1850s or '60s.

From the collection of the Monroe County History Center, 202 East 6th Street, Bloomington, IN, www .monroehistory.org, Faces and Places Collection.

chang for it was the greatest trial that I ever was called to endure I prise so highly her privileges I love so well the doctrains of holiness oh how I love her sweet communion feastes the privileges of the classroom could my dear husband have been satisfied I never could have left but I feel to praise the Lord I care not for the name religon is the same bless the Lord oh my soul[3]

Elizabeth's comment that she had "tarried back" from joining the Baptist Church for a year and six months already suggests that it may have been the attraction that brought C. C. to Bloomington in the first place. Sectarianism was so marked in the mid-1800s that it was quite unusual to "take one's letter" and move from one church to another. C. C. preached in a Baptist Church in a small community called Putnamville, south of Greencastle, Indiana, for a year or so. But Elizabeth's "strang impression" that she would return to the Methodist Episcopal Church was correct: C. C.'s involvement with the Baptists ended by January 1 of 1859, and he and his wife returned to the Methodists.

Elizabeth and C. C. had six children when they arrived in Bloomington. Several of the children were known by their middle names, a family custom that continued with many of the grandchildren, and several of those family names would be used and reused in subsequent generations, which makes it confusing to read the family tree. The first two children born were sisters, Sarah Elizabeth and Mary Eleanor (known as "Ellen"). Next came two brothers, James David and William Norton; and after them came two more sisters, Anne Manerva ("Annie") and Martha ("Lola"). The youngest child, born four years after the family's arrival in Bloomington, when Elizabeth Showers was about forty-three years old, was named Charles Hull for his mother's family and known fondly as "Hullie." Because of Elizabeth's extended years of childbearing, Hullie was nineteen years younger than his older brother James and twenty-three years younger than his eldest sister Sarah. A short while before the family's move to Bloomington, the eldest daughter Sarah had married John Sears in Orleans, Indiana, and the newlyweds relocated to the Bloomington area around the same time as Sarah's parents and siblings did. John Sears, the eldest son-in-law, was a workingman from rural Orange County who was skilled in the useful trades of blacksmithing, house plastering, and machine work; he is credited with having plastered the columns of the old Monroe County Courthouse in 1855.[4] In later years his descendents would play an important role in the Showers family business.

The three Showers boys, James, William, and young Hull, would become the Showers Brothers of later fame. Despite the five-year difference in age between James and William, the two were extremely close. In his memoir James recalled the birth of his younger brother:

> Mrs. Rhoda Metzer, the midwife of my Mother, called me into the house and told me I could see my little baby brother and if I would sit down on the floor and hold open my arms, I could hold him. Mrs. Metzer placed Willie in my arms and from that day on, all my life, I had my arms around him, and he was the same with me as soon as he was old enough to be my pal. During all our years of association, there was never a cross word between us. . . . William N. was destined to be the life-long playmate, pal, and business partner of James D.[5]

C. C. had learned the skill of cabinetmaking while young. In the early 1800s American furniture began to be manufactured with power tools rather than hand tools, and C. C. knew how to use this new technology. Steam power drove the machines that cut the boards and the tools that were used for shap-

James, the eldest son, eventually lived to the great age of ninety-seven. Late in his life he recorded a handwritten memoir of early life in his family. Approximately thirty pages in length, skipping back and forth in time, it was written during the last ten to fifteen years of his life and was an important historical source for the 1928 book written by Dale Dillon and published by Showers Brothers, *Thoughts Concerning the 60th Anniversary of Showers Brothers Company.* James continued recording his memories of youth long after Dillon's book was published, for one entry was dated 1938, the year before he died.

ing. All the power tools that can be found in today's home workshops—circular saws, drill presses, electric drills—had steam-powered equivalents in C. C.'s day. He undoubtedly owned at least a few of these necessary tools. Making furniture completely by hand, the old-fashioned way, was a remnant of America's pioneering years and now obsolete as a method of mass manufacture. Machines were the key to success when manufacturing a number of similar items for sale. During his years of living in frontier communities, C. C. must have built simple, utilitarian furniture for his family's needs, and he made and sold similar furniture to others. He taught his sons James and William to work with wood as soon as they were old enough to understand what they were doing. Years later James recalled that at the age of six he was able to build two-wheeled wagons, which he traded with other boys for marbles, pocket knives, and other trinkets, and that at the age of thirteen he did "a man's work, making tables, chairs and other articles of furniture."[6] William was removed from formal schooling "while still studying short division" and apprenticed (apparently to his own father) for $6 a month in order to learn the cabinetmaker's trade.[7] Both William and James received sufficient outside schooling to surpass their mother in spelling ability.

Elizabeth Showers, the matriarch of the family,
struggled against illness all her life.

Courtesy Nancy Teter Smith.

There was no mandatory schooling for children in most states during the mid-1800s. Children learned to read, write, and "cipher" at home, although if the parents could afford it, they might send their children to a school that charged for its services. Children from poor families often went straight to work as wage earners as soon as they could master the necessary skills, at which point their formal education was at an end. This appears to have been the case with James and William Showers. We have records of children as young as eleven or twelve working at the Showers Brothers factory in the early years.

At times during the early years, C. C.'s work required him to live away from home for prolonged periods of time, leaving Elizabeth in sole charge of the household. James recorded the following anecdote:

> When we were living in Owensburg (before moving to Bloomington) my father would go over to Orleans to do cabinet work, and on Saturdays I would ride our horse over to Orleans to get him, so he could spend the week-ends at home. One time in summer, when I rode the horse over to get him, I took sick on the way, at what we call Wood's ferry on the White River (East Fork near Bedford). You see, when we lived down south in Shreveport, La., I contracted malaria and it stayed with me several years. At times I would chill and fever would mount as high as 103 degrees to 105, and it would make me so deathly sick and delirium would follow. So, on this trip, I started out from Owensburg, wearing a linen suit and straw hat. I had not gone far till a rain shower came up and drenched me to the skin. It was soon over and then the sun came out and began to dry my clothes,—then again, it rained and I was drenched again. Then it turned quite cool. Soon I began to chill as I rode along and my fever began to rise. When I got to the ferry, it was noon, so the ferryman was in a hurry to go eat dinner and seeing only a boy on a horse, wishing to cross the river, he did not bring his ferryboat over on my side of the river to get me, but went into the house. By this time I was sick enough to die. As big as I was, I began to cry. Presently, two men came along and as they neared

me, I leaned over the side of the horse and began to vomit. They said, "Boy, you're sick." I told them "Know it." They took pity on me and turned around and took me to their house, put up my horse and fed it. They offered me some dinner, but I was too sick to eat and asked only for the privilege of lying down on their sofa. After a while, along about the middle of the afternoon, I got up and felt a little better. They offered me some coffee. I drank some and told them I must go on to Orleans and get my father but one of the men volunteered to go get him for me, and then my father could take me on home. So that night, father and I reached home. I could hardly wait to get there for my chills and fevering had begun all over again. The next day, delirium had set in and I was quite sick for several weeks.[8]

James reached competence as a woodworker early on. In his old age he remembered,

When I was about ten years old, my father had orders for a couple of cherry dressers that had to be finished within the week; he gave me the task of making them. Now, I have learned since then that making two dressers by hand within a week was a big job for a grown man. But, I had confidence in myself, so set about cutting my planks from the cherry wood—that smelt so good as I cut and dressed them down. Think of it! My only machinery was a hand-lathe & the saw-mill. After the boards were cut to dimensions, the rest of the work was done by hand. Just as I was ready to begin a dresser, my father came to me and said he had a more urgent order for a bureau and a corner cupboard, and would I make them instead of the dressers. A traveling carpenter who was in the shop said, "Boy, a corner cupboard alone is a big week's work for any man, let alone a bureau too!" That clinched my determination to get them both done on time. You can guess that I never idled away any time, but kept at it from daylight until dark, day after day. I took pains to not slight any part of the work, either. By Friday afternoon I had them both done—and was I proud! After examining them over my father commended my work, and told me I could take my brother Willie and Chub Edwards and go fishing out at Griffy's Creek—That was a great reward for me![9]

C. C. not only taught his sons how to shape wood, he also instilled in them a powerful work ethic and an understanding of incentives. James wrote,

My father taught us boys early in life to work. Even when two & three years old he gave us little tasks to do. If nothing else to pick up little pieces of boards & stack them in neat stacks, or to gather up shavings from his planing work. Toys were almost unheard of, but we had plenty of little wagons, & tiny benches & chairs & tables & bedsteads patterned after our father's furniture; at six & eight years of age we could make them ourselves. Wasn't he a good kind of a father to instruct us and permit us to use his finest woodworking tools? He instilled in us the love for work, that toil was honorable, that money requires work and planning to accomplish results. Father had a way of setting tasks for us boys to do and gave us a certain length of time to get those tasks done.

If all were completed on time and the finished work satisfactory, we were allowed a holiday to go fishing. How easy it was to work hard, when we knew we had a fishing trip coming as a reward! In later years, we would try that plan over at the factory! How the men would work if they knew we were granting them "time off" to go fishing when a certain amount of furniture was finished![10]

C. C.'s sons bore a lifelong reverence for their father. He was obviously an excellent role model and teacher to his sons, but one gets the impression that he was also a vacillating man given his constant relocations, his wavering between the Methodists and the Baptists, and his range of occupations over the years. For a short period he managed the large Planter's Hotel in Memphis, Tennessee, where his children were put to work; James later recalled washing dishes daily at the tender age of eleven for eighty to one hundred guests. We know that C. C. preached, made furniture, and kept shop, and that he was a kindly father to his children, but he does not appear to have been an effective businessman. However, his diverse range of professions might simply reflect the fluid and entrepreneurial nature of 1800s business: if one trade did not succeed, switch to a different trade and see if it would be better. At the time, this kind of flexibility was not necessarily viewed askance. In a periodical of the day, Ralph Waldo Emerson was quoted as saying:

> If your city young men miscarry their first enterprise, they lose all heart. If the young merchant fails, men say he is ruined. If the finest genius studies at one of our colleges, and is not installed in an office within one year afterward . . . it seems to his friends and to himself that he is right in being disheartened, and in complaining all the rest of his life. A sturdy lad [from the country] who in turn tries all the professions, who teams, farms it, peddles, keeps a school, preaches, edits a paper, goes to Congress, buys a township, and so forth, in successive years, and always, like a cat, falls on his feet, is worth a dozen of these city dolls. He . . . feels no shame in not "studying a profession"; for he does not postpone his life, but lives already. He has not one chance, but a hundred chances.[11]

Nevertheless, C. C.'s repeated relocations, combined with the number and variety of his business enterprises, create a strong suspicion that his aspirations outweighed his ability to succeed in business. This is exactly what would happen with the enterprise he was about to launch.

Chapter

2

SHOWERS & HENDRIX

AFTER THE SHOWERS FAMILY moved to Bloomington in 1856, C. C. established himself in business. It's unclear what led him to settle permanently in Bloomington instead of moving onward, but he remained in his adopted town for the rest of his life. The succession of enterprises that he launched in Bloomington was on a par with his previous work history. For a short while C. C. worked at a cabinet shop with Elizabeth's brother, Isaac Hull, where, according to James Showers's memoirs, he trained Isaac in cabinet building (C. C. is listed on the 1860 census as "cabinet maker"). The late Bloomington amateur historian Robert Leffler apparently had access to a trove of newspapers that no longer survive in the public collections; in his Showers pamphlet (preserved at the Monroe County History Center), he claims that the May 25, 1860 issue of the *Bloomington Republican* reported that Showers & Moffatt were making and selling bedsteads on the east side of the square, and that later that same summer Mercer and Showers were operating a grocery. By December 15 of 1860, Leffler states, C. C. was partnering with his new son-in-law, James Hendrix, who had recently married the second Showers daughter, Ellen.

Showers & Hendrix was the business that became the incubator for the Showers Brothers Company. The earliest advertisement yet located for the firm is found in the *Bloomington Republican*. Employing at least ten different fonts and type sizes, the notice states:

> FURNITURE Ware-Rooms. Showers & Hendrix, CABINET and Chair Manufactory, having taken the Shop and Warerooms formerly occupied by J. W. Bower, one door north of the Post Office, in Marsh, Cox & Co's New Building, Bloomington, Indiana, have on hand a large stock of FURNITURE of all kinds, such as Center, Card, Dining and Breakfast Tables, Bureaus from 9 to 35 dollars, Beadsteads [sic] from 2,50 to 12 dollars. Chairs, Presses, Safes, and all other furniture on hand or made to order, which we will sell as Cheap as any Other Dare!! All of our work warranted as represented. Lumber and all kinds of country produce taken in exchange for furniture. All kinds of Repairing, done on short Notice. Call and see us as we are determined to please in price and quality. COFFINS, Made in the cheapest and best Styles, and on short notice. We are the only owners of the Patent Cover for Coffins. Nov. 22nd, 1860.[1]

According to an account of the company's origins written sixty years later, the workshop for the company was located on the east side of the courthouse square, "approximately where the Wiles Drug Store now stands" (the center of the southern half of the block). "The building was . . . a frame structure. Owing to the location of this frame building, the neighbors were very skeptical as to the safety of their homes [because of the danger of explosion and fire from the steam-powered boiler] and constant pressure had much weight in bringing about the construction of a new two-story building. . . . built in 1864. The enterprising furniture manufacturers had hardly gotten started again until the building and practically everything contained in it was completely destroyed by fire."[2]

At the rebuilt business, Hendrix served as salesman while C. C. probably oversaw production and made trips in order to obtain or sell merchandise. A somewhat later advertisement had a slightly different approach than the first:

> Large Stock of FURNITURE! Showers & Hendrix, Bloomington, Indiana, Have an immense stock of Furniture which they offer to sell as cheap as good Furniture can be sold in the State; and having facilities for MANUFACTURING fast, and cheaper than others in this part of the state, we propose to sell Cheaper than any body else does, that sells GOOD FURNITURE. We shall not attempt to enumerate the articles we have, but will say that our stock is LARGE AND COMPLETE. And we can furnish you with anything you may want in the Furniture Line, from the commonest to the finest. We invite particular attention to our stock of Parlor Furniture, Which is the best assortment ever offered in this place. We ask you to come and look at our Furniture and ask prices, and you will be satisfied, that the place to buy your Furniture is One door North of the Post-Office, Bloomington, Indiana.[3]

The text continues:

SHOWERS & HENDRIX, UNDERTAKERS! Bloomington, Indiana, have just received a large assortment of Patent Metallic Burial Cases, For ordinary interments, depositing in vaults and transportation, they have no equal. They are made of the most imperishable materials, and are enameled inside and out to prevent rust, and the exterior has a fine Rosewood finish. When properly cemented the remains of the deceased are free from irruption of water or depredations of vermin, and may without offensive odor be kept as long as desired, thus obviating the necessity of hasty burials. Their long and successful use and the approbation given them, renders unnecessary any extensive notice of their valuable advantages. We also keep constantly on hand All Sizes of Wood, Cloth Covered and Plain Coffins. Showers & Hendrix, one door North of the P.O., Bloomington, Ind. May 27, 1864.[4]

An early advertisement for Showers & Hendrix.

In the twentieth century, when newspaper writers who were covering the Showers company searched for an eye-catching word to include in their headlines, they overemphasized the fact that Showers & Hendrix had got its start making and selling coffins, repeating the word ghoulishly again and again. This was done also in the commemorative book commissioned by the company in observance of its sixtieth anniversary. This gave rise to the widespread belief that Showers & Hendrix had operated a coffin factory during the Civil War. Those who repeated this misinformation should have stopped to consider how unlikely it was that the federal government would have contracted with a small workshop in a little midwestern community located hundreds of miles from the battle action. With tens of thousands of dead at every major battle as well as at the field hospitals, countless freight trains would have been required to accommodate the number of coffins that were necessary, but the rail lines were often intentionally destroyed as the armies passed over the land. A large number of the unhappy victims of war were buried on the spot in shallow graves or pits, without coffins.

But it's certainly possible that Showers & Hendrix may have sold several grieving Bloomington families the caskets that were sent south after the war to retrieve the remains of a loved one who had fallen in battle. The impervious metal caskets that were mentioned in the advertisement became extremely popular during the 1860s precisely because so many families were shipping bodies back from the South to be reburied at home. However, the advertisement makes it clear that these metal coffins were manufactured elsewhere. Records show that on the infrequent occasions when an inmate of the county poor home died, the Monroe County commissioners purchased plain wood coffins from Showers & Hendrix.[5] Bear in mind that all large furniture stores in the late nineteenth century stocked coffins along with chairs, beds, and tables. Advertisements for furniture stores that stocked coffins would continue to appear in Bloomington newspapers until the early 1900s, forty years after Showers & Hendrix first advertised their caskets. It's not a surprise that C. C. sold coffins; it would be more surprising to find a well-stocked furniture company of that time that *didn't* sell them. In any event, the advertisements of the period make it clear that Showers & Hendrix was not a "coffin factory" but a furniture company that sold coffins.

A later address of the business was on the south side of the courthouse square, just east of the central alley.[6] James and William, the two eldest Showers sons, worked at Showers & Hendrix under the direction of their father

The profession of undertaker was relatively new in America at this time, according to *The Sacred Remains: American Attitudes towards Death*, by Gary Laderman. Until the mid-1800s it was customary for each bereaved family to wash and lay out its own dead, which they dressed or wrapped in a shroud. Most carpenters maintained a stockpile of coffins of different sizes. Around the middle of the century the professional undertaker began to offer grieving families his services: assisting the family in a variety of ways, providing a casket and placing the body in it, providing the pall and the hearse, and placing the coffin in the grave or tomb. An undertaker who was also a minister, like C. C., had an advantage over competitors.

and brother-in-law. It's tempting to imagine Showers & Hendrix as a grubby establishment with a sawdust-filled workshop in the back room, but by the late 1860s it was an impressive and spacious business that carried a broad range of styles ranging from rustic to elegant, with prices to suit any budget. Customers were not only the residents of Bloomington but also the much larger number of citizens who lived in rural Monroe County and in the surrounding counties. Although Showers & Hendrix purchased a new location for its manufactory,[7] it certainly did not manufacture *all* of its wares, as company myth would later have it. James Showers recorded in his memoirs that when his father had operated a furniture store some years earlier in Shreveport, Louisiana, he found that local customers wanted furniture in a style that was more expensive (and presumably more ornate) than that which C. C. could build himself. Accordingly, C. C. had traveled to New Orleans to purchase and bring back the kind of goods that his customers preferred. Showers & Hendrix did the same thing by manufacturing a minority of its own wares and importing the rest. This imported furniture included many fancy and expensive items, as itemized in legal records stored at the Monroe County History Center. These show that in 1866 Showers & Hendrix, along with a third partner named Kimbley, opened up a branch location for their store in Vincennes, more than seventy miles

It's not clear whether this advertisement refers to woven wicker (very popular in the late 1800s) or the more rustic and less skilled bentwood technique.

Advertisements appearing in the *Vincennes Times* beginning December 8, 1866, read: "Showers, Hendrix & Kimbley would respectfully inform the citizens of Vincennes and surrounding county, that they have opened in Wises' old stand, on the corner of Main and Water streets, FURNITURE WARE-ROOMS where they will furnish all articles in their line at wholesale or retail. Our stock consists in part of Bureaus, Bedsteads, Sofas, Wardrobes, Sofas, chairs, &c. Having had years of experience in the manufacturing and sale of furniture, they flatter themselves that they can furnish any article in their line as cheap as can be bought elsewhere."

away from Bloomington. The company's letterhead read "Showers, Hendrix & Kimbley, UNDERTAKERS, Wholesale and Retail Dealers in Furniture and Chairs." In smaller letters to the side was added "Manufacturers, Wholesale and Retail Dealers in all kinds of FURNITURE AND CHAIRS, Prices as low as at any place in the West. All Orders Promptly Attended To."

To stock the new Vincennes location, the firm purchased a large amount of furniture made in Cincinnati. The concept of opening a branch location might seem both modern and optimistic, but it was an overreaching on the part of Showers & Hendrix. The aggrieved Cincinnati manufacturer, Henry Closterman, sued over their alleged failure to pay for a large shipment of furniture that they had ordered. The itemized list retained in the court records included one dozen "English cottage chairs," three dozen "slatback chairs," one dozen "balltop spindles," one dozen "round post," half a dozen "Boston rockers," one dozen "plain Grecian," one dozen "bent dining," one dozen "small office," two library chairs, one dozen "cane French," two "#1 piano stools," two dozen "slat rockers," one dozen "banister rockers," one dozen "child's cane" seats, three "brace arm" rockers, two "Fifth Avenue," two "oval backs," a single and extremely expensive "Elizabeth rocker," six "cane parlor," and eight "nurse chairs." Even if the merchandise had been divided between the company's two locations, two hundred chairs of different shapes and sizes is an impressive inventory that would have required a lot of space to display or store. Showers & Hendrix was obviously neither a small nor meager establishment. As settlement for their debt to Closterman, Showers, Hendrix & Kimbley offered to ship two thousand "hickory bark seats" back to Cincinnati. These hickory seats probably resembled the rustic "Old Hickory" furniture manufactured in nearby Martinsville, Indiana, from the 1890s onward. Showers & Hendrix probably imported its fancy wares while manufacturing only the more simply made and cheaper items. At least four men in addition to young James and William Showers were employed in making furniture for the firm: Ed Clark, Ed Coffin, Taylor Voss, and Henry Tourner.[8]

C. C. somehow found time amid all these activities to become a father for the seventh and last time in 1860 when Elizabeth—then in her 40s—gave birth to her third son, Hull. "Hullie" spent much of his childhood inside the family furniture workshop, watching his brothers and father making bedsteads, dressers, and chairs. At other times he would have seen how James Hendrix charmed shoppers into making purchases at the store. The teenaged elder sons were solicitous and caring toward their little brother. Because the town was only ten blocks long, most residences were only a few minute's stroll from the courthouse square. James recalled in his memoirs that "when brother Hullie was three years old word came down to the furniture shop that he was lost, so I hastened from the shop on Walnut St. (east side of square) over to Washington St., and when I got to Eighth St. I saw a small boy standing near on the corner crying, and when he saw me he came toward me crying, 'Jimmie a pig got after I'—He was heart-broken and scared but was only three squares [blocks] from home!"[9] In those days of free-ranging livestock, this was probably a common occurrence. The result could have been much worse than merely being chased and frightened; a newspaper account from the 1880s mentioned that a man walking down an alley had been badly gored by a cow when his dog menaced its calf. An enraged hog was easily capable of killing a small child.

James and William Showers honed their skills in the manufactory of Showers & Hendrix, building furniture, crating finished pieces in order to ship or deliver them, and hoisting these heavy objects onto wagons or into railroad cars. The brothers probably began as teen apprentices who worked under the direction of their father in return for their room and board. James recalled that his father successfully taught his sons to produce quality furniture at top efficiency:

The three brothers in the 1860s, from a much later
newspaper article about the company.
Left to right: William, Hull, and James.

Courtesy Nancy Teter Smith.

It took speed and skilled craftsmanship too to make a profitable turnout at the factory, and our father's training was profitable to us. One time he brought a skilled and experienced wood turner up from Cincinnati to help get out a large order of beds, on time. I was in my teens, and a turner if he was a good one could make about $2.50 a day. That was much more than twice the earnings of a common laborer . . . we were paying these wood turners 60 cents for the turnings on each bed, four posts and 2 stretchers. This man bragged that he could outdo any of our men but we let him talk

& we let him "show his stuff"—He threw up the job because he could not make turnings for 4 and a half beds each day, thereby earning $2.50 in wages! I am not boasting, but I have turned out eleven beds in a day many a time, that would have been $6.60 a day, if I had drawn wages![10]

WAR AND WEDDINGS

The Civil War significantly disrupted the everyday pattern of life in Bloomington. Rallies were held, flags were waved, and large numbers of local men mustered and marched away to board trains heading south. Heated public debates were held between those who were faithful to the Union and those who supported the right of the Southern states to secede, for many of Monroe County's residents were originally from Kentucky and remained faithful to their Southern roots. Neither James nor William heeded the repeated calls to arms. But in the summer of 1863 General Morgan led Confederate soldiers in a raid across the Ohio River into southern Indiana. Crossing the river at Brandenburg, Kentucky, Morgan led his men into Hoosier soil, passing rapidly through Corydon, Salem, North Vernon, and other small and defenseless towns, burning houses, looting personal belongings, stealing food and horses, and killing. The state had not expected a raid of this nature and was unprepared; Governor Morton issued an urgent plea for volunteers to group together to protect the farms and villages in the path of Morgan's Raiders. Salem was only sixty miles south of Bloomington, and Bloomington townspeople feared that the raiders would come closer during their swift march. As James recalled in his memoirs, "my mother was a pious woman, and war was against her religion. She would not permit us boys to go to war, but this new series of raiding by Morgan's men in southern Indiana, struck fear in her heart that the Civil War was getting very close to our home so she consented to let me volunteer in this new group of soldiers." He had just observed his twenty-second birthday.

Under the command of Captain Budd, James joined the First Regiment of Minute-Men. They assembled and departed for Sunman, not far from Cincinnati.

> A group of children collected at the station and made faces at us, & called us "Lincoln Hirelings," they were Southern sympathizers. We were to guard the food cellars, and places where ammunition could be bought, and to watch that Morgan's men did not steal horses from the farms. While guarding at a farmhouse near Sunman, a group of soldiers asked for some breakfast, and the housewife opened up a new barrel of flour & commenced to bake biscuits for them—just as she took some out of the oven,

down . . . came more soldiers, dozens of them—all of them were hungry—and believe me that poor woman had to keep on baking biscuits as long as there was any flour left in the barrel.—Some of the villages we were sent to guard from the raids of Morgan & his men, the people had been so tormented and feared the raids so much, that when we would enter the villages from one direction, the people [would] flee out of the village on the other, thinking us to be more of Morgan's men.[11]

Morgan soon passed on into Ohio and the immediate threat was gone. James returned to civilian life, but it could not have been pleasant to continue as a non-combatant during a war that engaged more than 196,000 fellow Hoosier men. One imagines both James and William keeping a low profile for the duration of the war.

Responsible young men of that era did not seriously contemplate marriage until they were making enough money to sustain a wife and a family. By 1864 James had reached that degree of self-sufficiency. In February of 1864, not long after his adventures with the First Regiment of Minute-Men, while the Civil War was still raging in the East and South, the twenty-two-year-old James married sixteen-year-old Loretta Fish and brought her to live with him. Sixteen years of age seems terribly young to marry by twenty-first-century standards, but James's parents, C. C. and Elizabeth, had married as teenagers, and the two eldest Showers sisters had married at eighteen and nineteen. Loretta moved in and commenced her housekeeping, cooking their meals on a wood stove, cleaning and washing, possibly planting a vegetable garden. But she miscarried in September during the early months of her first pregnancy. She died the following year in August of an unknown cause, the unhappy victim of either disease or another unsuccessful pregnancy. The couple had been married only a year and a half. Elizabeth wrote in her daybook,

August the 28th [1865]

Just haveing Returned from haveing consigned the Remains of a Loved one to the Narrow Limites of the cold grave while the people of god wher essembleing in the earthly sanctuary Our dear Lurettas spirit fled to god to the riper and Better sanctuary Sabbeth Morning August the 27th Farewell sweet spirite thou arte gon to swell the Number above who have Washt there Robes and made them white in the Blood of the Lamb though thou has been torn from us and the embrace of thy beloved Companion yet we sorrow not like those without A hope yet faire one it was hard to give thee Up Thou wast so wining in all thy ways so Meek in spirit O Thou are gon to join in that Heavenly musick thy ear caught the night Before Thou Left us Those Beautiful angels that came for thee And hovered over thy dieing couch whom thou spoke of Bore thy spirit to the paradise of god.[12]

No photos of the unfortunate young girl have survived, James never referred to her in his memoirs, and she is missing from all the summaries of the brothers' lives. But her grave and that of her miscarried infant lie next to his in Bloomington's Rose Hill Cemetery.

At the end of the next year, in December 1866, the twenty-year-old William married the young Lida Hanlon, but this marriage was also ill-fated. Lida died fourteen months after their wedding, but unlike Loretta, she left a permanent reminder in the form of a newborn daughter, Jennie. Elizabeth wrote,

> *February the 23rd, 1868*
>
> Death has again visited our familie circle taken away a loved one and deare Lida She has quit this vale of tears gon to the home of the soul she leves a companion Broken hearted. She ended Lifes Briefe story she reached her home in Glory O may the Lord suport her sorrowing Husband take care of the little Infant daughter She Leaves behind I take this Little Babe only a few hours old from a sence of duty O may the Lord Enable me to discharge my duty in Reference to it Faithfully Bring it up in the [illegible] and admonishion of the Lord if permitted to Live.[13]

Working men in those days were neither prepared nor willing to undertake the single parenting of infants, so the baby was turned over to Elizabeth. The newborn infant suffered constant seizures for several days following its difficult birth. Elizabeth may have initially taken over its care "from a sense of duty," having an eight-year-old son and two teenage daughters still at home to look after, but she soon felt true affection for the tiny baby girl:

> *Feb. the 29th [1868]*
>
> Feeling very feeble in Body from fetuige and loss of sleep our dear Little Baby has been sick ever since the death of its dear mother O what a love I feele this poore feeble Body is sinking under the Burden five days and Nights our Little Baby laid in spasmes scarce ever out of my arms during that Time on Friday Being the day set apart for selfe Examination and prayer while in my meditation with The little suffering I[n]fant In my arms just then going into another hard spasm it was suggested to my mind that in the days of the son of God when he Invest this Earth he heald the sick Restored the Blind and Raised the dead with these thoughts before I was hardly aware of it I fell upon my knees with the struggling Babe in my arms asking God to Restore it by healing it of these dreadful spasms or Release it by Taking it to himself Just then I felt the power Of God come upon me in a powerful maner never to be forgotten strang to say But nevertheless true When I arose from my knees the spasm had past off it was the Last all praise and Glory be to his holy name.[14]

Young William Showers in the 1860s.

Courtesy Nancy Teter Smith.

This unidentified photograph from the family
album was taken during the 1860s and is
most likely baby Jennie Showers.

Courtesy Nancy Teter Smith.

Elizabeth and C. C. kept their granddaughter until she was ten, according to a recollection written decades later by a descendant.[15] Lida was buried in February of 1868, and in October of the following year William married Hanna Lou Hendrix, the younger sister of his brother-in-law, James Hendrix. (If this sounds confusing, it can be explained as a brother and sister of the Showers family marrying a sister and brother of the Hendrix family.)

James married his second wife, Isabella Allen, known as "Belle," in January of 1867 in Greenville, near New Albany, managing to leave on the southbound train for his wedding just hours ahead of a snowstorm that shut down all rail traffic. A story related decades later described how James had met Belle.

> Capt. [John Wesley] Walker and J. D. Showers were life-long friends. They started their friendship as young Odd Fellows and continued it through the years. One incident that drew them close together happened when they were both young men. They went to New Albany together to attend an Odd Fellows reunion and decided to go across the river to Louisville to see the sights. Being burdened by their lodge regalia they stopped at a New Albany home to leave it for a few hours. The daughter of the house took it at their request—and made such an impression on young Mr. Showers that the lodge reunion was followed by a courtship and the New Albany girl became Mrs. Showers.[16]

Belle was technically from nearby Greenville, not New Albany; but it's certainly possible that one of her numerous brothers could have been an Odd Fellow, since lodge membership was an important social networking opportunity at that time. Belle was twenty-one or twenty-two when she wed James. She would be a loving and supportive wife to her husband and their marriage would last almost sixty years. The Allen family of Greenville was large and many of its men specialized in woodworking or carpentry. Two of Belle's brothers would work for James and William at the Showers company in later years.

The two brothers and their brides took up housekeeping together. James explained,

> As brothers Willie and I were very close to each other in working and saving we had contrived to lay aside $300. We had but one pocketbook, each of our earnings went into it, and we shared & shared alike. With this precious $300 we began business in 1868 in a little shed-like structure on the corner of Grant and Ninth Street, size 30 ft. by 40 ft., with two stories. Then we bought a lot and built us a cottage, Willie had taken himself a bride, and I had been married the year before, we had a home jointly . . . a few years [after] Willie and I had set up to housekeeping in our new double cottage, . . . a

minister wanted to buy it. He offered a cash sum of $150 and the remainder of payment in a half section of wild, unfenced land over in Jasper County. We traded off our little honeymoon cottage and each of us set up in a home of our own. In less than a year we sold the land for $2,700—then set to work enlarging our factory.[17]

With the proceeds from this real estate transaction in hand and their new wives settled into their new homes, James and William turned their attention to matters of money.

This collection of Bloomington faces was made by James Allison in
the 1860s. It is possible that the mustached man near the middle,
four rows down from the top, is C. C. Showers, flanked
on the left by James and on the right by William.

*Courtesy the Lilly Library, Indiana University,
Bloomington, Indiana.*

Chapter

3

LEGAL TROUBLES

WORKING MEN IN THE LATE 1800s toiled approximately ten to fourteen hours per day, six days a week. In his memoirs, James Showers mentions that the Showers & Hendrix woodturners were paid $2.50 per day. Working six days a week for fifty-two weeks a year meant an annual income of $780 for a skilled woodworker. That sounds like abject poverty, but a dollar went a lot further then than it does today. For comparison, ordinary untrained laborers such as haulers and diggers made about $1 a day, and the Showers brothers were earning more than double that amount. A surviving page from the company account book dated January 1868 shows payments of $21.50 to James and William, which was the same amount that C. C. himself drew.[1] If paid weekly, this would have meant an annual income of more than $1,100. By this point James and William, aged twenty-six and twenty-one, respectively, appear to have reached the rank of full partners in the family business.

Again the tantalizing question arises: just how much income did the Reverend Showers and his wife enjoy? In the 1928 book, *Thoughts Concerning the 60th Anniversary of Showers Brothers Company,* Dale Dillon implied that the family had little money and practiced a culture of thrift, referring to "the strain of those hard, hard times in that little Indiana town."[2] The part about thrift is

undoubtedly true, but it's unlikely that the family arrived in Bloomington in an impoverished condition. Any man with enough money to open a business (or a series of businesses) as C. C. did was better off financially than the majority of his fellow citizens. In an era when there were no trustworthy banks, C. C. and Elizabeth appear to have possessed sufficient money and/or investments to allow them to ride out rough times; James recalled one year when his father's furniture workshop in New Albany, Indiana, made so little money that C. C. decided to relocate his family northward to the town of Orleans. This move, like all the others, would certainly have entailed expenses that a truly poor man would simply not have been able to afford. Beginning in 1859, three years after C. C. and his wife had moved to Bloomington, they began buying and selling real estate, both together and individually. It's possible that Elizabeth had control of her own money through inheritance or family connections (the first of all the real estate transactions made by the Showers family was the sale of part of two lots to Elizabeth in 1859),[3] but it's also possible that C. C. registered properties in his wife's name to try to shield them from his creditors. Residential lots in the 1860s in Bloomington cost only a few hundred dollars, but some of the purchases made by C. C. and Elizabeth reflect multiple lots or commercial locations of Showers & Hendrix, which of course cost more. One transaction of this latter sort, dated December 15, 1869, was a sale by James Cookerly to Elizabeth Showers and her daughter Ellen Showers Hendrix of an undivided half of in-lots 163 and 164, for $3,500. That was an enormous amount of money for most ordinary people, far more than a whole year's income; the president of Indiana University only earned $2,500 per annum around that time.

Despite the lasting respect and affection that James and William felt for their father, we have no evidence that C. C. was a profitable businessman or that he exercised good judgment. Much of the newspaper record for most of the 1860s is missing. In the newspapers that survive, however, C. C. Showers

Wearing clothing typical for a furniture worker of the 1860s and '70s, this worker holds a can of varnish and a brush. The man is probably either Clarence or Thomas Allen, brothers of James Showers's wife, Belle Allen; both men worked at the Showers factory.

From the collection of the Monroe County History Center, 202 East 6th Street, Bloomington, IN, www .monroehistory.org, Faces and Places Collection.

On July 10, 1871, a number of indignant citizens petitioned the city council to pass an ordinance prohibiting swine from running at large. "They root up the ground before our doors; they rub their filthy sides upon our neatly painted fences; they leave their filthy ordures upon our sidewalks; they may be seen at times reveling in their filth even upon the side walks of our public square. For these and similar reasons we humbly and earnestly solicit your honorable body to shield us from this nuisance." A smaller number of citizens signed a counterpetition; C. C. Showers was one of them. Perhaps he kept one or more free-ranging pigs, but if so, his neighbors viewed them with loathing.

is barely mentioned, even though this was an era in which virtually everyone's doings were hailed in the local press. Of the main sources of information covering this particular period, James's memoirs, C. C.'s obituary, and the sixtieth anniversary commemorative book published by the Showers company were all either written or influenced by the Showers family, and all are uniformly respectful toward C. C. But the public records preserved at the Monroe County History Center tell a completely different story. The partnership of Showers & Hendrix appears to have collapsed beneath a flurry of at least ten lawsuits that accused the firm of non-payment on promissory notes, failure to pay off mortgages, or failure to pay for goods received. Suits were filed not only in Bloomington but also in Vincennes, where the branch location was. The names of C. C. Showers and James Hendrix appeared on advertisements for the Vincennes store for only two months, December and January of 1866–67; by February 1867 the business had been taken over by their former partner, John F. Kimbley. The final evidence of the financial disintegration of Showers & Hendrix is a bankruptcy notice that appeared in the *Bloomington Progress* late in 1869: "The books and accounts of the firm of Shower [*sic*] and Hendrix have been placed in my hands for collection, and all persons knowing themselves indebted to that firm will do well to call at the Law Office of [James] Hughes & [Nick] Van Horn, and settle immediately, and save costs."[4]

It is clear that the late 1860s and the first half of the 1870s were an extremely difficult period for C. C. Showers. For years after the furniture store had closed its doors, lawsuits pursued him and his partner, James Hendrix. Court records retained at the Monroe County History Center include a foreclosure on the property where C. C. and Elizabeth lived, a suit for nonpayment filed by Showers & Hendrix's Vincennes lawyers, and a poignant, misspelled pencil-written bill from an itinerant laborer who sued C. C. Showers for $3.80 for unpaid garden plowing and for "halling" (hauling) timbers all the way from Fairfax, a considerable distance south of Bloomington. The itinerant lumber hauler won judgment for $3.80 against Showers & Hendrix, but he had to sue the partners again the following year for nonpayment of the relatively trifling sum that nevertheless represented nearly four days' hard physical labor for him and his team of draft animals. In another action brought against the business, Showers & Hendrix asked the court to grant a continuance of trial to a later date because material witnesses who could testify in favor of Showers & Hendrix were not available. Those witnesses consisted of C. C.'s son-in-law John Sears and his brother Frank, who had evidently both been employed at Showers & Hendrix. Even if one is inclined to assume the best of C. C. because he was a minister of the church, the absence of the same witnesses in a second lawsuit as well makes one wonder whether C. C. had sent them away intentionally in order to delay proceedings. A different lawsuit was brought by a cabinet worker who sued the company for not paying him the promised wage of $3 per day; in their answer to the lawsuit, C. C. and James Hendrix answered boldly that his work was only worth $1.50 per day.[5] Most companies face occasional lawsuits, but the number of cases brought against Showers & Hendrix throughout this time period (persisting through 1876) probably indicates a classic business failure. A startling item in the *Bloomington Progress* dated August 9, 1871, reported that C. C. Showers had been arraigned and tried before officers of the Methodist Episcopal Church on charges of swearing to a false schedule of property and making false statements. A committee of three church members served as the jury and found him innocent. The *Bloomington Progress,* obviously partial to the defendant, stated that it was scarcely fair to presume that a man who had preached the gospel for twenty years could be guilty of such charges. It noted, "The friends of Brother Showers are delighted at his acquittal, and he has withdrawn from the church." This must have been another short-lived departure from the church. It was not a permanent split, for by the end of his life C. C. was once again a devout and observant Methodist in good standing.

One lawsuit was brought by Showers & Hendrix against a customer who had failed to repay a note he had written for the value of goods purchased at their store.[6] The purchaser acknowledged that he had signed a note for the balance that was due on a "hair mattress" (upholstered with woven horsehair) and a bureau. Showers & Hendrix had obtained the mattress for the defendant and told him that the cost, $45, represented only "cost and carriage" and affirmed that it was "very cheap at that price." "Relying solely upon the representations of said plaintiffs he took said mattress at that price" but learned afterward that the mattress was actually of inferior quality and only worth $15. The aggrieved purchaser also complained of the bureau, which Showers & Hendrix had assured him was made of "good seasoned lumber and put up in the best workmanlike manner and well veneered with a superior article of veneering." The man claimed that the bureau was actually made from green wood and that as it dried out, the joints came apart and the veneer fell off. The defendant claimed that he was damaged to the amount of $45, for which he demanded judgment from the plaintiffs. This does sound fairly damning, but the reader must remember that we are hearing only one side in each of these quarrels. (As a matter of fact, Showers & Hendrix won this particular lawsuit.) Nevertheless, there were far more legal actions filed against Showers & Hendrix during its relatively short existence than were brought against Showers Brothers over a span of years.

It is extremely unfortunate that most of the court records contain the complaint and the answer to a given case, but not the resolution. Only a few of the court papers record that Showers & Hendrix (or more likely, James and William) repaid at least some of the debts that had triggered several of the company's legal cases, and they appear to have won at least some of the lawsuits. But it must have been difficult to hold their heads high after the family was tarnished by bankruptcy in 1869, which in those days was viewed as an event of humiliation and shame. On February 10, 1870, not long afterward, Elizabeth recorded in her daybook, "Another week has past with all its anxiety and cares, temptation at times has ran exceedingly high, trials not a few O my heart sighs for retirement and rest O I am learning more and more that this public Life has not a good influence upon my family O I would to God it was otherwise but hush O my soul God knows it is not my wish that I am so situated."[7] Bear in mind that the final years of Showers & Hendrix, the years when the lawsuits began to stack up, was the same approximate period in which William lost his young wife during childbirth, leaving the family with an infant to care for as well as a heap of debts to attend to. Those years were not a particularly happy time for the family.

Beginning in 1928, the Showers Brothers Company would give its origin as 1868, although this date is difficult to verify. One source puts the date of the company's origin at 1866,[8] while a different one specifies the date as November 17, 1869.[9] Neither of these sources (local histories of dubious value) can be relied upon as accurate. Advertisements for Showers & Hendrix continued to appear in the *Bloomington Progress* until nearly the end of 1869, when the bankruptcy occurred. The official date of 1868 presumably marks the point at which James and William became full partners in the Showers & Hendrix business or purchased it outright, name and all—or it could be a misremembering, six decades later. It's more likely that the brothers took over the business in 1869 when its legal problems became severe, buying out their father in order to give him time and money to fight his law cases, but we have no evidence for this. Regardless of who now owned it, Showers & Hendrix continued operating as a business through the end of 1869. On September 8 of that year, a notice appeared in the newspaper announcing a startling career change: C. C. Showers and James Hendrix had bought the Bloomington House hotel and had renamed it the National Hotel, redecorating (possibly with Showers-made furniture?) and repainting it. After December 8, 1869, the furniture ads for Showers & Hendrix abruptly ceased; the two Showers brothers were now on their own, using a new business name: Showers & Bro.

It is extremely frustrating that immediately following the dissolution of Showers & Hendrix, James and William disappear from our sight for quite a long while. Throughout the early 1870s the newspapers provide virtually no news or advertisements of the brothers' new firm. Part of the difficulty is that much of the surviving newspaper record consists of a Democratic newspaper, the *Bloomington Courier,* which had no interest in publicizing or promoting staunch Republicans like the Showers family. The newspapers were all vehemently partisan at that time and never gave favorable mention to their political enemies. The *Courier* recorded a series of unusually jovial after-hours Republican businessmen's celebrations involving the Showers brothers in a highly disapproving manner: "The attention of the city Marshall is called to the continuous racket emanating from the back rooms in the second story of the building occupied by Smith's Jewelry store. The unearthly sounds would lead one to believe that a band of wild Comanche Indians are quartered there and the nuisance should be at once abated."[10] (Smith was a Showers in-law, as will be explained in chapter 4.)

Except for brief intervals of hilarity with their Republican friends, the brothers must have been working extremely hard to establish their own company and also to help their parents negotiate their legal morass. It's possible that James and William remembered these years long afterward as difficult ones because they were repaying their father's debts. For most of the 1870s our only glimpses of the brothers appear in the form of intermittent short newspaper items regarding the activities of the Odd Fellows, and various real estate transactions. We have only a few sketchy details for most of the decade in which they laid the foundations for their furniture empire.

DOMESTIC LIFE

James and Belle's first daughter, Mattie, was born in 1868, around the time the business was being started. An anecdote of her infancy was recorded by her father decades later, indicating how little the young couple knew about parenthood.

> When Mattie was a baby we proudly took her down to her [Allen] grandparents the first time one hot June day. We went down the New Albany and Salem railroad to Borden and Mr. Allen met us at the depot with horse and carriage.

> We were quite disappointed, Belle and me, that he did not pay any attention to the baby, at all, on the trip over to the home. However, after putting up the horse, he washed his hands and came into the living room and took the baby off of Belle's lap and laid it on the floor, and began to unwrap it, to our dismay he took off blanket after blanket, and its jacket and long dresses & petticoats, even its woolen stockings—and then said to it, "Now kick!" It was so relieved to get out of those hot clothes that it just kicked and gooed at him & Mrs. Allen. Now Belle & me were just sure that baby would be bad sick from being unwrapped that way and exposed so much, but it slept like a log all night, and never was sick a bit—The grandparents advised us to dress her lighter in warm weather and we took their advice, and the baby was healthy and soon began to play with her feet.

> Just notice now few clothes the children & babies wear nowdays. 1938[11]

Mattie's paternal grandfather, C. C., dived into his new job as landlord of a sizable establishment. The National Hotel that he had purchased with Hendrix stood for many decades on the north side of Kirkwood Avenue half a block east

James's eldest daughter, Mattie.
Courtesy the Helm family.

of the courthouse square. More like a boarding house than a true hotel, it had thirty persons living beneath its roof in 1870 according to the federal census of that year. These included C. C. and Elizabeth, their unmarried daughters, Lola and Annie, along with little Hullie and granddaughter Jennie. James Hendrix lived there as well with his wife, Ellen Showers Hendrix, and their young daughters, Laura and Nellie. Also residing at the National were nine male university students ranging in age from eighteen to twenty-three; a Mr. and Mrs. James Thompson and their two children; a sixteen-year-old lad who worked at the saddle shop; the grocer James Rogers; drugstore keeper William Fullerton; shop owner John Smith, who ran a furniture shop and then a jewelry shop and watch repair around the corner on the courthouse square; the county auditor, Perry Henry; Robert Leffler the miller (possibly the ancestor of Robert Leffler the local historian); and the thirty-seven-year-old Irish cook whose job it was to feed all these people each day, Annie McGuire.

A vivid description of a similar Bloomington boarding house was written years later by Edwin Fulwider. In his memoirs he describes the establishment run by his grandparents:

The two long tables sat about twenty-five boarders three times a day, and absolutely on schedule. Just prior to meal time the boarders would assemble on the front porch in the summer time, or in the front hall and parlor in the winter. At the exact hour Grandma would signal and all would file into the dining room. . . . Two young helpers . . . put the food on the table in big dishes which were passed so everyone could help themselves family style for as long as the food lasted. There was always plenty, no one ever left the table hungry.

The dining room was very large, the tables were covered by long linen table cloths changed twice a week. . . . It is staggering to think of the quantities of food that had to be brought together and prepared for three meals a day at the quality level demanded by my grandmother. Grandfather Robertson . . . did almost all of the outside work, bring[ing] in supplies, unloading delivery wagons, and above all keeping the fires going. All cooking was done on an old fashioned wood burning kitchen range. . . . These big ranges had to always be at the right temperature for baking, frying, boiling, at the right time. Breakfast required one kind of heat and noon dinner and evening dinner still different temperatures, summer and winter. Grandpa was an artist with the stove, and also the big boiler in the basement that provided heat for the house in winter, as well as fires in two grates. . . . Twenty-two tons of anthracite coal were consumed in this house every year.

Roasts were whole legs of pork or beef, sometimes the meat was boiled in great tubs with vegetables added in the final stages to make a tremendous stew. Beans, peas, and all other vegetables in season, biscuits and gravy for breakfast, ham or bacon and eggs by the ton. Seasonal vegetables had to be canned in summer to provide legumes in winter months when no fresh things were available.

Breakfast served, the dishes [were] washed by hand in the big sink and everyone started immediately on noon dinner . . . one meal ran right into another without a single minute of let-up in the routine. One continuous cycle: Peel potatoes, Cook, Serve, Wash Dishes. Peel potatoes, Cook, Serve, Wash Dishes. . . . And there was all that laundry: Imagine the table linens, napkins, bed sheets, towels, dish towels, wash cloths, plus their own personal clothing. All of this had to be laundered by hand, this was way before washing machines were invented for home use. Everything was boiled in an old fashioned copper boiler on an old coal laundry stove in the wash house. . . . In cold or rainy weather all the wash had to be hung up to dry on the back porch, back halls, or anywhere available. And then there was the ironing. Each of those bedsheets, table cloths, etc. had to be hand ironed with old fashioned flat irons heated on the stove.[12]

The National Hotel may have appeared to be a reasonable investment for a man like C. C. who had previously managed a hotel in Tennessee. But it's doubtful that the enterprise was profitable, with so many family members

Looking from downtown Bloomington toward the east, the National
Hotel is visible on the left. It did not have a front portico when
C. C. Showers and James Hendrix owned it.

Accession 7200, collection of Indiana University Archives.

living there instead of paying boarders. Perhaps sensing a bad investment (or possibly scrambling for cash again), the Showers and Hendrix families did not remain at the National Hotel for long. In November of 1870, less than a full year after the purchase of the hotel, the sheriff and local butcher, Lawson McKinney, bought C. C.'s share of the National Hotel, and by the end of the year he had bought out Hendrix as well and was sole proprietor of the place. C. C. was now compelled to focus his attention on the plague of lawsuits that were following him, while James Hendrix attempted a number of short-lived enterprises. Hendrix left town with his family for a brief period (possibly to avoid his legal difficulties), but in the early 1870s he returned with his wife and two daughters and began working for his brothers-in-law at their furniture business. At some point in the 1870s C. C. also went to work for his sons and became a traveling salesman representing their line of furniture; the 1880 census identified him as a "commercial traveler."

Some time in 1870, before the sale of the National Hotel by C. C. Showers and James Hendrix, an interesting handbill was printed on fine cotton bond.

The National Hotel had an untidy subsequent history. When McKinney sold the hotel to E. T. Taylor in 1872, the *Bloomington Progress* noted, "The property is now unencumbered (of liens and/or mortgages), for the first time in twelve years." The under-insured building burned to a shell in 1873, and Taylor killed himself with a gunshot through the heart eight weeks later. McKinney went on to become the city treasurer, taking the opportunity to embezzle a significant amount of city money and absconding to Texas. The National Hotel was rebuilt and enlarged, and continued under a string of different owners into the early twentieth century.

This handbill is unique in that it appears to be the earliest known effort to "boom" Bloomington: to glowingly paint the many benefits of the community in order to attract outside investors. It lists amenities such as the soil, the timber, the railroad facilities, and the presence of the university.[13] Up and down the left and right edges of the handbill are advertisements from the local businesses that underwrote the cost of printing it, including C. C. Showers and James Hendrix at the National Hotel. On the opposite side is the first known advertisement for Showers & Bro., who are listed as "Manufacturers and dealers in FURNITURE and CHAIRS. Also, Undertakers."[14] This is the only evidence we have that the sons briefly dabbled in their father's former coffin making and that they briefly sold retail furniture. But the handbill is significant because in the years that would soon follow, the brothers would pursue this idea of "booming the town" and would tirelessly promote the community to outside interests.

One final legal case is worth mentioning. In 1875, six years after Showers & Hendrix had closed shop, Mathew Campbell filed suit against C. C. Showers and James Hendrix, their wives, Elizabeth and Ellen, and James and William. Six years earlier, in 1869, Showers & Hendrix had executed a promissory note to Campbell that was secured by a mortgage on the furniture shop as well as by another property just northeast of the city limits, 63 feet wide and 150 feet

James's wife,
Belle (Allen) Showers.

Courtesy the Helm family.

William's wife,
Hanna Lou (Hendrix) Showers.

*From the collection of the Monroe County
History Center, 202 East 6th Street,
Bloomington, IN, www.monroehistory
.org, Faces and Places Collection.*

deep, "containing a furniture factory with a steam boiler (tools and fixtures) all to be included under the mortgage." In October of that year, shortly before the purchase of the National Hotel, James and William had purchased the factory property from the family consortium. Although the mortgage on the storefront had been paid off, Campbell argued that the mortgage on the factory property had never been fully paid. He sued, alleging a balance of $300 on the promissory note and asking for payment plus interest and foreclosure. James and William succeeded in defending their ownership of the property, located at what would later be called Ninth and Grant Streets. In the two decades that followed, this small piece of property purchased from their father and brother-in-law and preserved in the face of legal challenge would enable James and William to make their fortunes as industrialists.

Chapter

4

THE BROTHERS ENTER
BUSINESS

AT THE BEGINNING of their new partnership, the brothers were careful and did not repeat the errors of their father. They found a business partner in store-keeper Frank Rogers, whose investment resulted in a short-lived incarnation of the company called Showers, Rogers & Co. The firm's advertisement in the August 7, 1872 issue of the *Bloomington Progress* read:

> Planing Mill and Furniture Manufactory. Showers, Rogers & Co., Smith & Tuley's Block, Up-Stairs, in Smith & Tuley Hall, Bloomington, Ind., are prepared to fill orders for Furniture or Chairs, either at wholesale or retail. We have greatly enlarged and improved our manufactory, having added new machinery, and our facilities are such that we can sell as cheap at wholesale or retail, as any other house in the state. Carpenters and Builders are informed that we have procured the necessary machinery, and can now dress and rip lumber at very low prices. Good seasoned lumber always on hand and furnished very cheap.

The business was set up to provide millwork, claimed a 1922 profile of James Showers. Supposedly, the frames of all the doors and windows at the Central School building in Bloomington were manufactured by James and William's planing mill.[1] But the company manufactured simple furniture as well. Reminiscing on those early days decades later, William Showers noted that the company originally "did custom work for contractors and made cheap bed-

Planing Mill and Furniture Manufactory.

Showers, Rogers & Co.,
Smith & Tuley's Block, Up-Stairs, in the Smith & Tuley Hall, Bloomington, Ind.,
Are prepared to fill orders for Furniture or Chairs, either at wholesale or retail.

We have greatly enlarged and improved our manufactory, having added new machinery, and our facilities are such that we can sell as cheap at wholesale or retail, as any other house in the State. Carpenters and Builders are informed that we have procured the necessary machinery, and can now dress and rip lumber at very low prices. Good seasoned lumber always on hand and furnished very cheap.

may29 SHOWERS, ROGERS & CO.

Newspaper advertisement for the Showers planing mill, an early incarnation of the business.

steads which were sold unfinished to a jobber in St. Louis."[2] The sons would ultimately become extremely wealthy businessmen, but it would take the help of friends with money and many years of hard work. Rogers was one of many partners that James and William would have over the coming years; Samuel C. Dodds and Henry Henley were other early business partners. Rogers apparently sold or leased his "Furniture Ware Room" to the Showers brothers, which they stocked with goods for buyers.[3] In each case the partners brought money into the enterprise along with business contacts. When not doing business with partners, the enterprise was called Showers & Bro.

In those early years the brothers themselves manufactured the furniture, probably with the assistance of a small handful of skilled workmen. To increase their efficiency the brothers specialized in their tasks: although both were skilled cabinet builders, William was in charge of production while James took on the task of obtaining orders.[4] The brothers at some point decided that they were not interested in manufacturing furniture for retail sale or in operating a furniture showroom, as Showers & Hendrix had done. Instead, their new goal was to mass-manufacture wholesale furniture to sell in other cities. Technology and improved national infrastructure assisted them; in February 1870 a new railroad bridge was opened across the Ohio River, which meant that for the first time Bloomington products could easily be sent to Louisville and other points south. Rail transport was key to reaching wider markets. Rail service through Bloomington ran only north–south, between Louisville and Chicago, but another railroad intersected the line at Greencastle, running west to St. Louis and eastward through Indianapolis to the Atlantic coast.

RARE
CHANCE!

We the undersigned have bought the entire stock of Furniture of B. F. Rogers. Our stock, together with his, makes an immense stock of Furniture, at least three thousand dollars worth more than is needed in a store in Bloomington, we therefore conclude to sell off about three thousand dollars worth at nearly

WHOLESALE PRICES

At retail. Now is your time if you want Furniture. It is understood that all old contracts and Furniture on time, and for trade, remain at the old regular prices; the above is only

FOR CASH!

Wholesale men can also have a discount from regular wholesale prices. Now don't wait till we get our stock reduced to its regular size, for then this chance will come to an end.

Showers & Bro.

BLOOMINGTON, IND. OCT. 4, 1872.

An early broadsheet dated 1872 shows that the brothers were still selling retail furniture out of a storefront that year.

Accession 4417, collection of Indiana University Archives.

Any of the communities linked by these railways were now potential markets for Showers furniture.

Doing business on a large scale called for marketing and production skills beyond any that the brothers had experienced at Showers & Hendrix. James remembered difficult early experiences in his memoirs:

> I got an order from one man to keep us busy for a while. He wanted all the unfinished (not varnished nor painted) beds we could make, we were to deliver them just as soon as completed. There was no written order—and we were dumbfounded when the buyer went back on his order. Said he was over stocked! Here we were with 300 beds, and a lot of lumber on hand—a lot of money invested in workmanship and no customers at hand!
>
> Necessity drives folks to do things, they say, so Willie told me to get ready and start on a selling trip. He borrowed about $35.00 in cash from some friends and I went to Bedford in hopes of selling some there—but when I went into the store where I had hoped to sell there stood a rival furniture manufacturer trying to make a sale. Times were panicky and the dealer told our rival he couldn't use any beds just then, at any price. Presently our rival left, and I presented my case, telling him about our predicament (tried to make it sound humorous, to ease the lump in my throat). Adding that I believed we could sell him some really good bedsteads at such a price that he could make a small profit on selling them—and we could likewise get our merchandise in circulation. I left with a good-sized order, and that man was one of our very best customers, from that time on.
>
> The next passenger train leaving Bedford was not going out till the next morning. —So, I hopped on a freight train going to Shoals, and had just interviewed a customer and closed sale of a number of beds, when in walked my rival salesman.
>
> He tried his sales luck, but failed. "I guess the early bird got the worm that time"! He inquired which way I was going and I said I wasn't sure, he said he believed business was better over at Cincinnati, and he'd go there.—Well, I went to Washington, Ind. and sold some beds—and then on to Vincennes, but who should I meet in Vincennes but my rival salesman, he had come by passenger train, and I by freighters, and walking it part of the way, occasionally getting a ride by horse and buggy.
>
> By going from town to town, I sold a few beds here & there, after making a circle around in Indiana, I came back by way of Terre Haute and Greencastle.—My cash was gone, but I had orders for all those beds!
>
> When these were delivered and collected for we got busy & made another 300 beds, and sold them, many being re-orders from the previous "300" buyers. Business kept on and we had another piece of luck, an advance order for $1,600 worth of finished beds.[5]

A fanciful depiction of the first Showers Bros. factory shed, taken from the commemorative book *Thoughts Concerning the 60th Anniversary of Showers Brothers Company*, by Dale Dillon. The book's typography and engravings are charming but highly inaccurate.

But advance orders were not a guarantee that the brothers' new business would run smoothly.

Thus far in our business this was the largest order we had ever received, so Willie and me were quite joyful. We got the lumber ready and started the mill up. But to our dismay the boiler would not draw, we figured that the wind was "against it" that day. But the next day there was no wind at all, and still it wouldn't draw—Then we knew disaster was upon us! The boiler pipes had worn out, that meant buying a new boiler!

It was December, and we knew it would take a month to get and install a new boiler, and the ones ordering the beds were in a hurry for them. The biggest problem was the money—It would take at least $500, and how could we get it?

Willie said, "Jimmie you'll just have to go down to the Bank and ask for a loan!" My courage sank, but I mustered my courage & went to see about it—Now the head of this bank was never "on our side" when it came to business deals, and when he heard my request, he lamely replied, "Well, I'm sorry I could have let you have the money yesterday, but I don't have it today."

I left the bank knowing full well he had told me a falsehood; that hurt me worse than not getting the money.

So I tried another plan . . . snatching a few hours sleep, I arose very early next morning, rather it was about midnight—hitched up a horse and buggy and made the long, dark drive to Terre Haute in a December blizzard. My plan was to reach the office of the firm ordering that $1,600 worth of beds, as soon as the men came to the office that morning.

On getting to Terre Haute, I put my horse in the livery stable and went over to the office just as the office boy, Jim Ross, was opening the shutters & getting a fire in the stove. I enquired when his uncle E. W. Ross would come and he said, "Right away," so I was glad to warm myself by the stove, and wait.

Presently Mr. Ross came in, and I explained our situation at the factory, of the boiler's collapse etc. and our inability to deliver the beds on time.

He told me it "was alright," and was sorry we had the misfortune, etc.—"But," I told him, "we won't be able to deliver those beds at all, unless you or someone lends us $500 to buy another boiler!" Personally, I was pretty sure he had the money, and felt fairly sure of my ground, in asking him for the loan.

"What kind of a boiler do you expect to buy" he wanted to know. "We figure on getting a horizontal boiler this time," I told him—"Very well then, if you intend to buy a real boiler instead of another one of those infernal upright contraptions, I'll let you have the money!" So he gave me the money, and my thanks to him were sincere that morning—Then I rode home in the snowstorm to Bloomington.[6]

James broke the news to Belle that he had to leave her alone at home with baby Mattie in order to make an emergency trip to Cincinnati.

> Both of us were uneasy for me to leave so far away, for she was not feeling well. But necessity was upon us and time was precious in getting the new boiler so I finally decided to go, making the trip over the Big Four railroad. Going to the boiler yards of Jonas and Son, I bought a horizontal boiler that had been used slightly. It was out of a river packet or steamboat named the "Sultana." On completing the purchase, and making plans for it being shipped to Bloomington, I boarded the train back to Bloomington arriving home on Christmas morning. That day my boy Charlie, was born!
>
> When the boiler arrived we began installing it. Now to erect a 40 foot smoke stack, made of metal, was no small task in those days. There were no derricks so it was by dint of muscular exertion and ingenuity that we scaffolded up in the air and finished the 40 foot smoke stack. When we fired the boiler, it drawed fine, tho' it was a windy day. So the men set to work willingly, and, in a record time those beds were made and delivered.[7]

An account recorded more than forty years later noted that the firm did $80,000 worth of business in the first year following its initial "stepping out period," which provided the brothers with a net profit of $38,000. This seemed a fortune after their days of counting pennies and paying off debts. This account claimed that Showers Brothers was the only firm in the (Mid)west that manufactured cheap, unfinished beds, and because of this their business grew swiftly.[8]

BECOMING ESTABLISHED

From this point on (early 1871) business appears to have been less fraught with drama. The two brothers worked hard and their business continued to expand throughout the decade. Year after year, every bit of profit the brothers made was turned back into improving the factory.[9] The land around Bloomington abounded with cheap, high-quality hardwoods, but freight costs on the single north–south railroad line were extremely high and prevented the brothers from immediately profiting. "Within seven or eight miles of Bloomington, are hundreds of acres of land, that may be purchased at from five to seven dollars per acre ... upon which is an unlimited quantity of the best hard timber in the county," reported the *Bloomington Progress* in 1870. "If it were possible to get this timber to market without paying two-thirds of its value for transport, the trade from this one item would give our town new life."[10] The paper called for an east–west railroad through Bloomington (something that did not arrive until thirty years later) in order to break the monopoly and lower the costs of transportation. James and William knew firsthand about the quality of the local hardwoods; intermittent deed-book records of purchases outside the city limits show many parcels of land that they purchased and presumably logged. It's very likely that there were many more properties for which they simply paid the landowner for the privilege of cutting trees.

In the spring of 1871 the brothers' fledgling enterprise had its first mention in the local press: the *Bloomington Progress* reported that the Showers brothers had filled an order for nine hundred dollars' worth of bedsteads to go to Terre Haute, which according to the newspaper was a frequent destination for Showers products. By the spring of 1873, the *Progress* noted that the proprietor of the West Baden Springs had ordered twenty bureaus, twenty-two bedsteads, and other "chamber furniture," amounting to an order worth more than five hundred dollars. The proprietor, Mr. Kane, reportedly visited other factories at Connorsville and Indianapolis but chose to order from the Showers company because "he could do better [with them, price-wise] than at either of the other places." This must have pleased the brothers immensely. A contract for a noted spa like West Baden would reflect well upon them when they traveled to other cities to drum up business from other buyers.

The editor of the *Bloomington Progress* at the time, John Walker, was the father of James Showers's good friend John Wesley Walker. This personal connection ensured that the paper was kept up-to-date on the doings over at the new company. Wesley Walker was described in the 1870 census as a house carpenter. Both he and James were professionally linked by their involvement in different types of woodworking, and they were also Odd Fellows. The two had been traveling together when James first met his future wife, Belle.

William Showers poses with "the first bed made for sale."

Courtesy the Helm family.

By the middle of the 1870s the brothers were employing a handful of workers to assist with production. Work was sporadic; their "hands" worked only when an order came in and were let go when business went slack. They occasionally employed boys as young as ten or twelve to do tasks requiring less skill.[11] Nonetheless, by 1876 the brothers had made their mark; they were by that time accepted as prominent citizens and businessmen. They were keenly interested in the public welfare, and both James and William were among the 217 people who petitioned the local government to reincorporate as a city instead of a town.[12] Their factory had ceased doing millwork and was specializing in bedsteads. James was an officer of the Odd Fellows; William was elected to the brand-new city council and served on the city's Finance Committee in 1878. The city council was composed of prominent citizens and leading businessmen; William was now in politics as well as in business. Both of the brothers had young children at home: James's youngsters Mattie and Charlie had been joined by baby Maude; and William's children (in addition to the motherless Jennie) were Nellie and William Edward (later known as W. Edward).

James and William's sisters were not invisible as far as their brothers' growing company was concerned. Although the sisters did not directly participate in the functioning of the company, the husbands and/or children of all four Showers sisters found employment or profited in some way from the brothers' firm. The eldest sister, Sarah, had married John Sears in 1855 while her brothers were still boys; John and his brother had worked occasionally for Showers & Hendrix, and John's son and grandson would work in future years at the Showers company. The second Showers sister, Ellen, had married James Hendrix, C. C.'s former business partner who later worked with James and William. In 1872 the third Showers sister, Annie, married Henry Hewson, who worked for the company in later years in various capacities. In 1874 the fourth sister, Lola, dashed the hopes of many of the local maidens by marrying the handsome and popular John Smith, local jeweler and watch repairman, whom she had met while residing at the National Hotel. (Smith was the shopowner whose late-night revels were frowned upon by the Democratic newspaper.) Smith benefited almost immediately from his family connection by turning his shop into a furniture store that was stocked with Showers-made wares, which could be sold more cheaply than furniture imported from elsewhere that arrived by rail with a hefty shipping charge. For the better part of half

Young Maude with her tricycle.
Courtesy the Helm family.

a century, the Showers brothers' company could more accurately have been called Showers & Extended Family.

This leads to the question of the role of the Showers women. Contrary to modern readers' assumptions that women in the 1800s did nothing but care for children, run their households, and prepare meals, Showers women were extremely active in religious and philanthropic activities and belonged to a number of well-organized groups and clubs that would last for decades in

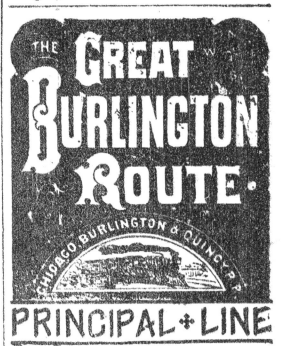

An advertisement for John P. Smith's furniture shop. He could sell furniture cheaply because his brothers-in-law made it locally.

Bloomington. Elizabeth blazed the path for her daughters and daughters-in-law. As early as 1865 she led what appears to have been a Sunday school class for the Methodist Church (this could have been either a children's class or a more demanding adult study group); on December 23, 1872, she recorded in her daybook: "By request of Rev. J. J. Hight I consented to take charge of Class No 2 the Cross seems very heavy but the Lord wonderfully sustains me with increasing admiration." And on February 16, 1873, she added, "Sunday met the class and the Lord was present to bless each one Husband said it was the best class he ever attende[d] to the dear Lord be all the glory." Elizabeth was active in the church-sponsored temperance movement as well as in the Methodist Church's mission society, and her daybook records that she traveled from Bloomington to attend regional conferences in other Indiana communities on behalf of the mission cause. In 1875 she took part in a difficult and demanding outreach mission: by request of the various pastors of different churches in Bloomington, she and several other Methodist women agreed to visit every single household in Bloomington in order to meet and pray with the inhabitants. Her daybook contains records of having visited anywhere from five to eight different families on different dates, each time discussing religion, praying, and inviting the inhabitants to attend church. On December 14, 1875, she wrote, "Sister W and myself visited to day 5 families had Religious worship with them kindly received by all Except the Catholicks they refused letting us pray with them O Soul pity them and bring them into the light." They ultimately met with a total of forty households. In February 1876, after the lynching of the habitual petty criminal "Crook" Mershon at the county jail, Elizabeth lamented his murder by the mob and wrote, "O I see now that we as Professt Christains have not done all our duty to that poor Criminal or we would have tried to gain admission to his cell and pointed him to the Savior the poor sinners Friend that taketh away the sin of the world."[13] She added regular visits to jail inmates to her activities.

Ultimately, Elizabeth's religious and philanthropic outreach wore her out. After a period of increased invalidism, she died in June of 1878, having barely reached the age of sixty. Elizabeth's death was presumably the reason that her ten-year-old granddaughter Jennie returned to live with her father and stepmother. The week after Elizabeth's death, the June 22 edition of the *Bloomington Courier* printed a statement that she wrote in her final days. Because her daybook ends where one or more pages have been torn out, this passage was probably the last she ever wrote. The statement displays the pious sentiments of a minister's wife, expressing resignation at her impending death and the hope of soon entering the kingdom of heaven. She ended by stating, "These few lines I write upon my sick bed. I have no fear of death. My will is in harmony with the divine will. One thing I regret: that my dear children, some of them, are not more religious, but I leave them in the hands of the Lord, hoping to

Another member of the Showers family was also inadvertently involved in the lynching of Crook. Elizabeth's son-in-law John Sears was working as the city's night watchman on the evening that the lynching occurred. Two masked men seized him, stripped him of his gun, and escorted him into the jail, where he was confined along with the jailer. A large band of masked vigilantes had assembled there and soon dispatched Crook with a couple of shots. Perhaps John's eyewitness account of Crook's pleadings for mercy were what so tugged at Elizabeth's heartstrings.

meet them in Heaven, hoping and trusting at last it will be said 'she hath done what she could.'" One wonders which of her seven children were lacking in proper religious sentiments. James and William were faithful churchgoers throughout their lives.

The brothers were not merely "Sunday Christians" but practiced high ethical standards and upright moral dealings throughout each week. They were men of their word; they were helpful to friends and strangers alike in need; they could be relied upon when they committed to anything; and in terms of character they were warm, engaging, friendly, and trustful of others. As a result, they achieved something extremely important during the 1870s, the decade in which they built up their business. From this point on, in whatever they set their hands to, they were completely supported by their fellow businessmen. The goodwill they generated would prove to be their salvation during their darkest days in the next decade.

Chapter

5

THE BOOMING '80S

THE YOUNGEST SHOWERS CHILD, Hull, joined the firm as a partner the same year that Elizabeth died, in 1878, although he was still a teenager. He had a pleasant face with an open, earnest expression, dark hair, and jutting ears. Some accounts claim that Elizabeth Showers gave Hull her interest in the company upon her death,[1] but there is no evidence to support this claim. He may have purchased a partnership in the firm with whatever inheritance he received after his mother's death.[2] The following year, Hull married Maud Ella Coatney on October 15, 1879, two days after his nineteenth birthday. His bride was only sixteen at the time, the precocious and intelligent daughter of a prominent farmer and landowner in the Bloomington area. A plump and pretty blonde, a staunch parishioner of the Christian Church, she was recorded in legal documents as both Maud Ella and Ella Maud. In years to come she would play an important part in the family business. At some point the name "Ella" became merely an initial and she primarily went by "Maud E." The addition of a second Maud to the family (the first was James and Belle's daughter) complicates the narration of the family story, as does the occasional "e" placed by the newspapers at the end of her name. In order to simplify this

Photos taken around the time of the marriage of Hull Showers and Maud Coatney. He had just turned nineteen and she was sixteen.

Courtesy Jim Holland.

narrative, "Maud" will always refer to Hull's wife, while "young Maude" (with an "e") will refer to James's daughter.

By the standards of the day, Hull was getting an excellent start in business and in life, thanks to his older brothers. "Hullie" apparently cut a dashing figure with his youthful marriage and handsome face, his work in politics, and his subsequent construction of an elegant new residence. Curiously, Maud purchased the building lot at the corner of Sixth and Lincoln Streets herself in November 1880, so it's possible that her parents gave her the money as a wedding present. Maud and Hull soon became a notable young couple in Bloomington business and society. When he ordered a studio portrait of himself as a young, well-dressed businessman, Hull did not pose beside an elegant piece of furniture but instead lounged in his three-piece suit on a bale of hay. Perhaps this was meant to represent the family's rise from humbler beginnings.

After Hull joined the firm, the manufactory at Ninth and Grant Streets became known informally as "the Showers Bros. bedstead factory." Business was excellent and the factory employed a score or more of workers. In a town of 2,800 people, it had become one of the largest employers. Frequent orders kept the machines in constant motion. The original shed that had housed the first business was long gone, and the structure that had replaced it was ambitiously rebuilt and enlarged in 1881 using brick. The prolific local builder H. J. Nichols, who was soon to construct the first two buildings on Indiana University's new campus in Dunn's Woods, designed and built the new Showers factory building.[3] The structure now had three stories, a tall chimney, and a metal roof. At the rear, a small frame ell with a shingle roof nestled against the taller brick structure and contained the machine room. Lumber was stored a short walk away, and the steam machines were fed from a nearby cistern that the company had excavated. In the tintype photograph of the factory in this chapter, the image is reversed (a quirk of that particular process) but when enlarged and viewed in a mirror, lettering along the entire street facade of the factory can be seen to proudly announce "SHOWERS BRO'S BEDSTEAD MANUFACTORY." Smaller lettering over the front opening indicates the entrance to the freight elevator; we can see the rear end of a freight wagon backed up to the doorway, heavily laden with crated furniture. At the back, along the roofline of the frame addition, water barrels are perched for ready access in case a spark landed on the wood shingle roof and began to smolder.

Hull Showers, the young businessman, lounges
casually in a studio portrait.

Courtesy Jim Holland.

Hiram J. Nichols and his son John Nichols were architects for two generations of the Showers family. The elder Nichols built significant homes for members of the Showers family throughout the 1880s and constructed some of the first houses in Fairview, the subdivision that was backed in part by Showers money. The younger Nichols in turn built elegant residences in the early 1900s for the next generation of the Showers family. John Nichols not only built for the Showers clan; he actually married into it. His third marriage was to Mabel Dunn, who was the granddaughter of John Sears and Sarah Showers.

The first Showers factory stood just north and west of Ninth and Grant Streets.
This tintype image is reversed, so the photographer would
have stood across the street to the northeast.

Courtesy the Helm family.

"The building . . . when first completed was looked upon as an accomplishment little short of marvelous," an account more than thirty years later remembered. "Friends of the three brothers knew well what extraordinary efforts had been essential to accomplish it. The brick structure was the means of giving employment to from 25 to 40 men and the townsmen had every confidence that the men piloting the growing concern would soon have it forging ahead of anything of its kind in the country."[4] Architectural historian Eryn Brennan points out that the physical form of the factory (brick bearing walls with small sash windows) meant that the interior of the factory would necessarily have had minimal lighting.[5] The city did not yet have electric lighting, so tasks would have been performed by lamplight or by the small amount of window light. The various aspects of furniture construction—cutting, shaping, assembly, sanding, finishing, and varnishing—were performed on different levels of the three-story building. Even if assembly lines had existed in those years, furniture construction is not necessarily conducive to that kind of manufacture. Varnishing and finishing must be kept separate from woodcutting because dust floating in the air will destroy the finish.

The builder who constructed the factory building, H. J. Nichols, also erected Hull and Maud's splendid new home on East Sixth Street. It was a towering two-story Victorian structure with a columned porch and decorative, fine, iron tracery along the rooflines. James and William Showers had known what it meant to live in financial uncertainty and to count every penny while they struggled to bail out their improvident father; they also had experienced frontier life and had missed out on much of their adolescent schooling because they were expected to work like men. Their younger brother, Hull, had completely different experiences. Although he had witnessed his father's humiliating financial setbacks, he never knew a time when the family business did not exist, and as a teenager he was fortunate enough to move straight into his own partnership in his brothers' company, marry a clever woman, and build his own elegant home. He never had to share a tiny cottage, count pennies, and drive buggies through blizzards on behalf of the company. Although he grew up familiar with his father's furniture shop and his brothers' young business, it's not clear whether he himself possessed any particular hands-on woodworking skills; his role at the Showers Bros. bedstead company was assisting with sales calls. Both James and William—but not Hull—were remembered in later years as having often worked in overalls alongside their men; James was the "master mechanic" and William was skilled at lathe turning.[6]

James and Belle's three children. From eldest to youngest:
Mattie, Charles, and young Maude.

Courtesy the Helm family.

Although James's and William's means had improved greatly over the past
fifteen years, they did not yet live in the affluent style that Hull and the next
generation of their family would take for granted. In fact, as recorded on the
1880 federal census, James and Belle Showers and their three children were
keeping boarders like any ordinary family. These included Belle's brother,
Thomas Allen, a cabinetmaker who worked for the Showers company for some

years, as well as five university students. Bloomington still had a marked shortage of residential buildings. Most of the available rooms in town were rented out to lodgers for extra money, even when the owner of a given home happened to be a factory owner. This made simple economic sense: if the bedstead company slowed or shut down for a few weeks between big orders, James still had income from his five boarders that would help with his own housekeeping costs. Anyone who possessed an extra room or extra house in those years could make an easy profit from it. Both James and William would benefit greatly from this lesson in the coming years.

"COASTING ON SHOWERS HILL"

The era of swift expansion for the company coincides with a sudden wealth of information available in the local newspaper record. The scarcity of information on the Showers family throughout the 1860s and '70s suddenly gives way to abundant mentions in the local press beginning in 1881. Many of these mentions were undoubtedly supplied by the Showers brothers themselves, since the newspapers of the day encouraged subscribers to submit their own news. The *Bloomington Courier* announced: "Anything calculated to interest the people of the town or vicinity, that would be a topic or even a subject of common remark, either in social circle or among a cluster of citizens on the street, is of such local significance and consequence as to be gladly received by the editor."[7] The city's newspapers were typically four pages long with about half of one page devoted to local items. This was where readers turned for news of marriages, fires, deaths, illnesses, new businesses, church revivals, and strayed livestock. Most of these one- or two-sentence notes were social—"Mrs. Smith has departed to spend a week in Cincinnati with her sister"—or noted the illnesses of citizens—"Mr. Wilson is suffering grievously from consumption and is not expected to live." Much of the content of the local press was not news at all but nevertheless paints a vivid picture of life in 1880s Bloomington; a brief wintry item published February 4, 1882, in the *Telephone* referred to young folks enjoying "some excellent coasting" on Showers Hill. The land near the factory rose sharply to the west and must have offered a thrill to those who possessed toboggans.

The three brothers, as good Republicans and the owners of a fast-growing local company, enjoyed frequent mentions in the local Republican press, including hearty endorsements for James when he ran (successfully) as city councilman for the Second Ward, replacing William when he stepped down from the council. The frequent newspaper write-ups of the early 1880s also offer valuable glimpses of the young Showers factory. Its success reflected the latest developments of the Industrial Revolution, which was only belatedly penetrating into areas of the Midwest such as Bloomington. Newspaper readers were fascinated with anything having to do with modern machinery and technology. In early November of 1881, Albert Seward placed an electric light atop the courthouse tower, and the following summer the Bell company installed poles and wires and placed the first telephones at the National Hotel, the post office, the Adams Express office, and Dunn & Co. The workshop of Showers & Hendrix had used small-scaled, steam-driven power tools, but James and William Showers needed large factory-scaled machines in order to manufacture mass quantities of furniture. They installed a series of new devices designed to speed the task of making bedsteads. The *Progress* reported that "Wm. N. Showers went to Cincinnati last week to secure a machine that has just been introduced. Showers Bros. are determined to keep up with the times."[8] "Showers Bros. are having the steam heating apparatus placed in their Bedstead Factory. Everything is first class in that establishment."[9] And, "Showers Bros. are putting in a new engine. A visit to the handsome new three-story factory building of Showers Brothers will repay any one. The *Progress* hopes that the Showers Bros. may make a million dollars—they have already made a nice start in that direction."[10]

In those days it was possible for interested people to step directly into factories to look around and to ask questions of the workers and owners. In a humorous mode, the *Progress* reported: "A Bloomington woman who was looking through the Showers Bros.' bedstead factory, last Saturday, was very much interested in the inspirator which is attached to the boiler [apparently a device that keep it fed with water], and was so pleased with the idea of its self-action in drawing the necessary supply of water from the well, that she determined to attach one of these handy contrivances to her husband's mouth so that he might draw his supply of liquor from the nearest saloon without absenting himself from home at night."[11]

Not all of the company's workers were adult men. William "Weed" Shaw began working for the Showers brothers when he was only twelve, which was common in that era. Sons of poor families had no expectation of higher education or of gentle treatment; it was their duty to go forth into the workplace and toil for their keep. Young Weed was put to work at a scroll saw; he was fortunate enough to escape serious injury on the machine and proved himself to be a valuable worker. He would still be employed by the Showers company four decades later, when the 1920 census recorded him as "Sup[erintendent], furniture [factory]," and he held the distinction of being the first Showers employee to hold shares in the corporation (he even made his way onto the board of directors, thus becoming a perfect example of the rags-to-riches paradigm). Many other boys came knocking at the Showers factory door seeking work. One of them was little Johnny Sears, aged only eleven and supposedly barefoot, according to an account written long afterward.[12] (This account did not add that Johnny was a nephew of the owners.) His brother Charlie Sears also began at the Showers company as a boy; both would go on to enjoy lifetime employment at their uncles' factory. Charlie was particularly clever with his hands and was the favorite of his Uncle William; in later years he would eventually work his way up from the machine rooms to become the respected general superintendent of the entire factory.

The factory's distance from the railroad was becoming a significant problem by the early 1880s. The company's production had grown such that it was transporting hundreds of crated bedsteads each week to the rail yards across town, a distance of some ten blocks. The brothers ordered a local builder to create for them an enormous wagon capable of hauling large loads of crated bedsteads, and even this merited a note in the *Progress*: "Showers Bros.' new wagon is a splendid specimen of what can be accomplished in this line by a thorough mechanic. The wagon was designed by James Alexander, the old reliable wagon maker and blacksmith, whose shop is located at the corner of Seventh and Dunn streets. Every piece of timber in the wagon is carefully selected, and the hard wood is of choice second growth. . . . Any individual who may take an interest in this class of work will be profited by giving it a careful examination."[13] The newspaper also reported each of the frequent occasions when William or Hull left town on business trips to secure contracts for the company.

The company was rightly concerned about the ever-present danger of fire. Fire engines were pulled by horses (or men) and were simply mobile pumps with hoses attached. There were no hydrants, and the firemen pumped from whatever water source was available: cisterns, wells, or ponds. An 1881 petition signed by thirty-two "citizens" (business leaders with clout) respectfully asked the city council to pass an order permitting the construction of a cistern on the west side of Grant Street fifty feet south of Ninth, the construction of which would be partially underwritten by the Showers company.[14] This appears to be the first evidence of the company's involvement in obtaining an adequate water supply for the city, a venture that would span the next forty years.

The brothers had built up their business by specializing in bedsteads, but they felt the time had come to include a new item. On November 9, 1881, the *Progress* reported, "The new chair factory building is to be erected east of Showers Bros. bedstead factory. The contract has been awarded to H. J. Nichols, and the factory will be three stories in height, 60 × 40." The newspaper followed this item by calling for lower freight rates for manufacturers; perhaps William or James had expressed frustration to the editor at the continued high cost of shipping their goods. That same day the *Progress* added, "Wm. Showers went to Michigan City last week, and purchased a building pattern entire, dressed and fitted, for the 3-story chair factory, and but three weeks' time will be required to erect it after the material arrives." This was apparently an early example of a building kit. Kits are invariably associated today with those manufactured by Sears, Roebuck & Co., which would arrive pre-cut and ready to assemble, but the concept was not original to Sears and predated their own catalog sales by several decades. The concept of kit building, then as now, was innovative and efficient. The Showers brothers were serious about anything that could save on labor costs. A month later, on December 7, the newspaper reported that the chair factory was being constructed more rapidly than any three-story house ever built in Bloomington. "It will be a success," it predicted. And early the following month, on January 10, 1882, the *Progress* announced, "Chairs manufactured by our own factory are now exposed to sale at John P. Smith's. They are more substantially and smoothly made than those brought to this place from other factories." This new chair factory would soon be supervised by James and William's new business partners and friends, local businessmen John B. Waldron and S. C. Dodds, who had invested money in the enterprise. Although the factory was known as "Dodds' chair factory," the Showers brothers remained co-partners in the enterprise.

The Showers brothers hired both white and black workmen. The two races did not ordinarily socialize freely together in the greater community, yet the Showers brothers appear to have encouraged their workers to do just this. "On Friday last an exciting game of base ball was played by employees of Showers Bros. bedstead factory, between a picked nine of colored men and an equal number of whites. The game was called promptly at 1½ PM and the 'colored nine' went in to win, their score being 20 to the whites 8. Prof. Gray of Louisville was the impartial umpire."[15] The black community in Bloomington was small, so there were only three black workmen at the factory in the earliest days, although more would join the workforce later. These three were George Walker, "Cap" Anderson Johnson, and Jefferson Drake; the latter two would remain steadfast Showers employees until the end of their lives. Relations between the Showers family and the black community of Bloomington were always friendly; C. C. Showers frequently preached for the black Methodists.[16] The Showers company in the 1880s had no idea how long it might endure as a business, but it treated men of both races in an exceptionally kindly manner and offered jobs when the time came to the sons of faithful workmen.

The newspapers commented repeatedly during most of the 1880s on the scarcity of dwellings and rentals in town. The Showers brothers decided to do something about it, as they believed that if their employees were well housed, they would have good morale, work harder, and become better citizens. "On Saturday last Showers Bros. bought of James Ward, his dwelling house, east of their bedstead factory, and seven town lots, for the extremely low price of $1000 cash. It is the intention of the firm to build a number of cottages in the spring, to be rented to the men who work in their factory."[17] This practice of building humble employee dwellings near the factory was presumably the genesis of the small and racially mixed neighborhood between North Dunn and North Grant Streets later called Bucktown. In those early years the area must have presented a striking appearance: a tall brick factory directly on the edge of town, towering over adjacent workers' cottages, with woods and farmsteads visible in the distance. This investment in homes for workers would become a template for decades to come as the brothers continued to buy land and develop it for the benefit of their workers. This would ultimately lead to the creation of building and loan associations that would enlarge Bloomington by adding entire new neighborhoods.

In addition to building homes for their workmen to live in, the Showers brothers provided workers with a standard of living sufficient for at least one employee to insure his new home, a practice that was slowly becoming more common. Insurance was not something that every ordinary workingman took for granted and would have possessed, yet the June 7, 1882 edition of the *Progress* noted that "George Walker, a colored employee of Showers Bros., lost his residence by fire, on Wednesday forenoon of last week. The fire, it is presumed, was communicated through a defective flue. The furniture in the

In the spring of 1896, when the local Republicans (including William Showers, Charles Sears, and Joe Smith) gathered to choose delegates to the party convention, they assembled at the African Methodist Episcopal (A.M.E.) Church in Bucktown and were jeered at for doing so by the *Bloomington Courier.* "The candidates so loved the Colored Brethren that they took up a collection for the church," the paper scoffed (March 24, 1896). The *Courier* was a Democratic paper; the Republican party had opposed slavery and supported suffrage for blacks.

house was saved, but the house was burned to the ground. Fortunately Walker had $300 insurance on his building."

The Showers company and the products it generated were now being noticed by other Indiana towns. In 1882 the city of Greencastle invited the brothers to relocate the business there. An item in the *Greencastle Banner* was reprinted by the *Telephone* with a certain degree of indignation: "If a furniture factory can make money at Bloomington, it ought to much better here, with our east and west railways and other advantages."[18] Several weeks later the *Telephone* followed this up: "This week the Showers Brothers received from the Mayor of Greencastle a letter asking if $10,000 and release from taxation for ten years would be any inducement for them to move their factory to that city. We are glad to re-affirm . . . that it will be no inducement. Evansville offered to erect two large brick buildings enclosed with a lot of five acres if the Showers would move to that place, but the offer was respectfully, but firmly, declined."[19]

The new technology was speeding production and bringing wealth to the company owners, but the machinery that sawed and planed the wood was loud, hot, and extremely dangerous. Any man who worked around this kind of machinery was aware that the probability was high that he would eventually incur an injury. "On Friday last Bill McPhetridge (the house mover) and Andy Gordon, both met with accidents at the Chair Factory," the *Progress* reported on May 17, 1882; "McPhetridge was working at the 'frizzer,' and the revolving knives caught his left thumb and tore it off at the second joint. Gordon then took the machine, and it wasn't long till the two fore-fingers of his right hand were cut off at the first joint." Knowing each of the workmen by name and knowing in some cases a little about their families as well, the Showers brothers were concerned for their well-being. At most factories, when a man could not work due to injury, he received no paycheck. As a response to men being maimed at their factories, James and William organized a laborers' union with themselves as officers.[20] Any workman who paid a dollar a month into the union fund would receive compensation for time lost due to any injury on the job. The brothers also occasionally offered their workforce the incentive of a five-day work week instead of the usual six days if the laborers were able to meet production goals by a given deadline. "As late as 1910—forty-two years after the founding of the business—weekend holidays of this nature were sometimes earned by the entire employee group."[21] Supposedly this practice had its origin in the incentives C. C. offered his sons in the early years to hone their skills and do their work more swiftly. The practice of earning vacation days by meeting production goals early was a Showers company policy by the 1880s (hence the Friday afternoon baseball game mentioned earlier, along with a separate fishing excursion to Bedford that also made newspaper mention). This practice may even have been a company custom as early as the 1870s. A happier workforce was a more stable workforce, and loyal workers would stay on instead of drifting without notice to new jobs elsewhere. Benevolent factory owners were not unknown in the 1800s, but they were not common, either. Capitalists of the Gilded Age were not particularly distinguished by kindness or generosity to their workers, but the Showers brothers were among the exceptions. They appear to have been outstanding men to work for, judging from the large number of men who worked for them for the rest of their lives.

James and William had become humane owners of a thriving business that promised to continue growing for the foreseeable future. They were participants in city government and were on excellent terms with other businessmen as well as with the mayor. Their energetic young brother, Hull, was assisting with landing contracts and making a name for himself in social and political circles. To celebrate their fifth wedding anniversary in 1882, Hull and Maud threw themselves a party at their elegant new house to which fifty guests were invited. During the presidential election campaign in 1884, Hull proudly and publicly hoisted the flag of the Republican candidates on a twenty-foot flagpole atop his home. C. C. had relinquished his other enterprises and was now content to work for his sons as a traveling salesman. His skill with words must have been an asset when making sales. After Elizabeth's death he had married a local widow, Sarah Harrison, and was listed on the 1880 census as a "commercial traveler." But in the late afternoon of January 16, 1882, terrible news arrived by telegraph from Greencastle. C. C. was dead.

Chapter

6

DEATH AND FIRE

C. C. HAD DEPARTED FOR OHIO on the morning of January 16, 1882, on a sales trip on behalf of his sons. Because Bloomington then had only a single train line, which ran northwest toward Chicago, passengers who wished to go east needed to take the northbound train to Greencastle, where they could transfer to the other rail line. C. C. had gotten off at Greencastle with his valise and had some hours to wait until the eastbound train arrived. He walked into the town to look up a friend and presumably found a place at which he could order a meal. Then, drawn by professional interest as a former woodworker, he stepped into a local planing mill to have a look around. It was snowing heavily.

While there, he heard the whistle of a locomotive. Believing that it was his train, he rushed off in the direction of the depot. He hurried through the falling snow with his head down, holding his hand up to the side of his face to ward off the cold snowflakes. The yards of the intersecting train lines were complex and were made more confusing by being blanketed in snow. As C. C. picked his way through the snow on the tracks past a parked train, the prolonged hissing of escaping steam from the nearby engine masked the sound of an approaching express train. C. C. stepped past the parked train and onto the rail directly in front of the oncoming express before he realized his mistake. Either in confusion or resignation, he turned his back on the approaching engine. He was struck and carried along for nearly forty feet. At some point one of his feet caught on an obstruction, and he was wrenched beneath the engine.

"The engine and forward trucks of the baggage car passed over his legs severing one of them and badly crushing the other," reported the *Progress* and the *Telephone,* which ran identical accounts of the tragedy.[1] "Mr. R. A. Fulk and others immediately carried the mangled form into the depot. Here an effort was made to have him speak, but he did not. Once he raised his head and glanced around him and then sank back. He died in about 20 minutes." A telegraph was sent to Bloomington informing the three brothers that their father had been run over by a train and "badly cut up," followed a short time later by a second telegraph announcing his death. William and Hull left immediately for Greencastle on a special train and arrived that night. An undertaker took charge of the body and the next afternoon the brothers returned to Bloomington.

"People seemed paralyzed by the news of Rev. C. C. Showers's death, Monday a week, and only words of sorrow and regret could be heard," reported the *Progress* on January 25. "It was the general topic of conversation. It had been so short a time since he left his friends and family, and seemed in unusually good spirits. He was well-known in Ohio and IL where he solicited orders for the bedstead factory of his sons in this place, and was respected everywhere." His death was marked in the newspapers with expressions of shock and dismay. C. C.'s obituary was far longer than those of any other citizens who had died before him, rivaling that of former Indiana governor Paris Dunning, who had been a leading citizen of Bloomington for years. It seems odd that a man who was scarcely ever noticed by the newspapers in life would be blazoned across their pages in death, but the bereaved brothers were immensely popular and everyone was sympathetic toward them in their loss.

Because obituaries invariably praise the dead and ignore their faults, it was assumed for decades afterward that C. C. was a virtuous and profoundly religious patriarch of the family rather than a man who had once been accused of misrepresenting overpriced mattresses and selling bureaus made of green lumber, a man who had been bankrupted and had a shaky relationship with his own church. But whatever his financial failings, he created a lasting influence on his sons in terms of their work ethic, religious belief, and kindness. His obituary also noted that C. C. Showers "was especially a friend to the colored people and was much beloved by them. They are now among the chief

The elderly C. C. Showers,
taken not long before his death.

Courtesy the Helm family.

mourners of his loss. He frequently preached for them in their churches and was always ready in every other way to lend them the right hand of Christian fellowship." None of the other obituaries of leading citizens of that era made any reference to the deceased having helped people of color, so this small detail shows how unusual it was for white people to treat black people in a kindly and decent manner. It shows also that this was important to the Showers family.

The obituary noted that C. C. had mentioned the day before he died that he had dreamed he was dead, and "was ready to go at any time." On February 15 the *Progress* printed an enlarged account of the premonitory dream that C. C. had experienced two nights before his death. The article was written by the Rev. J. W. Webb and was reprinted from the *Western Christian Advocate*, a Methodist publication. (Rev. Webb was one of several who spoke at C. C.'s funeral.) "Here is the remarkable part of this terrible affair," the account read.

> On Saturday night, at his home, he had a strange and impressive dream which awoke him. He told his wife, and at an early hour told one of his sons, and related it to him. He also told it in Brother W. F. Browning's class, at the church of which he is a member. He dreamed that he suddenly died, and a guide escorted him among high mountains until they came to a deep ravine and large cave, into which a great throng of people were entering. As each one entered and was ordered to advance, he fell on his knees and begged for mercy; but a deep and solemn voice would say it is "too late!" "too late!" "too late!" repeating it thrice to each. His guide told him this was the entrance to hell, and

In 1886, several years after C. C.'s death, the *Republican Progress* printed a list of leading citizen pioneers, "those who laid out and built up the town," who had died during the past nineteen years of the newspaper's publication. Reverend Showers made the list even though he was a relatively recent arrival, having come in 1856, while "pioneers" were regarded as those who had lived in Bloomington since the first decade or so of its existence. Despite the plethora of lawsuits and his bankruptcy, C. C. still could have been an exemplary citizen who, through no fault of his own, was falsely accused by a number of litigious men and suffered economic reverses as a consequence.

they who entered were worldly church members, and that the fault was largely owing to the preachers who preached more to please them than to save souls. The guide told him that this was not his doom, and that he would soon take him to his heavenly home. He was so impressed with this strange, bright vision, that he spent all day Sabbath in reconsecrating himself to God. On Monday he was to start on a trip, and did so. One of his sons was to go that same day to Louisville, on important and urgent business, to be absent a day or two. The father entreated him not to go, saying "William, do not go today." "Why not, father?" said the son. He said, "[D]o not leave home until you hear from me." At this the son promised to remain, and did so. About 5 o'clock that evening he received the dispatch telling of his father's death. This is truly strange, and by many would have been regarded as superstition before the accident, but surely not afterward. The morning he left home he told his wife he knew not where or how soon he should fall, but for her to be assured he was ready. On the train he spent most of the time reading a beautiful Bible, which he carried in his valise, and talked long with an old friend, reading and expounding the third chapter of first John, to prove that one could live a holy life without sin. His favorite theme was sanctification, and had been for seven years. He preached it, talked it, and professed the experience wherever he went. Many thought he made his "hobby" too prominent, but surely it was a splendid hobby for such a death.

If sanctification had indeed been the sole topic of his conversation, fellow citizens who were less devout than C. C. might have grown weary of listening to him. But undoubtedly C. C. was able to converse with many different people about things that engaged and concerned them.

The death notice in the newspaper referred to C. C.'s widow, Sarah. "The bereavement will be the more painful to the widow from the fact that we hear this is the third time she has undergone the suffering consequent upon the sudden death of a husband," it noted. "Her first husband, it is said, was killed by an accident, the second died within a few days after marriage, and the fate of the third is a mournful reality of the present. She will find many sympathizing friends to comfort her in her almost unbearable burden of sorrow." Three times widowed, Sarah never married again. C. C.'s broken body was buried in Rose Hill beneath an obelisk of limestone, with his first wife, Elizabeth, beside him. The couple lies there today in a family plot surrounded by raised curbs of native stone, but most of their children were laid to rest elsewhere.

C. C. left a life insurance policy for $2,000 to be divided equally between Sarah and his three sons.[2] Adjusted for inflation this roughly equals $44,000 in modern currency, or $11,000 each. That was certainly not enough money to get by on for the remainder of one's life, but William, James, and Hull were extremely loyal to their stepmother and helped her out financially, as they always did with their extended family. And Sarah would have needed familial assistance in that era, when women were dependent upon men for support; the 1880 census listed a ten-year-old boy named John Campbell who lived in the household and was described as C. C.'s stepson. John, the child of a former marriage, was probably what we today would term a special-needs child, and in later years he was sent on two different occasions to the asylum in Indianapolis.[3] The Showers family appears to have looked after Sarah to the end of her days. When she finally died in 1910 at the age of seventy-seven, her six pallbearers were all members of the extended Showers family.

With C. C.'s death, an era had ended for the company. The man who had taught his sons to shape wood, to assemble furniture, and to work hard was now gone. But he had imbued them with an excellent work ethic that would guide the family for decades to come. His sons had gratefully received his lessons, applied them with determination and hard work, and were in the process of creating a furniture empire.

One more painful bereavement was in store that summer for James and Belle. In August, their eldest daughter Mattie died of typhoid at the age of fourteen. The *Progress* described her parents as worn out to the point of sickness from nursing her night and day during her illness.[4] The *Telephone* printed

The *Republican Progress* recorded how Sarah made ends meet during the next few years, in a report from March 11, 1885: "James Showers has swapped houses with Mrs. Sarah Showers. The trade included furniture, as Jas. D. had his house furnished and arranged to accommodate 'roomers,' and Mrs. S. intends to make that business a specialty." Renting out spare rooms to boarders was a respectable way for an older woman to make ends meet. There was no provision for retirement pensions for the elderly at that time, and a single older woman needed some form of income to survive on. All ordinary people in the 1800s did something to earn money throughout their lives, until they became too feeble to do so.

a long obituary, which it did not generally do for most children's deaths; but it did so in this case to show respect for a citizen as important as James. The *Telephone* also noted that the grieving parents had sent away to a studio in New York City to have a large framed portrait made of Mattie.

UP IN FLAMES

The most unexpected shock of all fell upon the three brothers two summers later, in 1884. The *Republican Progress* described what happened:

> It was just 4:15 PM, Saturday [August 8], and in Showers Bros. bedstead factory the whirr of machinery and the escape of steam from the heavy boilers could alone be heard. In the office, William and Hull Showers, and James Hendrix were beginning the work of paying the employees. Money was piled up in rows on the table, and as each man was handed the amount due him, it carried with it visions of contentment and plenty at each laborer's home. Suddenly the cry of fire was heard, and the money was hastily swept into convenient baskets, the books were taken from the safes, and the men who were in the office rushed to the west side or ell of the building, only to find that long tongues of flame were reaching out in every portion of the upper story.[5]

The fire began in the attic of the frame ell that abutted the main brick factory and housed the company's finishing department. Sparks from the tall chimney settled on the wood-shingled roof and caught fire. Workmen were

James's two surviving children, Charles and young Maude, looking somber
a year or two after their sister's death. Charles, named for his grandfather
C. C., was already struggling with the early stages of tuberculosis.

*From the collection of the Monroe County History Center, 202 East 6th Street,
Bloomington, IN, www.monroehistory.org, Faces and Places Collection.*

still at their jobs inside and barely had time to get out of the building before the entire structure was ablaze. The building was so packed with combustible materials and various chemicals used for varnishing that once the fire had started, it raged without any possibility of being extinguished. Because the building burned so swiftly, workers had no time to gather up their tools or their coats, and those who were surprised on the upper stories had to escape through the windows.

"An alarm brought the fire department and an immense crowd of people to the factory, when everything possible, under the circumstances, was done to save the building, but it seemed to be filled with flame, and in less time than is required to tell it, the entire structure was consumed, with all of its valuable and costly machinery," continued the *Progress*. "The firemen and citizens worked heroically," the *Saturday Courier* reported on August 16. "It was with great effort that the residence south, and the colored church opposite the factory were saved. Had the latter taken fire, the chair factory, just east, would have been in great danger." And the *Telephone* reported,

> The large number of citizens on the grounds and the fire department were soon at work. For a time they carried out what was moveable in the factory, but this was soon stopped by the nearing flames. In the meanwhile the fire department was using every effort to save adjoining property. The wind had changed and now sparks were flying thick to the south-west, threatening to burn out a block or more. The residence of Enoch Berry, just south of the factory, was in great danger, but water was soon pouring upon it and it was not long till it was safe. In the rear of the factory, to the west, James Manley's barn had caught and also that of William Millen, and to the north large piles of lumber were burning. It was impossible to save either of the stables, but through heroic work the fire in the lumber was extinguished. It required constant work to save the residence of William Millen, that was done by pulling down a part of the stable to keep the fire from spreading. By five o'clock the factory was in ashes, and all danger was over, more than eighty thousand dollars having been destroyed in a single hour.[6]

Toward the end of the conflagration the brick walls of the factory collapsed onto the top of the boilers, which fortunately did not explode, because the safety valves had been knocked open by the falling bricks. Others feared a calamitous explosion of the benzene stored at the factory, but there was less on hand than thought (only three barrels, stored in a pit). Unprocessed lumber was wisely stored a block away from the burning building. Although one or more of the stacks of piled lumber caught on fire at least once, the firefighters managed to quench the flames each time, which kept lumber losses at a minimum.

The *Saturday Courier* summarized the company's progress up to that date:

> About eight years ago the Showers brothers, James, William and Hull, began the manufacture of bedsteads in a frame building where the one burned last Saturday stood. They had no capital but energy, honesty and a firm determination to win. What they have accomplished in eight years is told by the fact that in February last their factory property invoiced $82,000. Besides this each of the brothers have handsome residences of their own. The number of hands employed was from 80 to 100 and upwards, and no employee was ever heard to utter a word of complaint against one of their employers. The Showers boys were always kind and liberal with their men, and to get a job at Showers' was considered to be a very good thing. They have the warmest sympathy of the community, and whatever our people can do for them, as citizens, will be cheerfully done. The employees should not be forgotten. Many are now without means of supporting their families. It should be seen that they do not want for anything, by extending them financial aid, and assisting them in getting other employment.

The newspapers also noted the following: there were over one hundred workers on the payroll at the Showers company; the roof fell in less than twenty minutes after the alarm was issued; all that was saved was the company books and papers along with a few bedsteads; the factory's capacity at the time was between 800 to 1,000 bedsteads per week; and 2,500 finished bedsteads were stored in the factory and burned. "John Beatty went back after his watch and

The city had a single fire engine in the 1880s. Firefighting was problematic, for in the days before telephones, someone needed to run and alert the firemen, who would haul the fire engine to the endangered building. If the streets were deep with mud, the engine often failed to arrive at the scene until the building was hopelessly consumed by flames; on several occasions the engine arrived on time but malfunctioned. The *Telephone* reported on July 8, 1882, that a new fire engine had been imported from Elmira, New York, for testing purposes and had thrown a jet of water almost one hundred feet high before malfunctioning. It threw water over the fish weathervane atop the courthouse tower, and was taken to the three-story Showers factory for testing.

had a narrow escape," stated the *Courier*; "In an adjacent garden, a lot of cabbage, potatoes and apples were roasted." "Bert McGee had his left hand and arm, and his neck terribly roasted, and will be unfit for duty for some time," added the *Progress*. James Showers had been unable to come to work for two weeks owing to a painful and draining abscess on his knee, but when he heard that the factory was on fire, he asked to be driven to the scene in a wagon to witness the scene firsthand.

The *Telephone* offered another instance of the humane treatment of workers by the Showers brothers and the regard in which they were held by their workforce. "The alarm of fire was given just as the hands were being paid, and those that did not get their allowance were asked to come around to William Showers' late in the evening," said the *Telephone*. "As the workmen came in for their pay it was a touching sight, and when it was handed out they pushed it back saying they wanted to give them that much. But William told them they had worked six days for that money and they must keep it. Not one came in but that went away crying. The Showers boys have always treated their men as if they were a part of the firm, so this common sympathy is only natural." The *Progress* observed, "Showers Bros. have built up their business within the past ten years, beginning on nothing. Last January an invoice showed that the factory building, machinery, lumber, and manufactured goods, were worth $90,000, upon which they did not owe one cent. Each member of the firm (William, James and Hull Showers), own good residences, and no three men in Southern Indiana could be more prosperous than the Showers Brothers. There has been a lull in business during the month of July, but within the past ten days favorable contracts had been made and some very heavy orders had been secured."

The night of the fire, a "citizens' meeting" was held after the regular meeting of the Blaine & Logan Club (James G. Blaine and John A. Logan were campaigning on the Republican ticket in the 1884 presidential election, and the club was made up of their local supporters). Despite the name of the meeting, it was not attended by ordinary citizens but by prominent Republican business leaders who also happened to be good friends of the Showers family. During the meeting they expressed sympathy and concern for the three Showers brothers and passed a resolution (mindful of the recent inducements by Greencastle and Evansville) that would encourage the three to rebuild immediately and continue their enterprise in Bloomington. Speakers included the Methodist leader W. F. Browning, postmaster Dr. McPheeters, and business owner J. G. McPheeters. They called on their fellows to meet again on the following Monday night to discuss the best ways of proceeding. The group considered several options, including the possibility of the Showers brothers rebuilding on land south of town that had been given to the rail company along with $1,000 in exchange for promises to build there (which agreement the railroad had reneged upon). Another possibility was suggested: McCalla's planing mill had stood empty for some time and could be easily reconfigured to meet the Showers company's needs.

"Railroad officials . . . were met by the committee appointed at the citizens' meeting," reported the *Courier*. "They said they wanted to hold onto the ground south of town, as they intended building the shops there next spring. The $1,000 cash they are willing to release. They also said that when the Showers brothers rebuild their factory they would make them good rates on their freight. The Showers brothers do not want the ground below town, but ground in the neighborhood of the hoop factory, in the northwest part of town, would suit them. In all probability they will rebuild in that location." By August 27, nineteen days after the fire, the *Progress* reported cheerily:

> On Saturday, Showers Bros. closed a trade for the Graham lots, west side of town, and the deed is to be made today. Three buildings are to be erected for the Bedstead Factory, and work will begin at once. Two of the buildings will be of brick—the third will be encased with corrugated iron. Each building will be 140 feet long, and all the latest improvements in construction and machinery will be adopted. Citizens contributed $1,200 as part of the purchase money for the ground. The east side of town grew and prospered just as rapidly as Showers Bros. business grew and prospered, and the west side will take on a boom just as soon as the buildings for the factory are begun.
>
> Note: It's possible that the $1,000 relinquished by the railroad comprised the major part of the $1,200 contribution, but the record is unclear.

Another item that same day noted: "Showers Bros. are preparing to build two dwelling houses on the old factory grounds, with the brick and stone saved from the burned buildings." The new Bucktown dwellings were now a fifteen-minute walk from the new factory instead of just around the corner. The distance represented the entire length of the small city from east to west. Within the next few years a number of workers would begin to relocate to the west side neighborhoods, closer to their new workplace.

It has passed into Bloomington legend that "the city" assisted Showers Bros. in its move to a better location, but it would be more accurate to say that it was the business community. The city council of Bloomington simply passed a special ordinance to permit a new railroad switch at the new location. (James was a councilman at the time and voted in favor of his own ordinance.) Modest funds for the relocation appear to have been provided by the Showers family's business friends and by the people who subscribed to have their names placed on the Showers ladies' fundraiser quilt, but the biggest help probably came from the hefty loan issued by the First National Bank, which was under the direction of their friend Nat U. Hill. A later newspaper account recalled that

> there was not enough money in sight to rebuild and enlarge, and the Showers Bros. with N. U. Hill and Mrs. Martha Buskirk,[7] for the First National Bank, met to talk it over. Both J. D. and W. N. Showers started on long explanations of the situation and how they had hoped to have a bigger and better factory—now the fire had wiped out all prospects. Before they had gotten through, Nat U. Hill . . . with big tears filling his eyes, replied, "O, you boys are all right: the old First National will back you to the limit and we'll all sink or swim together"—and then they all cried.[8]

The new location on Morton Street facing the railroad tracks was superb for a factory. The fire that destroyed the old factory building was a blessing in disguise, an opportunity for the company to grow faster and larger than the brothers had ever imagined. The insurance settlement would enable them to construct spacious and modern buildings directly next to their freight carrier. On September 3, 1884, the *Progress* reported: "M. D. Griffy & Co. have secured the contract for Showers Bros. Bedstead Factory Buildings. They will be 100 feet apart, three in number, and each 50 × 132 feet. 102,000 bricks and about 70,000 feet of lumber will be used in the construction. The building for the machinery will be on the north end of the grounds; the next building south will be the finishing and varnishing departments; the third building will be the wareroom and shipping department. The firm have enough seasoned lumber on hands to supply their factory during the next twelve months." J. G. McPheeters, the same Republican businessman who had spoken at the citizens' meeting on behalf of the Showers brothers, owned a hardware store and was awarded the $1,300 contract for roofing the new factory buildings with tin, a choice contract, but also a way for the brothers to thank a businessman who had supported them.

On October 9 the new factory buildings were opened with a ceremony that included hoisting a flag to the top of a tall mast, performances by a band, and speakers who made brief comments. "On last Thursday at 4 o'clock the machinery in the new factory on the Graham lots, one square west of College Avenue, was put in motion for the first time, and the occasion was seized upon

Composite photo of the three Showers brothers.
Left to right: James, Hull, and William

Courtesy Nancy Teter Smith.

by the many warm friends of the Showers Brothers as the proper one to show their gratification over the fact that these energetic men were again on their feet, better prepared in every respect to meet the requirements of their rapidly growing business," reported the *Republican Progress* on October 15, 1884.

> The Riley Dramatic Band headed a procession of citizens that marched over to the grounds at 3:30 PM.... The machinery building was then crowded with people curious to see the whirring machines. Everything moved like clockwork, showing that the Showers brothers are complete masters of the situation, let them be placed where they may....
>
> The brick layers finished the last of the three buildings on Saturday evening, and everything will be in running order this week. Providence seems to have smiled upon this enterprise as the weather, usually rough at this season of the year and unfit for outdoor work, has been phenomenally fine, thus enabling the builders to push to completion the work begun only some four weeks ago.
>
> Among all of our acquaintances, the *Progress* does not know of three men more deserving of their good fortune than the Showers Brothers. They are not drones but active workers in the hive, and with sleeves rolled up they lead in every department of work that is done in the factory. Mr. James Showers, the eldest of the brothers, is a skillful machinist and has no superior in this department, while William and Hull give special attention to the general details of the business in sales, shipment, etc.

Two months after their devastating fire, the Showers brothers were back in business, stronger than ever.

Chapter

7

PROSPERITY AND LOSS

HENRY HEWSON, Irish born and a soldier in the Civil War, had married the youngest Showers sister, Annie. He had been a Bloomington shoemaker since at least 1869, as shown by advertisements in the *Bloomington Progress*. An advertisement some years later read, "Henry Hewson, just east of the old Greeves Corner, has purchased a handsome, carefully selected stock of Ladies, Misses and Children's Fine Shoes, and asks an inspection of them before you purchase. Also, best Low Button and Congress Shoes for Men EVER OFFERED in this Market."[1] This all sounded promising—the Showers family was now connected to another Bloomington businessman—but the following month a new item appeared: "Owing to a dull trade, etc., Mr. Henry Hewson, the well known boot and shoe maker, next to the Greeves Corner, has been compelled to close his retail department. His assets are about $1,400, with some $2,400 of liabilities. Showers Brothers hold a mortgage on the stock for $600. This misfortune of Mr. Hewson's does not interfere with his custom business, and he will continue to manufacture the best boots and shoes in Bloomington, for his old customers. Don't forget Hewson when you need something in this line."[2] Hewson had obtained a loan from the First National Bank with James and William as his sureties; in return they had taken a mortgage on his stock and fixtures. He defaulted on his bank loan and then failed to pay off the mortgage within the time agreed upon.[3]

His brothers-in-law actually sued him for foreclosure; the court papers record that Hewson was given notice of the lawsuit and was called three times but "came not." The court found for the plaintiffs and ordered Hewson to pay $829, which included interest and attorney's fees; this represents about $19,500 in today's currency values. The following year, 1886, the *Republican Progress* announced that Henry Hewson would be joining Cyrus Reed as a traveling salesman for the Showers factory.[4] Perhaps he lacked the skills necessary to succeed at sales, for a few months later the newspaper announced: "Henry Hewson and family left Bloomington for Tuscola, Ills., where they will hereafter reside. Jas. Showers bought Mr. Hewson's house."[5] Five months later the *Progress* reported, "The wife and children of Henry Hewson, of Paxton, Ills., are visiting Bloomington friends. Mr. Hewson has not succeeded in Paxton as well as he expected, and is hunting another location."[6] One can imagine how humiliated Hewson must have felt at this public admission of repeated failure. Fortunately, his powerful in-laws were willing to help him out a third time, and in January 1887 he accepted a position as lumber inspector at the Showers factory. He worked in various positions for them thereafter until he retired.

The two elder Showers brothers were both in their forties by this time, but they still took an active part in the work at their factory. After working all day together, they chose to be near each other in their free hours as well and purchased adjacent building lots on North Walnut Street. The brothers hired H. J. Nichols to build them identical homes with large verandas, high ceilings, and imposing staircases. The business was doing quite well and the *Telephone* reported on July 2, 1886, that the company would be running all summer long with a full force of hands and had ordered $3,700 worth of "glass plates" (probably mirrors) from a specialty firm in Berlin, Germany. "This Berlin firm only sells to large manufacturers," noted the *Telephone,* "and the size of the order shows that Showers Bros. are going in the business in earnest." The amount spent on the order equals approximately $87,000 in today's money values. The American mirror industry must have lagged badly behind that of Europe if the company was forced to order from Germany, but the Showers brothers would never have procured glass abroad if it were available at this price in the United States. Approximately twenty-five years later the Showers company would build a glass factory next door to its own plant in order to have easy access to mirrored plates.

James Showers's house on Walnut Street. William's house was identical but is hidden from view on the immediate right. Both houses have been torn down.

From the collection of the Monroe County History Center, 202 East 6th Street, Bloomington, IN, www.monroehistory.org, 1986.077.0196.

The Showers brothers were working with other local business leaders to promote the growth of industry as well as the physical growth of the city. By 1884 the papers were filled with news items about local houses being built; a building boom was happening for the first time in Bloomington history. A front-page article in the *Bloomington Courier* on September 25, 1886, noted that the city was bustling with business and was nearly unrecognizable as the dusty little town of former days.

> The improvements taking place . . . in Bloomington are a matter of fact with our citizens and pass almost unnoticed; but when we stop to consider what rapid strides we have made within the past twelve years the result is surprising. Twelve years ago our Court house was a perfect old rookery. Since then it has been remodeled and greatly

improved by the building of additions, vaults, a steeple with town-clock, slate roof &c. Besides this a handsome iron fence around the yard has taken the place of the old board one, also a hitching rack of iron posts and chains. Some of the other important improvements during the twelve years may be summed up as follows: First of all in importance is the handsome new college buildings; eight new business blocks with large store[s]; several new manufacturing establishments, such as [the] chair factory, Dolan's stave factory, two more flouring mills, a large hub and spoke factory and the extensive Showers Brothers' furniture factory; five new and very handsome churches; another hotel; a city hall and steam fire department; three fine livery stable buildings, a post office furnished with all the modern improvements; several more secret societies; fully five miles of macadamized streets; at least twenty very fine residences; the electric light plant; besides . . . many minor improvements "too tedious to mention."

The Showers company was integral to the economic life of the community at this point as a major employer. The three brothers were pleased to be able to both contribute to the healthy local economy and reap the benefits therefrom. An excerpt from the February 1886 issue of the trade magazine, *The Furniture Worker,* was quoted in the newspaper:

> The recent fire in the extensive bedstead factory of Showers Bros., Bloomington, Ind., even though they lost much money by it, was a blessing in disguise. Mr. J. D. Showers, the senior partner . . . made the following statement: "Before the fire, I thought we were well fitted up, and we ran about 200 men. After our great misfortune in having our factory completely destroyed, I came to Cincinnati, and bought a full outfit of the latest improved machines from the Egan Company. I have been running my new factory for the past six months, and have about 125 men, and I turn out twenty-five per cent. more work and do it better than before the fire. I attribute this great saving to my improved machinery, and the proper handling of it, thus dispensing with many of my cabinet makers, and finishing my work more thoroughly and economically in the machine room." They are now building a large addition to their works for the manufacture of chamber suits. These gentlemen, by close and strict attention to business, have built up the largest trade in their line in the State. Their buildings and lumber yards cover a space of thirteen acres of ground. They are now running thirteen hours a day, and are thirty days behind with their orders. Their sales of bedsteads for the last two months have exceeded 5,000 per month, and we think it safe to say they manufacture the cheapest line of goods in the State.[7]

The same newspaper quoted *The Furniture Worker* on another occasion:

> The factory is situated on seven acres of ground. They have fifty-six thousand square feet of floor room, and for convenience cannot be excelled. Their immense dry-houses, of the latest patents, give them unlimited facilities for drying stock. They have side-tracks running through their immense lumber yards, packing rooms, etc. All furniture

This photo shows the Showers Brothers factory at some point after the original three structures built in 1884 had been joined into one, probably during the late 1880s or early '90s.

Accession 7200, collection of Indiana University Archives.

This fanciful bird's-eye view shows the same building as in the preceding photograph, but enlarged and lengthened for dramatic effect. Carriages, trains, bicyclists, and pedestrians are shown passing through what was actually an unpaved and scruffy industrial area.

Collection C174, collection of Indiana University Archives.

———————————————————

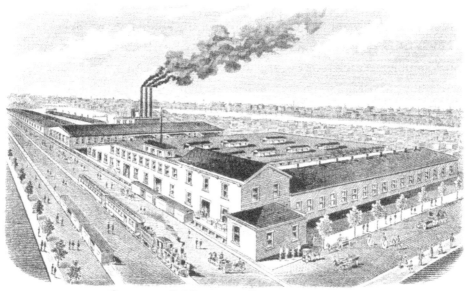

OFFICE · 348 WEST EIGHTH STREET

is loaded on cars set on their own side track for that purpose. When we look back at the past and stop to think that but twelve years ago these gentlemen started with a capital of less than one thousand dollars, we wonder and are lost in amazement. . . . By the books of this firm we see that they have shipped, in the eight months just past, 30,312 bedsteads, and 8,673 bureaus, dressers, and wash-stands. We think the little city of Bloomington very fortunate in having the wide awake and enterprising Showers Bros. as citizens. Well, good luck, boys, and may you live long and continue to prosper.[8]

However, during the mid-1880s, relations between manufacturers across the nation and their workforce began to fray. Although the Showers factory continued to shut down intermittently in order to give the employees some well-deserved rest time after meeting production goals ahead of schedule, there are hints of unhappiness on the part of at least some of the industrial workers of Bloomington. A wave of labor protests swept the nation beginning May 1, 1886. The Haymarket Riot in Chicago a few days later on May 4 became a turning point in the labor movement. Police at Haymarket Square attempted to break up a labor protest when an unknown person in the crowd tossed a dynamite bomb at them. Enraged by the blast, the police then fired upon the crowd. The event inflamed workers across the nation and made many employers assume that there were sinister connections between strikers and anarchists.

On May 11, 1886, one week after the Haymarket Riot, the *Bloomington Telephone* ran a lengthy article describing an attempt to form a local chapter of a national workers' union called the Knights of Labor, explaining the union's rules and aims. "Any female of the age of sixteen, or any male of the age of eighteen, whether manufacturer, employee of any kind, wage-worker or farmer is eligible to become a member of the Order, EXCEPT lawyers, bankers, professional gamblers, stock brokers, and any person who either makes or sells, or derives any part of his support from the sale of intoxicating drink," explained the unknown organizer for the Knights. The group's goals were to "advance the interests of the wage-worker, morally, socially or financially," and also "to abolish as rapidly as possible the wage-system, substituting co-operation therefore" and "to educate its members to an intelligent use of the ballot." The Knights were also opposed to monopolies involving land, transportation, currency, and anything else that would affect the interests of the masses. Unsurprisingly, the Showers brothers found the idea of a socialist workers' union to be deeply threatening. "The Showers Bros. . . . believe the order of Knights of Labor can do their workmen no good in any way and have so informed them. At 4 o'clock Tuesday evening all the hands were ordered to stop work and report at the office. This was done at once, when Wm. Showers explained to the workmen that the company had always refused to combine with other organizations and they would ask of the workmen the same. Here a petition was presented for the workmen to sign that they would not become Knights of Labor, and without exception it was signed."[9]

The *Republican Progress* reported, "The Showers Bros. have entered into an agreement with their employees to keep out of the manufacturers' union if the employees will refuse to join the laborer's union. This looks fair."[10] The "manufacturers' union" mentioned in the article was the Knights of Capital, a loose national confederation of factory owners that had formed in response to the Knights of Labor. Factory owners who participated in this federation kept a blacklist of workers who were known to have joined a union, in order to refuse employment to those men if they applied for a job elsewhere. The 1880s were not easy times for workingmen, and the new unions were agitating nationally for an eight-hour working day. But the prospect of shorter working hours did not please factory owners, who had known only an era in which men worked six days a week for ten to twelve hours each day. William, James, and Hull must have felt they were already accommodating their workforce sufficiently through their various incentives. The elder two brothers may have felt aggrieved and affronted, reflecting that they themselves had endured long hours of manual labor with their own hands while establishing their business. They saw little reason why the new generation of workingmen was not willing to do the same. The *Telephone*'s editorial on July 9, 1886, could easily have been written by a Showers brother instead of the publisher:

> I am glad that the effort to organize an assembly of the Knights of Labor was a failure; it could not possibly have worked any good to our workingmen. Contented labor is better than discontent and if left alone the first is almost certain to be the result; if a man is contented he is as wealthy as if he was a millionaire. In a place the size of Bloomington, where [there] is so much work to do, the competition for labor keeps the prices up and no organization of any kind on the part of laboring men could change the rate of wages one iota. Strikes and boycotts can not be defended; the courts are now ruling that boycotting is the same as blackmail and those who participate in them are being imprisoned. I think no one will disagree with me that in the time men strike they lose ten times as much as if they had kept on working.

The immediate threat of a workingmen's union dissipated in Bloomington, and it would be another half-century before the specter of strikes would return to haunt the company.

There were far more pleasant things to think about at that time, for in June 1886 William's eldest daughter, Jennie, married Joseph M. Smith, the son of local businessman Tobe Smith. Because the Showers family was by this time considered to be "society," the newspapers covered the wedding closely. The ceremony was held at the Walnut Street home of William and Hanna Showers, who had thrown open their two largest rooms for the occasion and decorated them with flowers. Jennie wore cream satin with lace and her cousins Laura and Nellie Hendrix served as her bridesmaids. The 8:30 PM ceremony was followed by a feast that did not end until late that night. The newspapers printed the entire list of gifts to the new couple. The most magnificent gift was given by William and Hanna Showers, who presented their daughter and new son-in-law with a handsome new house. The parents of the groom, Tobe Smith and his wife, provided all the new furnishings inside the home. James and Belle Showers gave their niece a new stove (an expensive item in those days); Jennie's Uncle Hull gave "a fine sofa" and his wife Maud gave a hand-painted toilet set. W. F. Browning, who had been the close friend and associate of the Rev. C. C. Showers, presented the couple with a large Bible. Many of the extended family's gifts were quite modest: Jennie's Aunt Annie (Mrs. Henry Hewson) gave a sofa pillow while her little daughter Bessie presented her cousin with a pincushion. Aunt Lola and the Rev. C. C.'s widow, Sarah, each gave a pair of towels, and Aunt Ellen Hendrix gave a set of twelve napkins. Jennie's teen-aged cousins Charles and young Maude, the children of James and Belle, each gave a rocking chair.[11] The combined Showers and Smith families all set out afterward for Cedar Lake for hunting and fishing.

Early that September Hull and Maud's third child, Clide, was born. "Hul. [*sic*] Showers in obedience to the scriptural command to increase and multiply, has written a new name in the family record," reported the *Republican Progress* on September 8, 1886. But the family's happy times did not continue for long. In mid-December Hull came home from work with a sore throat. Over only a few days, his throat grew worse and his tonsils became infected, resulting

H. J. Nichols built this substantial house on the southwest corner of Sixth and Lincoln Streets for Hull and Maud Showers. The site is now a parking lot.

Accession 7200, collection of Indiana University Archives.

Two of the Showers siblings married two Hendrixes; likewise, two of the Showers married two Smiths. Jennie was the second Showers woman to marry a Smith; her Aunt Lola had married Joseph's Uncle John P. Smith in 1874. He ran a furniture shop and also a jewelry and watch repair shop. Jennie and Joseph had grown up close to each other during childhood because of the friendship of the two families, and their marriage formed a second link between the Showers family and the Smiths. The Showers family would eventually ally itself to several more of the leading commercial families of Bloomington as well as to two physicians.

in the condition known as quinsy. A high fever developed; he was far too ill and weak to go to work, and for several days he remained in bed with Maud anxiously tending him. His infected tonsils swelled to a point where he could barely swallow or breathe, and pneumonia set in. The newspapers covered his illness and reported darkly that because a brief rally had been followed by deeper illness, he was not expected to live. Reverend Peak of the Christian Church came by the house several times during his illness to visit the sick man; Hull was unable to speak but painfully whispered, "Pray for me." But prayer was useless by this point, and drugs that could counter his condition would not be available for another sixty years. Early in the morning of December 15, 1886, Hull died, aged only twenty-six. In addition to his bereft wife Maud, he left behind their two little children, Erle and Beryl, and the three-month-old baby, Clide, who himself was dangerously ill with whooping cough at a time when all the adults around him were distracted with grief.

The Knights of Pythias, of which Hull had been a member, took charge of the grand funeral at the Christian Church that Hull and Maud attended. "The remains were encased in a handsome metallic casket, heavily trimmed with silver, and looked so natural that the dead appeared as if he had only been over-taken in peaceful sleep," the *Telephone* reported.[12] The Showers factory was closed in memory of its young partner, and ninety members of the Knights of Pythias accompanied the coffin to the cemetery on foot, joined by a hundred or so factory workers and countless private carriages.

The day before his death, Hull had summoned his lawyer and made a will that left his one-third interest in the Showers company to his wife, Maud. The young woman needed time to adjust herself to the new realities of widow-hood and single motherhood, but she was now one of the wealthiest women in Bloomington. The Showers company conducted an inventory to assess the value of its debts and liabilities; her one-third share was reckoned to be more than $27,000, which is approximately $637,000 in present-day values. Maud was about to do something that was a great step forward for a woman at that time. The Monroe County History Center has preserved a partnership docu-ment from the Monroe County Circuit Court that reads, in part, "Ella M. Showers proposes to become an equal partner with said surviving partners in the business of said firm, and to put into said new firm the share of her deceased husband . . . said new firm to assume and pay all the liabilities of the old firm." William and James apparently welcomed the partnership since they did not buy out her share; they knew that an intelligent partner is an asset, regardless of gender. Even if Maud were nothing more than a silent partner, the new arrangement was not merely a case of the Showers men wanting or needing her money. Maud was a born organizer who possessed good financial sense.[13] Although it's not known whether or not she took an active hand in the company's management, it's very likely that she contributed her opinions. She would remain an integral part of the company for the next twenty-six years, serving later as vice president of the board of directors after the company incorporated. And Maud proved her many merits by becoming soon thereafter one of Bloomington's most prominent women.

MAUD TAKES CONTROL

Maud Ella Showers had married Hull at the age of sixteen. His death left her a widow at twenty-three, the single mother of three young children, and in possession of a considerable fortune. One might assume that Maud, a farmer's daughter who had received limited formal schooling and who had taken up housekeeping and family life at such a young age, would lack intellectual development, but she was to prove herself superior to most Bloomingtonians of her day in terms of personal growth, organizing talent, and philanthropy. She

The company assets following Hull's death in 1886, recorded in the collection of the Monroe County History Center, included shares in the Monroe Building and Loan Association and the Working Men's Building and Loan company; a half interest in Dodds' chair factory worth $6,500; factory buildings and machinery assessed at a value of more than $18,000; large amounts of itemized types of hardwood lumber; a team of horses, feed, and stabling; various real estate; five railroad cars; a section of railroad track; and finished furniture. Liabilities included more than $5,600 in unpaid bills and promissory notes to James Hendrix and Cyrus Reed. The total value of the assets of Showers Bros. at that time was $81,573.60, equivalent to more than $1.95 million in modern currency.

was not a Methodist like the rest of the Showers family; instead, she was active in the Christian Church and associated herself with its missionary work and temperance campaign. Maud was a member of many different women's clubs; but before the reader imagines a group of ladies gossiping over their teacups, a word about these clubs is necessary. The 1880s and '90s witnessed an immense proliferation of clubs in Bloomington for men and women both, and this was a national phenomenon as well. The city's newspapers of that era are filled with countless items about the meetings of the Commercial Club, the Good Time Club, the Ladies' Foreign Missionary Society, the Oolitic Club, the YMCA (at that time more an uplifting religious organization and less a provider of gymnastic facilities), the Women's Club, the Commercial Club, the Monday Afternoon Club, the Wednesday Club, and Sorosis, among many others. These clubs, along with secret societies such as the Masons, the Odd Fellows, the Red Men, and the Elks, plus the various church societies, were the means by which citizens met, mingled, discussed ideas, and accomplished things. Social organizations were the most significant way that people took part in networking, and the importance of these groups is not to be underestimated. Bear in mind that after the fire of 1884 had destroyed the Showers factory, funds to help relocate it had been raised by members of a club composed of Republican businessmen. Membership in clubs like these was how a person engaged with his or her peers, and every active citizen in those days belonged to a number of different clubs.

Maud was a progressive who was deeply committed to improving society and bettering women's lot. She made lifelong friends and valuable connections through her activities in various women's clubs. By the age of twenty-two she had become closely involved with Bloomington's Equal Suffrage Club, which was composed of thirty or forty local ladies. This was a significant number in a small community like Bloomington and is evidence that the town was paying close attention to national progressive causes. At the time that Maud became involved in the suffrage movement, women in the United States—except for the few who lived in the Wyoming Territory—had no right to vote. The suffrage movement throughout much of the 1800s and early 1900s was also linked closely with the temperance movement. In an era when alcoholic men often abused their wives and children and destroyed their families' economic stability, many women believed that female suffrage combined with reduced alcohol consumption would dramatically improve and enhance the quality of American life.

Through club membership Maud learned to address groups, engage her listeners, and convince them of the value of her stance. In February 1887 the Equal Suffrage Club and other similar clubs around the state submitted petitions to Indiana's Senate and House of Representatives, calling on them to enact a law that would allow Hoosier women the right to vote in all municipal elections in towns and cities. (If reported correctly by the newspapers, the suffrage proposed would not have applied to federal elections.) When modern readers think of the suffrage movement they tend to envision white-clad ladies who marched with banners in the early twentieth century and went on hunger strikes while in jail, but the suffrage movement of the 1880s was so powerful that in 1887 a proposed constitutional amendment that would have given women the right to vote actually reached the United States Senate and was heatedly debated. In her new capacity as a co-partner of Showers Brothers, Maud solicited signatures among the working men of the factory for the Equal Suffrage Club's petition. James and William must have supported the cause of women's suffrage or they would not have allowed their female junior partner to enter the factory to pass around her petition. Impressed by Maud's eloquence, or perhaps merely concerned for their jobs, all but one of the 131 workers signed the petition. It is not known whether the refusal of that one man to sign Maud's petition did any lasting harm to his employment at the factory.

Members of the Equal Suffrage Club wore yellow ribbons, the badge of the suffrage movement. The group scheduled public lectures to dramatize their cause; speakers included the president of Indianapolis's Equal Suffrage Society, Mrs. Zerelda Wallace. This active old lady was a prominent feminist and lecturer as well as the stepmother of General Lew Wallace (author of *Ben Hur*). In May 1887 Maud traveled with other members of the club to Indianapolis to attend the state Equal Suffrage convention, where she was introduced to other influential suffragists and feminists.[14] Soon thereafter the club threw a celebration to observe its first anniversary, to which sixty invited guests showed up to enjoy conversation, ice-cream, and cake. In November of that year the famous Susan B. Anthony and many other women activists came to Bloomington to attend a suffrage conference hosted by the club; several of them stayed at Maud's home.[15]

In December 1887 Maud suffered another loss: her baby Clide sickened and died, almost a year to the date of his father's death. Although mourning, she was too engaged with her mission to drop from sight for long. In April 1888 Maud went farther afield for the suffragist cause, traveling to Washington to

Susan B. Anthony was elderly but still active at this time. She visited Bloomington at least twice; the second time she spoke as part of the effort by Hoosier women to lobby the state legislature to grant votes to women. "A half century hence in turning back the leaves of time, those looking up [the] history of woman's suffrage in Indiana will find that the first general convention of women in Monroe county was held in Bloomington on the 10th and 11th of November, 1887," the *Telephone* wrote on November 15, 1887, noting Anthony's appearance. "At that time it will be as much a wonder that we moved so slow as it is remarkable to-day that in 1840 it was not considered proper or right for a woman to attend a public meeting of any character."

attend the opening convention of the brand-new International Council of Women, which was attended by all the leading feminists of the day, including Susan B. Anthony, Elizabeth Cady Stanton, and May Wright Sewell. It must have been an exciting moment for Maud to stand in the same room with so many prominent women who had devoted their lives to changing the essence of American culture. This was in fact an epochal event, for the fledgling organization would thrive in coming years and in fact still exists today, with a website in three different languages. The *Republican Progress* understood the significance of the international convention and gave it detailed coverage that included portraits of each eminent speaker and a digest of their remarks.[16] This long and careful article was mailed back to the Bloomington newspaper by Maud herself, for the newspaper printed an item on April 4 that read, "The *Progress* is under obligations to Mrs. Maud Showers, who is in Washington City in attendance upon the Equal Suffrage Convention, for interesting papers published at the National Capital." It is quite possible that Maud wrote the article.

Bloomington's Equal Suffrage Club focused its gaze not just on women's rights but also on Bloomington's civic beautification. The group petitioned the county commissioners to remove unsightly obstructions that included signs, agricultural implements, and the privy from the courthouse lawn; they were successful in eliminating all of these objects except the essential privy. The Suffrage Club seems to have disbanded once it was evident that the national move for a suffrage amendment had failed, and the tasks of civic beautification were picked up by the new Local Council of Women. Maud moved from one group effortlessly to the next, never stopping her work to improve Bloomington. But not all her involvements were political: she regularly hosted church socials and was also very much interested in civic, artistic, and dramatic events. She took her two remaining children, Beryl and Erle, on vacations to Cedar Lake and to Bethany Park, a Chataqua-type summer community near Martinsville, Indiana, that was run by the Christian Church and on whose board of directors she served for several decades. She purchased a little cottage at Bethany Park and stayed there each summer for many years. The fledgling incarnation of the Bloomington "Y" (it's unclear whether it was the YMCA or the YWCA) met regularly at Maud's home for discussions.

In May of 1888 Maud became the first woman to address a Bloomington organization. This came about because Maude had joined the Bloomington Real Estate Association, which her brothers-in-law had co-founded with other local business leaders. The Real Estate Association celebrated the first anniversary of its founding with a luxurious banquet at the National House hotel, accompanied by music provided by the Bloomington Orchestra. After sampling a menu that included beef à la mode, fricandeau of minced veal, boned turkey, lobster salad, wine jelly, tea biscuits, French rolls, fig cake, lemon cake, silver cake, strawberries, oranges, lady fingers, and French kisses, toasts were made, followed by addresses. J. C. Dolan rose and teasingly stated that "the ladies present were not aware that they came pretty near not being there," but after examining the bill of fare the men had decided that their wives ought to be invited as well in order to help enjoy the delicacies. This was droll, since the members' wives presumably furnished much of the fare on the table that night. Maud Showers humorously replied that the only reason the men had invited the ladies "was because they had heard that their wives were going to get up a banquet of their own."[17] Although her reply was light-hearted and short, no other woman before this night had ever been recorded as speaking before a Bloomington business group, and the newspaper faithfully reported it.

As a leading citizen of Bloomington, Maud was constantly mentioned in the newspapers; she received coverage that was almost equal to that of her brothers-in-law James and William. Bloomington was no longer a sleepy, old-fashioned town but was moving into the dawn of the modern era. Women in Bloomington were riding bicycles and were frolicking at the new roller skating rink. More importantly, they were attending Indiana University in growing numbers. A small number of women were even seeking law degrees or medical diplomas. Any woman who was as vigorously active in social and civic groups as Maud was no longer expected to have her name published in the newspaper only when she married or died, as was the old custom. Maud was written up in the newspapers in a less welcome connection when she and a woman friend were robbed as they walked along the courthouse square, as the *Bloomington Courier* reported on October 19, 1889:

> Last Saturday night as Mrs. Maude Showers and Mrs. O. B. Clark were on their way home from the [horticultural] fair, about 10 o'clock, as they were passing the alley by the old Christian church, a boy dashed out and snatched Mrs. Showers' pocket book from her hand, and quickly disappeared. The cries of the ladies brought Charley Mobley to the spot but the young thief had made good his escape. He had no doubt seen the ladies at the Fair, and lay in wait for them. The pocket book contained about $23.00. Two boys, by the name of Hendricks and Mershon were arrested upon the charge, and had their preliminary trial before the Mayor Tuesday. They were bond [sic] over to court in the sum of $300, and upon failure to give bond were placed in jail. It is thought that there were four who took part in the robbery and it is likely that other arrests will follow.
>
> *Note: $23 in 1889 would be the equivalent of more than $500 in today's currency.*

Mershon strongly asserted his innocence in the matter. This was the second time the Mershon and Showers families had intersected. This boy was a relative, probably the son, of the incorrigible "Crook" Mershon who had been lynched a decade earlier at the county jail. This man's abject death had inspired Elizabeth Showers to begin making visits to prisoners in order to pray for them. In this particular case, young Mershon was eventually acquitted of the robbery while Hendricks was sentenced to two years.

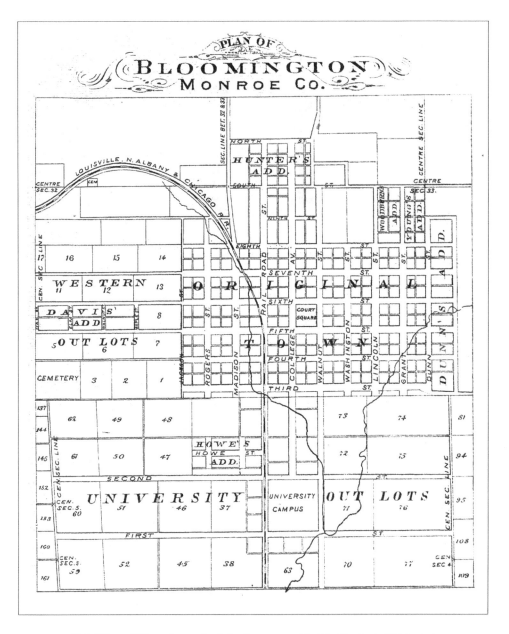

This "Plan of Bloomington" originally appeared in *The Illustrated Historical Atlas of the State of Indiana 1876* published by Baskin, Forester & Co.

From the Maps Collections of the Herman B Wells Library at Indiana University, Bloomington.

Chapter

8

BOOM AND BUST

THE SHOWERS BROTHERS were involved with their own progressive alliances. James and William were committed to modernizing Bloomington and enhancing its economic vitality in order to attract immigration and outside investment. William took Hull's place on the board of the young electric company; James joined the new waterworks committee. And both brothers helped to launch the Bloomington Real Estate Association, which specifically addressed the perennial shortage of housing for workers. For years the newspapers had complained about the lack of housing, noting that it was so scarce that anyone who built a new house would be able to rent it out with no trouble before it was completed. The Showers family's activities in this area would soon transform Bloomington.

The Real Estate Association was a win–win situation for the businessmen backers and the workingmen who borrowed money to build cottages. The wealthy men received a good return on their money and the workingmen moved out of the boarding houses and became property-owning citizens. It was easy to make money in those years by addressing an obvious need. Real estate development—creating all-new neighborhoods where farmsteads used to be—yielded much more money than simply renting spare rooms to boarders or constructing individual houses here and there on existing vacant lots. As employers, the Showers brothers were happy to have their workers buying homes because it created a larger pool of "steady" men to hire from, men who would not walk out on a job if they had a house they needed to make payments on. Workers' housing, the brothers felt sure, would have a beneficial impact upon local industry by stabilizing the workforce.

"The Bloomington Real Estate Association is frequently disposing of some good building lots," observed the *Saturday Courier* on September 29, 1888. "It is the best opportunity we know of for a poor man to get a home, as they not only sell property but are connected with a Building Association which loans money on the property, and thereby gives a poor man a start." It was now possible to obtain lots for a small down payment and only a few dollars a month. Lots cost from $300 to $350, depending on location (about $7,770 in modern currency values). The Bloomington Real Estate Association purchased open land south of the city from Showers Brothers' partner in the chair factory, Mr. S. C. Dodds, and divided it up into lots. This addition, South Park, was Bloomington's first subdivision, located at the southern end of Walnut Street on the outskirts of town, a short distance from the old university campus. The lots were sold at a widely publicized auction; one of the purchasers was Tom Allen, a woodworker at the Showers factory and brother-in-law to James Showers.

South Park was only the beginning. "A syndicate of capitalists—Collins & Karsell, Louden & Rogers, R. C. Greeves and James Showers—have purchased the property of J. C. Whisnand and James Williams in the northwest part of town for $6000 and will plat the twenty acres included in this purchase into lots," reported the *Republican Progress* on May 4, 1887. "The ground will make about one hundred lots, its location is high and very desirable, and the syndicate will make a good profit, besides furnishing good homes to many mechanics and laboring men." This northwest neighborhood on high ground was dubbed "Fairview" by the association. The architect H. J. Nichols, who had constructed the Showers Brothers factory at the old location, secured the contract to build the new workingmen's homes. (A number of the sturdy houses built at that time along the south side of Seventh Street still stand to this day.) Real estate development became heated as other businessmen followed suit and invested their money in new houses. Another new neighborhood was Maple Heights, located northwest of the Showers factory, on a hill overlooking the railroad and the factories below. This was offered by the Bloomington Improvement Company, one of the six real estate associations

"Cottage Row" on South Walnut Street. Although these are called cottages, they are upscale examples, as shown by the architectural trim. These homes typify middle-class housing in Bloomington during the boom years of the 1880s–1900.

Accession 7200, collection of Indiana University Archives.

that sprang to life around that time. Bloomington had entered a sustained period of impressive growth. Kenwood, on North College Avenue, was the next development, offering larger and more expensive lots sold by an out-of-town investment consortium.

The move to "boom the town" succeeded wildly. Even though hundreds of new homes sprang up like mushrooms, there were still not enough to accommodate the large number of people who were flooding into town. Bloomington's factories ran constantly and the sound of carpenters' hammers never stopped. Most of the new houses that were built were located on the west or northwest fringe of the little city, since growth to the east was blocked by the double obstacle of Indiana University and the surrounding Dunn farm. Wealthy homeowners purchased expensive lots and built gracious homes along Walnut Street and Kirkwood and College Avenues, and choice new lots were sold and developed on North Washington Street by the Showers brothers themselves. Beyond this central core district were the areas where the families of ordinary workmen lived George Walker, the black worker at the Showers company who had been noted in the newspapers for losing his home to fire but insuring the contents, sold his Grant Street home in the Bucktown neighborhood and moved to a new home on the west side in Fairview in order to be closer to his place of employment. Around that time Walker was listed in the paper as being one of the officers of an otherwise all-white building association;[1] he was obviously a prominent citizen of color and was also noted in the press for his musical ability[2] and his talent at cooking.[3] Walker's relocation to the west side was soon followed by a much larger entity: Dodds' chair factory, which had stood across the road from the original Showers factory building. It had not been harmed by the 1884 fire and had continued production under combined ownership of the Showers brothers and their friend and fellow investor S. C. Dodds. Nevertheless, it had suffered from the same problem that had bedeviled the Showers bedstead factory: the physical distance from the railroad. Any first-rate manufactory needed to be located alongside the railroad tracks. The chair factory finally relocated in 1892 to a new address along the railroad tracks in Maple Heights, a short distance northwest of the new Showers Brothers factory.

> The chair factory plant, just north of Showers Bros. furniture factory, has changed hands. One-half of it was owned by Showers Bros., and the other half has been purchased from S. C. Dodds. The inventory of the chair factory amounted to $31,000. It is understood that the manufacture of furniture will be conducted in the old chair factory and a quantity of the latest machinery will be purchased at once for it, and a dry kiln will be added. The newly arranged establishment will do business under the name of the "North End Furniture Company," and it will be placed in charge of [James's son] Chas. T. Showers, a competent young business man. Mr. Dodds has real estate and stone quarry interests to look after that will occupy his time, and this is given as his reason for disposing of the factory, which has always done a satisfactory business.[4]

Satisfactory indeed; on April 1 of the previous year the *Republican Progress* had noted that the chair factory had shipped an average of one rail car filled with completed chairs and tables every week. The Showers brothers and their sister-in-law Maud now controlled two separate factories.

A description of the bustling main Showers factory at this time is provided by the *Republican Progress,* April 9, 1890:

> While in the northwestern portion of the city last Wednesday the Progress stopped at the bedstead and bureau factory of Showers Bros. for a brief visit. This immense establishment has been described so often that it is useless to go into many details, yet

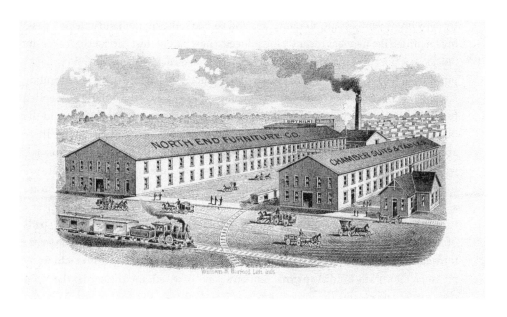

This trade card shows the short-lived North End Furniture
Factory, with the factory on one side of the card and
decorative graphics on the other side.

Courtesy Nancy Teter Smith.

the new improvements are so numerous and so marked as to demand at least a passing mention. The firm has recently introduced a new patent dust carrier that takes the blocks, saw dust and shavings from each machine and carries them into an immense pipe through which they are conveyed to the furnace, and fed into it in a never-ending stream, making the labor of the engineer comparatively light. The buildings are piled full of bedsteads, bureaus and washstands in various stages of completion, and the machine rooms are crowded with hurrying, busy men who work on the jump. There are 137 men on the pay roll. The engine, a Corliss, is as handsome as a picture, and works without noise or jar, while everything about the buildings (of which there are four or five) gives evidence of the watchfulness of the careful competent men who are at its head—Jas. D. and Wm. N. Showers. While in the factory that day there was a furniture dealer in the warerooms from Nashville, Tenn., who bought five car-loads of manufactured goods from Wm. N. Showers. One of the new machines recently introduced takes the place of the men who used to carve by hand—this machine, by pressure, makes any kind of an ornament on a panel of wood, and the harder the wood the sharper and clearer the impression, and it is done on a five foot board while you could count five. It will give the reader an idea of the business done by this firm when we state that during the year 1889 the firm of Showers Bros. shipped from this station 727 car-loads of their manufactured goods.

The family leadership at the company was subtly altering. Charles T. Showers, James's only son, had attended business school and had grown up knowing that he was destined to take his father's place in the family business. His younger cousin, W. Edward Showers (William's son) was still a teenager at this time and had hopes of going to medical school. By 1892 Charles was a young married man with a pregnant wife, living in a house that had been built for him and his family on North Washington Street directly behind his father's lot on North Walnut, eager to take the reins of the newly relocated chair factory. His close friend Harry Orchard was accountant at the company and the two spent much time together, both at work and outside the company walls. Charles was assisted at work by Sanford Teter, a handsome, hardworking, and intelligent young man who rose swiftly in the management of the Showers company. Teter was a former captain of Indiana University's football team and was a gentleman as well as an athlete; his analytic ability to solve problems was invaluable, and he was pleasant and helpful to all.

The Showers brothers carefully diversified their holdings at the beginning of the 1890s. In addition to real estate development and the savings and loan company, they purchased interests in several local stone quarries. Beginning in the late '80s, the Indiana limestone industry had experienced an enormous burst of profitability. It was the Midwest's equivalent of gold mining: quarries

This lad is probably Nellie's brother, the young W. Edward Showers.

From the collection of the Monroe County History Center,
202 East 6th Street, Bloomington, IN,
www.monroehistory.org, Faces and Places Collection.

across southern Indiana reaped unbelievable profits due to the introduction of new technology that allowed massive slabs of limestone to be neatly cut out of the earth, hoisted up by steel cranes, and loaded onto waiting railroad cars. Twenty-five miles to the south, the city of Bedford clattered with the sound of quarry machinery, and the population of Stinesville jumped to one thousand inhabitants almost overnight due to the presence of its high-quality limestone. The Monon railroad operated a special "stone train" that passed through all three cities and carried the valuable product north to Chicago and east to New York City, Philadelphia, and Washington, D.C. Indiana limestone was incorporated into the facades of the New York Times Building in Manhattan, the original 1889 Shoreham Hotel in Washington, D.C., Chicago's City Hall, the state capitol building in Indianapolis, and the residences of William and Cornelius Vanderbilt in New York City, along with countless churches and civic buildings all over the eastern half of the United States. Quarry owners became wealthy men almost overnight. Indiana University's new Kirkwood Hall was built using local limestone; the Adams brothers, from whose quarry the stone had come, built themselves handsome matching stone mansions near the old university campus using the same rock. The Hunter Valley northwest of town was pockmarked with massive quarries that saw constant frenzied activity. Any man who owned property adjoining the railroad, even the smallest lot, appears to have bored into the bedrock hoping to strike it rich as a prospector. Soon twenty-two quarries were operating within the city limits,[5] and new workmen were constantly being hired for the dangerous work of cutting and hauling limestone, which frequently resulted in maiming and death. The widows of men who had been crushed to death were paid minimal compensations and the dirty work went on without pause.

Fortunes were made very swiftly by men who happened to be in the right place at the right time. Investors could become extremely wealthy if they were able to invest in the channeling machinery and were lucky enough to obtain property that lay atop the geologic formation now known as the Salem limestone layer, a flawless layer of seamless, fine-grained oolitic stone six feet or more thick. This smooth and gleaming stone could be quarried into pieces of enormous size, which made it useful not only for the faces of buildings but also for columns, monuments, sculptures for pediments, and cemetery obelisks. A large number of spur lines were constructed along the Monon railway to serve the quarries a short distance away. The railcars were often only able to carry a single massive block of stone each.

The Showers brothers lived next door to each other, as did the wealthy Adams brothers, who had made a fortune by quarrying. The Showers men lived in identical frame homes on North Walnut Street and the Adams brothers lived in matching stone mansions on South College Avenue near Second Street. Because of the coincidence of the city's having two sets of matching homes built side by side by wealthy businessmen brothers, local legend became confused, and one hundred years later many people mistakenly believed that the Showers brothers had built and lived in the Adams brothers' houses.

The Showers brothers recognized the profits to be made from limestone and decided to join the action. They purchased a large property across Rogers Street from their own factory grounds, adjacent to the Monon tracks, and announced they were forming the new Central Oolitic Stone Company. They then co-purchased the Star Stone Company with the help of other prominent businessmen friends, and invested in the Star Quarry, the series of Hunter Valley quarries, and the Matthews stone quarry. Each company was a separate corporation with separate stockholders, but the same group of men effectively owned all five quarries.[6] Collectively, these five quarries made up nearly three hundred acres. James and William also invested in the downtown business block owned by their friend and fellow businessman, department store owner W. W. Wicks, when he updated his clothing store with a new fancy front and a skylight inside.[7] Home construction continued at a fever pitch; carpenters worked non-stop all year long except for the two or three coldest months of winter, building countless numbers of new houses. The *Republican Progress* reported on September 14, 1892, that forty homes were either being built at that moment or were being contemplated. By December 14 the same paper noted, "New [buildings] are projected and contracts let every day. There are so many buildings under construction now that there are not enough carpenters to do the work, because they work on one building a few days then go to another, and so sometimes one force of men will be working on three or four jobs at one time." The Real Estate Association was making good profits by issuing loans to home builders: in April 1893 it announced a return of 13.4% on its investments. So many people were now living on the west side that a new elementary school had to be built along Fairview Street.

A slender album was produced around this time to promote Bloomington to outsiders who might be interested in investing locally. It was filled with rotogravures that depicted its public buildings, typical Bloomington homes of not only the wealthy but also of workingmen, churches, streetscapes, the picturesque "North Pike" (Old State Road 37) with its small river gorge and waterfalls, and scenes of the Indiana University campus with handsome brick and stone buildings. It is probable that the Showers brothers and their business partners were in some way connected with the advancement of this album, since they had much to gain from attracting additional citizens and outside investment. (They were members of the Commercial Club, which was the forerunner to the modern Chamber of Commerce.) The album prominently mentioned the furniture and chair factories as well as the local stone quarrying industry. The introduction to the book explained:

> The past four years, since the spring of 1887, has [sic] been a period of unusual prosperity. Values in real estate have been established, and many handsome and substantial buildings erected. . . .The streets are broad, well-shaded avenues, almost all of which have been macadamized, and the sidewalks on either side well paved with brick, no less than about seven miles of brick pavement having been laid the present year. Three well-conducted building and loan associations have made it possible for a growing number of the laboring people to become possessors of their own homes, so that an unusually large proportion of the citizens own their residences, and exceptional good taste has been shown in their building, resulting in neat, comfortable and attractive cottages, which are to be seen all over the city, with all the conveniences within the means of an intelligent and industrious people.[8]

The book noted that Bloomington had three considerations of paramount importance to those thinking of relocating or investing: "the sanitary condition . . . , the educational, and the commercial and industrial advantages." It then described the local industries:

> The furniture factory was established on a small scale in 1868, and since that time has steadily increased until it is to-day the second largest manufactory . . . of medium

priced beds and chamber suites in the United States, the annual output of their products being about 750 car loads, the value of which is $275,000, and the amount of lumber consumed in its production about 5,000,000 feet, and their goods are marketed in every State and Territory in the Union. The average number of men employed is 190, and the average weekly pay-roll is $1,600. . . . The chair and table factory employs fifty men, and manufactures about 400 chairs and 300 tables per week, which are sold in all parts of the United States.[9]

It went on to describe the quarry industry, which had attracted "a considerable amount of foreign capital as well as a part of the surplus capital of the resident citizens." The Central Oolitic Stone Quarry and mill owned by the Showers brothers and their partners was cited as an illustration of this industry. "It is located within the city limits and has been in operation only a few months, and its estimated annual output is 2,250 cars of sawed and 750 cars of rough stone at a value of $40,000." This period of growth was one of the most vigorous in Bloomington's history.

PANIC STRIKES

But one of the worst economic depressions ever experienced by the nation was just around the corner. The Panic of '93 struck at a moment when the country gave every appearance of vigor. Like many other economic reversals, it was caused by unsound speculations that led to bank failures and created ripples that devastated the economy. The collapse of a single large Chicago bank resulted in the failure of dozens of smaller banks across Indiana. By early May the effects were being felt in Bloomington. The Worley Bank in Ellettsville failed and despite the owners' pledge that they would repay every last penny of investors' money, they hastily decamped to Chicago, leaving ruined people in their wake.[10] An attempted run on Bloomington's First National Bank was thwarted by the new time lock that the management had presciently installed on their vault. The bank's officers claimed the lock was malfunctioning, but it is very possible that they thought it best to lock up the money and sit on it until the financial panic leveled off. Summer saw little improvement in conditions. With money short, construction nationwide came to an abrupt halt. Quarries began to close down as the demand for limestone dried up, and Monon cancelled the special stone train since limestone was no longer moving between states. Quarry workmen were forced to seek new jobs because most of the quarries and stone mills had been idled. Even the Fulwider lumber mill and the Showers furniture factory turned off their machines and sent their men home owing to lack of orders. Temporary shutdowns had often occurred in previous years whenever the company rewarded the men for hard work with a few days off, or closed for a week or two between orders. But this time the closure was much longer. Unalarmed, the brothers set off for the opening of the Columbian Exposition in Chicago but reported back with some surprise that the grounds and structures at the famous Exposition were not yet fully finished. Even Bloomington's Fourth of July observance, a modest affair consisting of speeches and fireworks underwritten by local businesses, was cancelled due to the economic crisis. "Business men do not feel like going into such an enterprise again at this time for various reasons that are obvious," wrote the *Telephone* on June 20, 1893.

A month later, the July 28, 1893 *Telephone* observed optimistically,

> In these financial flurries, it is a matter of congratulation that Bloomington has escaped thus far, and now that the worst is over the indications are that our little city will experience no trouble. Bloomington's splendid condition is largely by reason of the high standing of its banks on the one hand, and also in the fact that it has never been a place for speculation. While property commands a good price, yet there are no fictitious values and real estate is generally worth what it costs. Merchants and business men can do much to assist each other, and instead of decrying and tearing down in these close times, the effort should be to encourage and build up.

It's true that life for the six-thousand-odd citizens of Bloomington was not as adversely affected as it was in other larger and more vulnerable cities, but the worst months were still to come. That summer Indiana experienced a serious drought followed by a crop failure, and Bloomington's factories and quarries ran only sporadically, often on half time and with reduced workforces. Banks in the western United States continued to collapse. Thousands of workers across the nation found themselves without jobs, although the newspapers noted wryly that the already-rotund President Cleveland continued to put on weight. Bloomington's First National Bank was issuing paper money in the name of its president, Nat U. Hill. It was a painful summer for many people.

Things did not improve the following year. The United Mine Workers called for a nationwide strike to protest the wages that had been slashed. Without steady supplies of coal for their boilers, factories and quarries could not continue to function. Hundreds of unemployed workers banded together in a large group known as Coxey's Army and headed across the country on foot for Washington, D.C., to lobby the government for jobs. Kelly's Army, another large group of unemployed working men who hoped to join with Coxey's Army, was traversing Iowa. By July of 1894 labor unrest had spread across the nation, with passenger trains disrupted by the Pullman strike and unemployed workers battling the police. Chicago was placed under martial law. Years later in his memoirs, James Showers recalled the difficulties of those years:

> Some of the boys who worked in the factory were there. They wanted to know when we would get up steam again. "We can't sell furniture at prices people won't pay," I said. One of the workers spoke up. "What if we work for less money?"
>
> We were paying them 15 cents an hour, which bought a lot of things in those days. "How much less would you be willing to work for?" I asked. The men agreed they'd be willing to work for half of what we'd been paying them. "Half a loaf is better than no loaf at all," one of the men said.
>
> So we got up steam again and gave the furniture buying public a bargain they couldn't turn down even in a panic. It was a three-piece oak bedroom suit and it sold for $10—the whole thing. In a few months wages of the men had been restored to their former level.[11]
>
> Brother Willie had a way of looking on the bright side of life, while I was far less optimistic. During the panic of 189[3] times were critical ever at the factory, just like they were all over the whole country.
>
> Willie was president of the business then, and his optimism was certainly an asset.
>
> Firms owing us money for furniture, simply could not pay. One furniture store owed us over $18,000. One day after we had renewed and renewed note after note for them and they had payed [sic] about half of the $16,000, word was sent us, the firm had closed its doors & gone into the hands of the receiver. Neither of us boys made any comment on the situation that day, till after dinner I chanced to meet W. N. alone in the finishing room.
>
> I remarked, "Well, Willie, it's pretty tough to lose $9,000 all in one lump, isn't it?" —"Yes it is," he said, but added, with a burst of his optimism showing, "Aren't we glad they didn't go broke, while they owed us the whole eighteen thousand?"[12]

The sudden slowing of the economy could not have struck at a worse time for the fledgling waterworks into which the brothers had already invested much time. Bloomington never enjoyed any large body of water. Only a few of the streams ran reliably year-round, and from its earliest days the town had suffered from cyclical water shortages. Violent thunderstorms are common through the spring and early summer, but from August through early October the weather is generally dry, and every six to ten years a genuine drought occurs. The population of Bloomington made use of wells and subterranean cisterns fed by downspouts on gutters, but this was not reliable as a permanent solution. Factories needed large amounts of water to operate their steam machinery; the city of Bloomington needed water to sprinkle on its dusty graveled streets; and the fire company needed water to fight the fires that periodically ravaged private dwellings or destroyed entire business blocks downtown. The solution seemed simple: organize a modern waterworks company that would dam a permanently flowing stream outside the city limits to create a reservoir, and then the water could be pumped into Bloomington and made available through hydrants along the streets. This apparently simple plan resulted in five years of ongoing problems and turned out to be a disaster for all involved.

The city council began by contracting with one Jesse Starr to create a city waterworks, and James and William Showers became directors of the new waterworks company. Land a mile west of town was purchased for a reservoir, but the earthen dam burst, carrying everything away. Starr absconded with more than $2,200 of funds (more than $51,000 in today's values) and was replaced by a Mr. Coon, a reputable man who had installed other waterworks in various locations across Ohio. Coon hired more than one hundred men to dig mains beneath the Bloomington streets, which required sinking the pipes sufficiently far beneath the surface to avoid freezing. This meant that the limestone bedrock had to be blasted, and one of these explosions shattered the large and expensive plate glass window in Mr. Wicks's storefront. Although Coon promised on his honor that water would be flowing through the Bloomington hydrants by the Fourth of July, 1893, he had taken over the enterprise just when the banks began to fail. He could not issue bonds to pay his workmen because no one would buy bonds at a time when good money was scarce. At least fifty liens were filed against the waterworks company and the well-intentioned Coon ended up leaving town under cover of darkness with only his horse, his buggy, and one trunk. The manager who was hired to replace him, Mr. Erlund, worked so hard and conscientiously that he suffered a complete physical collapse. And when the mains and hydrants were finally tested, the threads on the hydrants turned out to be incompatible with those on the city's fire hoses, for in order to save costs, the first of the three directors had purchased leftover hydrants that used nonstandard threading. But that was not the end: many of the mains had to be replaced (which meant that the streets had to be dug up a second time) and the pump-house boilers proved to be worthless. In November two "good homes" burned to the ground because the fire company was unable to get water out of the hydrants despite twenty minutes of effort. By November 17 the *Telephone* reported that the waterworks company had already invested $50,000, with no end in sight. The city council declared the waterworks franchise to be null and void, since the service that had been originally agreed upon had never been rendered. Water finally began to flow in the summer of 1894, although the newspapers complained that the reservoir was unfenced and that cows frequently could be seen standing in the city water up to their bellies. That same summer an unknown person sabotaged the reservoir by cutting the embankment.[13] The damage was repaired but the waterworks were ordered sold in 1898, the waterworks company having failed to live up to the requirements listed on the franchise contract.

James and William were caught up in the middle of this. At some point they resigned their positions as directors of the waterworks company in order to distance themselves from the malfeasance, but they remained committed to bringing water to the city of Bloomington. In the best of faith they had invested much time and energy and had earnestly tried to do the best for their community. James later recalled his involvement in the sale in his memoir:

> The waterworks plant was put up at auction by the sheriff. On the day of the sale a group of public-minded citizens counseled together and decided to buy the plant. I was asked to do the bidding.

> Companies from Chicago had sent representatives to Bloomington to bid for the plant, so the local group had stiff competition. When the rival bidders had bid above the amount of the liens $15,000, I asked the auctioneer if he could halt the sale for a few minutes and he replied "Certainly, Mr. Showers." Knowing that our group was waiting at the rear of the courthouse, I slipped out to inform the men that we were out bid by the Chicago companies and asked them what I should do. I was instructed to go back and buy that water works plant even if it took a bid of $100,000. So back I went and the auctioneer knocked it off to our local group for $21,500.00. Among this group were P. K. Buskirk, Van Buskirk, Nat U. Hill, W. N. Showers, Wm. T. Hicks, Major Perry and several others.

> These original organizers each bought $300,00 worth of stock and the city became the owner of the remainder. A 12 in. main pipe was installed and other features were completed according to specifications. The plant was bonded for $60,000, paying off all the original obligations. It was operated about 3 yrs by the city, accumulating enough money in that time to buy all the stock held by our original organizers. The water works then became the sole property of the city. This was the first step in our present waterworks system.[14]

It was no easy matter to scrape together this much money during an economic depression, but the group of Bloomington businessmen were nevertheless able to do it, most probably because their local banks did not fail and because of their foresight in investing in real estate. It is notable that during a coast-to-coast depression that left almost one in five American men out of work, the real estate market in Bloomington remained strong and homes continued to be built despite the hard times. Although area quarries shut down one by one as the price of limestone dropped to less than half of its former value, and the Showers factory stood idle more often than not for several years between 1893 and 1896, James and William were nevertheless still able to afford new carriages, to travel out of town on business trips, and to take personal vacations with their families in other states. The income from their real estate investments continued to come in even while their factory was closed down. The family entertained guests in style; young Nellie Showers hosted a huge party for her fraternal organization, Kappa Kappa Gamma, for which 150 invitations were sent out. Newspaper mentions of the Showers family depicted them living lives of ease. The *Telephone* reported on May 28, 1897, that W. Edward Showers was driving "a handsome horse and buggy that is not excelled by anything in town. It is the present of his father." Unemployed Bloomington workingmen were probably not sympathetic when they read in the *Telephone* on June 29, 1894, that "Charlie Showers is confined to his home with a very bad injury on his knee. He was swinging in his hammock and holding in his hand a lead pencil. The hammock swung against the side of the house, driving the sharp point of the lead pencil into his knee cap. He is unable to walk." As in most American economic depressions, the poor were affected far more profoundly than the wealthy.

THE FEDERATION OF BLOOMINGTON CLUBS CLEANING UP THE CITY.

An unidentified civic leader joins forces with local women
to clean up Bloomington's courthouse square.

The Bloomington Courier, February 16, 1897.

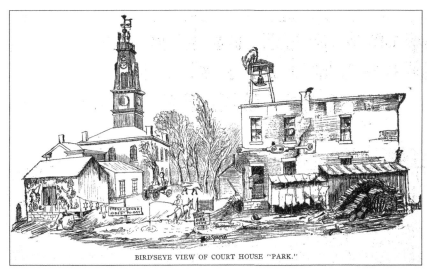

BIRD'SEYE VIEW OF COURT HOUSE "PARK."

The fire company's headquarters on the north-east corner of the square.
Note the piled wood, the heap of manure, the crack in the
building, and the goat on top of the bell tower.

The Bloomington Courier, February 23, 1897.

Chapter

9

MOVING TOWARD
MODERNITY

NOTWITHSTANDING the shaky national economy, Showers women were instrumental during the 1890s in improving the town. From the elder generation, these included William's wife, Hanna Lou; James's wife, Belle; and James Hendrix's wife, Ellen. Maud Showers came next in age, then those from the younger generation: William's daughters, Jennie and Nellie; and James's daughter, young Maude. Several Showers women served on the Ladies' Cemetery Association, which had the goal of improving the city cemetery west of town, which had fallen into a sad state of disrepair. Despite the financial depression the association succeeded in collecting enough modest donations to be able to enlarge the cemetery through the purchase of a large adjoining property, and the group even built a small cottage for the sexton. They arranged for a graceful archway at the gate to the cemetery, covered the drives with fine crushed stone, arranged for the grounds to be kept well mown, and installed a decorative iron fountain in the center of the grounds. They renamed the burial ground "Rose Hill" and planted flowers among the graves. Funds were raised by means of a pleasure excursion by train to Louisville, a special performance of the Gentry Dog and Pony Show, and a baseball exhibition between "lean" and "fat" players. "The ladies deserve great credit for their energy and determination in this enterprise, and have certainly pushed it to successful completion, hampered by circumstances under which a like organization of men would have failed," remarked the *Republican Progress*.[1]

Similarly, a group of ladies led by Mrs. E. M. Seward beautified the Monon train depot with flowerbeds, urns, and mounds of colored plantings that read "Welcome" and "Monon." The May 12, 1893 *Telephone* noted that it was difficult for men of the town "to secure attention to a mere aesthetical proposition, when their busy minds were engrossed with more important monetary concerns." Because of the serious financial depression, these ladies' achievements are noteworthy. They managed to improve the quality of life in Bloomington at a time when men either considered such activity unworthy of their interest or believed that it could not be done.

Within a few years the women's group had planted scores of trees across town, and the city now bore a very different and pleasing aspect. "WOMEN'S Work.—Progress of the Movement to Beautify Our City," read the April 13, 1897 *Telephone*. "Bloomington has indeed taken on a new life this spring. Everybody is making needed repairs and improvements. About three hundred shade trees have been planted along our streets. The lawns are being looked after more carefully than ever before and there is a spirit of progress throughout the city." And yet there was still more to be accomplished. The women turned to the problem of the manure and garbage that lay in the public streets and alleyways.

"CITY STREETS.—They Are Not Rose-Beds by Any Means.—" declared the *Bloomington Courier*.[2]

> Undoubtedly the streets of Bloomington are today in worse condition than ever before in the history of the city as regards cleanliness. They are the dumping grounds of all the ashes and trash that can be accumulated in the city. Yet the city ordinance strictly prohibits such evils. It has reached such a point that the main streets about the public square are but the receptacles for wood piles, old boxes, coal and barrels. It is high time the proper authorities get down to business and place the city streets in a respectable condition. Spring is upon us and by a concerted action we may clean up ready to receive visitors that will soon begin to arrive in search of a location.

There was no municipal garbage collection in Bloomington in those days. Every household that could afford to do so paid to have its refuse hauled away at intervals, but the poorer households simply threw their rubbish into their privies or onto trash heaps behind their homes. The odor of the city must have been unbearable, particularly in mid-summer. Clouds of flies rose up from

PRESENTED BY
MONROE COUNTY STATE BANK
BLOOMINGTON, IND.

MONROE COUNTY'S OLD COURT HOUSE

The pre-1906 courthouse, showing the trees that were planted
by the united efforts of the local women's clubs.

*From the collection of the Monroe County History Center, 202 East 6th
Street, Bloomington, IN, www.monroehistory.org, 1998.082.0001.*

manure piles outside homes and flew in through windows and doors to settle
on food and cooking surfaces.

The campaign for garbage removal was not merely a case of genteel ladies
turning up their noses at filth. This was part of a larger overall campaign to improve civic sanitation and health. The concept of germ theory had finally pen-
etrated to the American Midwest and struck a nerve there. Each year the same
infectious diseases swept through the city, typhoid being the chief danger. The
women wanted to alert the citizens to the fact that the lack of sanitation was
the cause of many dangerous diseases that could be avoided through simple
preventative measures. The various ladies' clubs hosted at least one public in-
formational lecture on sanitation by a doctor. The Federation of Ladies' Clubs

petitioned the city to abolish the hitching racks on the courthouse square because of the filth that lay around them. The city refused to do so, citing the hardship that this would impose on rural residents who rode in to town with their wagons and buggies. The ladies objected that no one took responsibility for cleaning the area around the racks:

> A committee of ladies from the Federation of Clubs called upon the city council last Tuesday night. It was composed of Mesdames J. D. Showers, etc. . . . The ladies asked that the sanitary ordinances be more carefully enforced, and that a sanitary policeman be appointed. Also requested that the local laws against throwing paper and trash on the streets be carried out. This ought to be done as a matter of pride, without compulsion.[3]

The city was preparing to lay down new brick pavement on the downtown streets, a potentially slick surface that needed to be kept swept and clean. Nevertheless the city fathers refused to do anything about the problem of manure lying in odiferous piles around the hitching racks. To the annoyance of the city government, the women appealed to a higher authority, petitioning the State Board of Health in Indianapolis, which investigated and then ordered the city of Bloomington to clean up the hitching areas. The city requested an injunction that would put everything on hold until the matter could be examined in court. By December the ladies had won. The city of Bloomington conceded that the space around the hitching racks would be kept clean at all times.

As the Equal Suffrage Club had done before it, the Council of Women lobbied the city to clean up the unkempt courthouse grounds, which were littered with unsightly junk and contained a dilapidated bandstand and a filthy public latrine that could be smelled at a distance. "[The courthouse yard] will be graded, filled up in low places and sodded," said the *Telephone* on April 14, 1899. "Flower beds with blooming plants will take the place of the present unsightly barren portion and speakers' stand. The ladies are determined to make the park a vast contrast to what it has been in past years, and Sheriff Kinser will lend his assistance in making it a thing of beauty and joy forever." A team of men was sent out by the city to begin collecting dirt and rubbish from the city streets. The newspapers were filled with praise for the women's achievements. An article in the *Telephone* on June 14, 1898, entitled "Cost of the Cleaning-Up Campaign," commented:

> Once on a time some years ago when a U.S. Senator and wife from the Pacific slope [Mr. and Mrs. Leland Stanford] visited our city for the first time, their opinion of the place was expressed in the statement that Bloomington was nothing but a dirty,

muddy, little town. Several weeks ago when the convention of the Indiana Union of Literary clubs brought about 400 strangers to our city, it was heard repeatedly from them, "what a clean, pretty city Bloomington is!" Both opinions at the time stated were true. Bloomington was changed from a dirty to a clean, pretty city by the thorough and systematic cleaning in April. The idea of such a cleaning originated with the Local Council of Women. This council presented the matter to the city council and by the mayor's proclamation, one week of April was given to city cleaning.

Such a complete transformation could not be wrought without considerable expense. The entire cost was $167.34; of this amount the Local Council of Women paid from its own treasury $106.79. The city treasury of Bloomington paid $40.30; Hon. A. M. Hadley donated a team at $2.25 a day for eight days, making $18; Hughes Bros. donated a team one day at $2.25, all of which made the entire expense $167.34.

Note: the sum would be equivalent to at least $4,200 in modern currency.

Many histories have overlooked the significant contributions made by women's organizations to civic improvement during the 1800s and early 1900s, but it is evident that even without the right to vote in elections, Bloomington women had impressive organizational and lobbying skills. Their struggle to improve the town would continue for many more years, and Showers women were invariably found in the center of the action.

FAMILY ADJUSTMENTS

In 1890, at the age of twenty-seven, Maud Showers had married again. The groom was Ambrose Cunning, a prominent judge who later ran for Congress. Maud did not withdraw from her business involvement with Showers Brothers even though the newlyweds moved to Martinsville to live while the judge was working there. Maud retained her own property, including her house on Sixth Street, which was rented out. She maintained close ties to the Bloomington clubs and organizations that she had belonged to. In addition to money concerns, other personal matters made 1893 a very difficult year for Maud. Both of her parents died within three months of each other while she was pregnant. Her baby girl, Gwen, was born while Maud was still grieving. Little Gwen appears to have been born with a chronic ailment and died in November, aged only four months. With these three losses coming in close succession (possibly combined with postpartum depression), her marriage began to unravel. Bloomington was startled to open the *Republican Progress* on October 10, 1894, and learn that Judge Cunning's wife was suing for divorce, claiming "nonsupport." The flabbergasted judge told the reporter, "The charge that he has at no time contributed to the support of the household is simply preposterous. He says that J. H. Smyth, J. S. Knight, both of Morgantown, rented store rooms of him and furnished all the coffee, sugar, tea, rice, soap, peaches, apricots, starch, prunes and lard used by the family, and other articles occasionally." The judge gave a list of other local grocers who had supplied food and household necessities to his home.

> He thinks the charge that he has contributed nothing to the support of the family must sound ridiculous to those men. The Judge says his current expenses for the support of the family, were about $7.50 each week. In regard to his wealth Judge Cunning says he is worth from thirteen to fifteen thousand dollars and that his wife is worth anywhere from fifty to one hundred thousand dollars. He states that his wife kept a little blank book in which she set down every nickel she spent for the family. This little book was a constant source of irritation to her and consequently a fruitful source of discord in the family. She wanted him to bear all expense of living and he had made up his mind to do so. For a year or two his wife has desired to move into a smaller house with white hard wood finish; and after he came here to attend court, he opened up negotiations with J. Howe to trade for the Alexander Robinson property in Bloomington, intending to furnish it in every particular himself. . . . He says their courtship was delightful, pure and sweet. He says that for the most part their married life was peaceful and happy. That his wife is a good reader, and together they read a whole library of the best books ever printed, and that she did nearly all of the reading. He says they had one of the sweetest girl babies born to them that ever came into this world. This little angel of the household died when she was four months old and left their home in darkness and gloom. He thinks if this sweet child had lived, all evil influences and petty cares would have been chased away by the light of her bright baby face and their home would have been a haven of rest, joy and sweet happiness.

The reporter also spoke with Maud, who with great dignity refused to go into specifics.

> The lady declined to talk on the subject, beyond a few expressions as to the fixedness of her purposes with reference to her suit pending in the circuit court. Mrs. Cunning stated that she did not think it worth while to take up space in the columns of the papers with any narration of the facts connected with her domestic troubles. . . . She did not think any of his publications could injure her or her cause in this community, where she has lived all her life; that at the proper time and place she would in the proper way make known all the facts in her own behalf and the public could then see who is to blame.

> *Note: The judge's weekly grocery expenses of $7.50 would equal approximately $186 in contemporary currency. And assuming $75,000 as a mid-range, Maud's holdings were equivalent to at least $1,860,000 in modern values.*

Divorce at this time inevitably entailed blame on the part of one party against another; there was no concept yet of a no-fault dissolution of a marriage. The judge and his wife reached a temporary truce and she withdrew her suit, only to suddenly resume her legal proceedings a day or two later. She was granted her divorce on January 9, 1895. Maud was thirty-one years old and had once again become single. In a move that might have surprised many people she chose not to keep her recent married name. She reverted to Maud Showers, the name by which she had been known for so many years, and perhaps partly to avoid the taint of gossip, she relocated temporarily to Indianapolis while her daughter Beryl attended May Wright Sewell's Classical School for Girls in Indianapolis.

Sewell was an active suffragist, lecturer, and educator who had helped organize the International Council of Women in 1887; Maud probably met her during Indiana's suffrage drive at that time. Sewall also founded what is today known as the Herron School of Art and the Indianapolis Art Museum, and maintained her famous progressive school for young women for many years. Each day of study was divided into a strict schedule and included mathematics, geography, grammar, foreign languages, and gymnastics, a subject that was uncommon for female students at that time (it was regarded as injurious to a young woman's health). "Until its closing in 1907 the school offered Indianapolis's girls an education equal to that found for boys in the Indianapolis Classical School and one based on the entrance requirements established for admission to such nationally known women's colleges as Smith, Vassar, and Wellesley."[4] By the time Maud and Beryl returned to Bloomington a few years later, Beryl had earned the distinction of co-founding the Tri-Kappa philanthropic organization while still a student at Sewell's Classical School for Girls. (Kappa Kappa Kappa continues an active existence to this day.)

As one marriage fell apart, another lasting union took form. Nellie Showers and the handsome young partner at the North End Furniture Company, Sanford Teter, had met several years earlier as university students and had fallen in love. Their wedding in April 1895 was the first of its kind in Bloomington, recalled the *Star Courier* years later:

> The window shades in the home of the bride's father were pulled down tightly during the ceremony and for a particular reason.... At the time of his daughter's wedding to Mr. Teter, W. N. was president of the local electric light company and his home was one of the very few in the city then equipped with electric lights. Town lighting had already been attempted at strategic points, such as atop the tower of Central school

Nellie Showers at the time of her wedding to Sanford Teter.

Courtesy Nancy Teter Smith.

building and the United Presbyterian church for example. But . . . many people then had never seen electric lights in homes. It was the practice to have the current turned on only after dark.

W. N. Showers thought it would be nice to have his daughter's wedding by "electric light" in mid-afternoon. As president of the local light company he ordered the current turned on during the ceremony. So with the shades tightly drawn to keep out the afternoon sunshine, Sanford Teter and Nellie Showers exchanged vows and Bloomington had its first electric light wedding![5]

But the family was soon to suffer another grievous loss. James's only son, Charles, the manager of the North End Furniture Factory, had been increasingly unwell. A serious illness at the age of ten had afflicted him with weak lungs, and the problem had developed into tuberculosis, known at that time as consumption. The family had done everything it could to protect his health, including sending him on long restorative trips to the dry air of the far West. Charles was still young and was enjoying his first years of married life with his pretty wife Leila and their baby, but he had suffered a series of hemorrhages in 1890 that almost killed him. After a period of remission, by February of 1896 he was again in desperate physical condition. "Jas. D. Showers, accompanied by his son Charles, left for the south on Monday," reported the *Republican Progress* on February 25. "They will go to California via Texas, and expect to remain away till sometime in April or May. Charley's health is not good this spring, and a change of climate was thought to be necessary." To describe his health as "not good" was an understatement; the young man and his father had left town in a desperate attempt to save his life. Less than a month later, by March 17, they were home again. Charles was dying.

"The hardships of the journey was [sic] too much for his weakened condition," the *Telephone* reported, "and he was compelled to return home, since which time his condition has been very critical. With a last hope, Dr. Lowder, the family physician, went to New York to secure the late Edison treatment, and it was tested only the day before death came."[6] Charles died on March 31, two weeks after returning home. He became the second Showers man to die a premature death. As James's only son, he had been raised since his earliest days to carry on the business after his father; but with Charley gone, Sanford Teter did his best to step up to bat for the family. The North End Furniture Company continued operations for another year or two but ceased doing business before the end of the decade. It's likely that the chairs it produced could be manufactured more easily in the larger factory just a block or two away, and at some point after 1898 its operations were shut down and given over to the larger factory.

KEEPING UP APPEARANCES

Charles's death led to major management changes in the next few years. In the late summer of 1899, the Showers Brothers Company filed incorporation papers. In a partnership, the partners personally assume all legal risk and divide any financial reward, but incorporation transforms a business into a separate legal entity that conducts trade, protects its shareholders from legal liability, and distributes rewards for investing. The first board of directors of the new Showers Brothers Company was composed of James Showers (president), William Showers (treasurer), their close friend P. K. Buskirk (vice president), William's son-in-law Sanford Teter (secretary), and Maud Showers. Capital stock was set at $50,000, divided into one thousand shares of $50 each. The president and treasurer each drew a salary of $100 per month (the annual equivalent of at least $31,000 in modern currency), while the secretary earned $15 per week. The economic conditions were extremely good at the time of incorporation and by May 1900, the very next year, a dividend of 10 percent was declared on the capital stock. By 1901 the dividend had climbed to 45 percent; by 1903 it was 50 percent. All stock at that time was held solely by members of the Showers family and by Buskirk. Earnings were turned back into company improvements or carefully invested in profitable ventures outside of the furniture factory. William lobbied (successfully) at the state level to run another railroad through Bloomington in order to further boost local industry; James invested in coal mines in neighboring Greene County. Both James and William helped found the new Citizen's Loan and Trust Company. Partners in this new banking company included P. K. Buskirk, attorney and businessman Ira Batman (who had boarded in 1880 during his student days at James and Belle's house), and Fred Matthews, who owned many profitable quarries around Ellettsville and Bloomington.

These men and their families, along with the other bankers and businessmen in town, constituted Bloomington's equivalent of the glittering New York society dominated by the Vanderbilts and Carnegies. These were the men who controlled Bloomington's commerce and finance. Their children grew up together, attended the same functions, and joined the same groups. Quarry

All the corporate information contained in this chapter derives from notes made by John Bendix in the early 1980s while researching the Showers company for the Monroe County Historical Museum (later the Monroe County History Center). At the time of Bendix's research, the company books of Showers Brothers Company had not yet been lost. These books contained the fiscal history of the company from its earliest days until the end, along with the minutes of the board of directors, but at some point the books were either misplaced or accidentally thrown out. This loss was a great blow, but it's fortunate that Bendix recorded data from their pages in his notes.

owner Fred Matthews's daughter Bertha had attended the same Indianapolis school as Maud Showers's daughter Beryl; Bertha was being courted by William Showers's son, W. Edward. Their union was supported and encouraged by the two prominent families, who enjoyed being linked by marriage as well as by investments. Although James and William had started out as ordinary workingmen with no higher education to speak of, they were by now two of the most influential men in town. They lived in spacious homes and their children were given university educations and were expected to wed others of similar status. Even though James and William continued to look after the needs of their workmen, they would not have relished their daughters' falling in love with any of the hundreds of ordinary men who toiled and aspired at the family factory.

In 1902 W. Edward and Bertha wed. The *Bloomington Courier* of July 18 called it "the most fashionable wedding ceremony ever witnessed in Bloomington," ignoring the fact that Nellie Showers's wedding only seven years earlier to Sanford Teter had been hailed in the same terms. The Showers family grew more influential every year, and their weddings accordingly grew more sumptuous. Bertha's wedding gown "was a dream of beauty, of the costliest chiffon, over taffeta, with lace, white trimming and a train of fan tulle."[7] She wore a brooch of diamonds and pearls, a gift from the groom. The times were changing and it was no longer fashionable to be married at home in the parlor; the era of impressive church weddings had begun. Although the bride was Catholic, the wedding was the first to be performed in the new Baptist chapel, probably because the new chapel could accompany a larger crowd of guests. For the occasion it had been filled with palms and white roses; on every seat were little posies consisting of white sweet peas tied with dainty ribbon and smilax. At the elaborate reception afterward at the bride's home, the entire ground floor of the large mansion was decked with white roses and pink and lavender sweet peas (the colors of Phi Psi, the groom's fraternity). In 1886 Jennie Showers's bridal gifts had included a new Bible, sofa pillows, and tea towels, but by the time W. Edward and Bertha married, wedding gifts had become more extravagant. "The gifts were of unusual value and occupied two rooms of the Matthews home. In addition to many cash presents, they consisted largely of costly and rare jewels, objects of virtu, works of art and brac-a-brac of every description." The wedding cake was monogrammed "M" and "S," and the ice-cream was molded in lily-shaped forms. The bride and groom were accompanied to the midnight train by friends who threw rice, and the young couple departed to spend a three-week honeymoon at one of the luxurious resorts on Mackinac Island in Michigan. They then set up residence in Chicago, where W. Edward was completing his studies at Rush Medical College. At that time he planned on becoming a doctor and did not realize that very soon he would be helping run one of the nation's largest furniture companies.

Sanford Teter, the highest-ranking person at the factory apart from William, James, and Maud, was as active in civic doings as William and James had been, and he served as city councilman just as they had done. Teter was commended by the *Bloomington Courier* when he employed detective work to solve a series of frauds that had been committed by men presenting themselves at the office to receive their pay who were actually outsiders impersonating workers.[8] In his dual capacity as councilman and businessman, he appeared before the members of the Fortnightly Club to deliver his careful assessment of the pros and cons currently faced by the city of Bloomington. The tremendous growth of Bloomington during the past fifteen years appears to have slowed, and professional men were debating what to do. As Teter put it, the advantages of the city included the presence of Indiana University, which continually drew in new students and visitors from elsewhere in the state and the nation; the

The young and handsome Sanford Teter in the 1890s.

Courtesy Nancy Teter Smith.

stone industry, which had again become extremely profitable; and lastly, the fact that Bloomington was not a suburb of a larger city but stood independent. The disadvantages included the presence of only a single railroad, which hindered industry (this was soon to change); the unusual expenses in extending or repairing the streets due to the rolling terrain; and the fact that much of the urban architecture was aging. Anyone getting off the train at Bloomington for the first time in thirty years, Teter pointed out, would see the old station, would stroll on the old flagstone sidewalk past the old levee, and would see the antiquated county livery stable and the old courthouse. "No wonder he feels like it were but yesterday instead of 30 years ago," he quipped.[9] The entire extended Showers clan felt similarly about the unsightly old urban architecture. As real estate investors, they had a strong belief that new buildings would bring a renewed sense of civic pride, which would increase prosperity. Teter called his listeners to action:

> Bloomington stone is shipped throughout the length and breadth of the land for federal and public buildings, yet we tolerate year after year an old relic of a courthouse which is totally unfit for longer use. Valuable records and files are stored in halls and attics and wood-rooms while the cramped condition of each office is a reproach to our county. Our city hall has not yet blown down, although it has repeatedly been condemned by building experts. The city has paid out enough in rent for City Clerk and City Treasurer's offices to have built fair buildings for their use. . . . We could use a stately government building to good advantage. We have a great need of a large railroad station with separate buildings for freight and passenger business. . . . Our needs are without number.[10]

He ended by calling for a city plan to be implemented, as "scores of beautiful cities" were doing elsewhere in the nation. Teter ended by reminding his listeners that "Bloomington is full of men of the highest ability in matters relating to public affairs; men whose names are familiar in connection with almost every enterprise intended to better our civic conditions. Such men, armed with the fortune of our location, and the opulence of our resources will work out the bright destiny of the 'New Bloomington.'"[11] It's clear who Teter had in mind: the Showers family and its close-knit group of fellow industrialists, who were by this time pulling strings not just in Bloomington but also at the state level.

CHANGING OF THE GUARD

In 1903 an epochal event occurred. James Showers was by this time sixty-two years old and had devoted forty-some years of his life to the family enterprise. He resigned as president of the company in July and sold his entire interest and stock in the Showers Brothers Company to William. He also stepped down as a director of the board, thereby completely divesting himself of any remaining connection with the company. Perhaps he was disheartened following the loss of his son to tuberculosis and saw no reason to persist in the family

James and Belle Showers inside their home on North Walnut Street.
Courtesy the Helm family.

enterprise, or possibly he was simply tired and worn after so many decades of making furniture. In any event, James quietly strolled away from the company that he had co-founded in order to pursue different interests. But he was not heading for retirement; he was still closely involved with the savings and loan company, the school board, and the telephone company. William became the president of the Showers Brothers Company and Maud Showers became vice president. By 1905 stockholders multiplied as other family members joined the board; these included William's son, W. Edward Showers, who had been successfully lured away from a medical career and back into the family business. Other stockholders were William's daughter Jennie Showers Smith and her husband, Joe M. Smith, and Maud Showers's son, Erle Showers. Joe Smith was no longer running his own store on the courthouse square as he had done at the time of his marriage; he had sold his business and joined the corporate enterprise of his in-laws, becoming superintendent of the Shipping Department. Erle was managing the Sears, Roebuck & Co. department, for sales to Sears were now a significant part of Showers Brothers' annual output. Erle's sister, Beryl, soon joined him as a stockholder; she would remain a company stockholder until the very end.

William was the eldest Showers left at the helm of the family business. He went each day to the factory and greeted workmen by name; he continued to beam upon his employees and appears to have been regarded with true affection by them. At Christmas of 1904 his workers gave him a lovely gift:

> A platform had secretly been constructed in the new annex, and as the whistle blowed [sic], the 250 employees by previous arrangement collected within the new building. Mr. Showers was induced to start to see about some machinery and was escorted to the platform and faced the happy workmen. He stood almost dazed while "Governor" Walker presented him a beautiful gold-headed ebony cane. Almost overcome, it was some time before Mr. Showers recovered sufficiently to respond. He heartily thanked the men for their esteem, and said that in his declining years, as he aided his tottering steps with this magnificent cane, he would always remember his 250 friends.[12]

In the early years, the Showers company had been owned and run by two brothers who allowed their sister-in-law to join them. As a corporation it expanded to draw in daughters, their husbands, and nephews. In 1906, when board president William Showers addressed a New Year's message to the directors, he emphasized the close bonds that united them:

> My dears, all of you are my own flesh and blood and before submitting the report for final action I wish to say that in all the 38 years of my connection with this business, this has been the most pleasant and . . . the most profitable year of them all. The New Year dawns with the brightest of prospects and when I look over one and all of you and knowing your ability as I do and your energy and push, and feeling in a measure that I have in my weak way helped to inspire and encourage you, I am proud to say that I now consider you the equals of any men in the furniture business and that your superiors have not yet been born. . . . I feel that you will uphold the standard that I have been so proud to bear for the last 38 years. . . . Go on as you have and your future is assured. Good morals, good citizenship and the knowledge that you have the unlimited confidence of your fellow men is a heavy asset, and with the energy, push and ability that good fortune has endowed you with, you have unlimited possibilities.[13]

Sanford Teter and his father-in-law, William Showers, play-
fully posing with one of the company's dressers.

Courtesy Nancy Teter Smith.

Showers Brothers Company was entering a golden era of growth, prosperity, and recognition. William's two sons-in-law, Sanford Teter and Joe Smith, soon became general business manager and first assistant, respectively. Teter held "the responsibility for all financial matters; the selling of the product; the buying of supplies for the shipping department; and of all duties and responsibilities of every nature connected with the office work of the firm."[14] W. Edward became general manager of production, including at the veneering plant and sawmill, as well as of quality control. Erle Showers managed the shipping departments. Dividends continued to be lucrative, ranging from 3 percent per month to 12 percent annually. The two largest shareholders were William and Maud, who held 36.6 percent and 23.4 percent, respectively, of all shares between them (half the worth of the company). W. Edward and Sanford Teter owned 10 percent each; Beryl, her brother Erle, and Joe Smith held 5 percent or less. Corporate control was thus maintained chiefly between the sole remaining Showers brother and his capable sister-in-law, Maud Showers. The "Industrial Edition" of the *Bloomington Courier* on April 26, 1904, profiled the company and observed first of all that Showers was the largest manufacturing plant in Monroe County and the largest employer, and that it had contributed more than any other industry toward the development of the city. The profile ended by emphasizing that "the best of feelings has been maintained" between the workers and the company owners.

The company instituted a sea-change in its production method that year when it added the capacity to do veneering. Veneer, the decorative wood facing that can be as thin as a sheet of paper, transformed the furniture lines of Showers. Instead of having to seek out top-quality wood and then laboriously sand and finish each flat surface in order to enhance the grain, thin decorative sheets of smooth veneer were glued onto the tops and fronts of bureaus, tables, dressers, and sideboards, all of which had been made of less expensive wood. The veneer enhanced the overall appearance, ensured that each piece would closely resemble the next, reduced the cost of materials, and eliminated a lot of work. As hardwood lumber became scarcer, the company turned to laminating several thin layers of wood. The elegant surface veneer was impressive and purchasers were frequently not aware that the wood beneath was not of the best quality. Sanford Teter became erroneously known in later years as having invented the word "lamination," but what he did was simply introduce the word to the workmen, many of whom had been unaware of the word or the technique.

Statistics from the profile in the April 26, 1904 *Bloomington Courier* stated that the Showers Brothers Company employed 240 men and was expecting to employ another twenty shortly. Three-quarters of those men were considered skilled labor. Shipments averaged seventy rail carloads per month. The sawmill daily cut 25,000 feet of timber at that time and secured its lumber by purchasing large tracts of land and then logging them. This is undoubtedly part of the reason that so much of the land around Monroe and surrounding counties had been completely clear-cut early by the twentieth century.

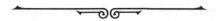

A Christmastime summary of the company in December 1905 painted the enterprise in glowing terms:

> The industry has continued to increase year by year until this plant now stands third largest of its kind in the United States, and its present output is three times that of any other furniture factory in the State.... The plant at present employs 300 men and by careful calculation 1100 people in the city of Bloomington receive their support from this plant. In addition to this number hundreds of people in this and adjoining counties receive a part of their support by furnishing logs and lumber to this institution. Many thousands of dollars are each week received by this company from out of the city, and are expended here for labor, logs, and lumber, thereby contributing enormously to the continued growth and prosperity of Bloomington.
>
> The management is exceedingly proud of its employees and attributes the larger part of their success to the faithfulness and untiring energy of these men. The large majority of these live in their own homes, which are unencumbered, and in addition have snug sums laid aside for a rainy day. The association between the management and the men is of the most intimate nature, and no joy, no sorrow is felt by one but that each shares his part.
>
> While it is a great comfort to the management to know that the business has been a financial success yet they are more proud of the morals, industry and good citizenship of their employees than of any other phase of their business, and believe that the secret of their success is due to the character of these men who have remained steadfast in times of adversity as well as prosperity and to the feeling of brotherhood that has always existed between employer and employee.[15]

Chapter

10

HOUSES AND A
HOSPITAL

W. EDWARD AND NELLIE had each enjoyed luxurious weddings, and now it was the turn of their cousin, Maud Showers's daughter Beryl. She and her new husband, the osteopath Dr. J. E. P. Holland, celebrated an enormous "society" church wedding in September 1903 "in the presence of about 400 friends," as the paper reported.[1] The church was artfully adorned by a professional floral decorator, who observed a red-and-green theme using asparagus ferns and roses; the family home, where the huge reception was held, was similarly decorated. Maud herself, dressed in white moiré silk with lace, gave away the bride to her new son-in-law. The wedding gifts occupied four entire tables. This lavish wedding was in stark contrast to that of young Maude (James's daughter), who married Dr. Burton D. Myers on March 3, 1904, with little public warning. "Surprise wedding this morning," read the paper. "Miss Maude Showers becomes the bride of Dr. Burton Myers.—Wedded at 10 o'clock this morning. Left on 11 o'clock train for Chicago." This young couple was united the old-fashioned way at the residence of the bride's parents, James and Belle Showers, with only the immediate members of the family present. "The bride is one of Bloomington's most popular and beautiful women," the paper noted, adding that she was an Indiana University graduate of the class of '01 and a member of Kappa Alpha Theta. "The groom is the head of the department of anatomy at the University and is an excellent teacher. . . . He came to IU last fall term when the School of Medicine was established here."[2]

Burton Dorr Myers had studied at the University of Leipzig and earned his MD degree in 1902. In 1903, when Indiana University established its medical school, Myers came to teach anatomy and help organize the new department. His marriage to young Maude was the first between the powerful Showers family and a faculty member of Indiana University. Organizing the new medical department was neither easy nor simple, and it took several years to become accredited. When it finally happened the *Bloomington Courier* noted, "Application for recognition was made to the State Board of Recognition and Examination some time ago. Dr. J. E. P. Holland, the successful osteopath of this city, is a member of this board and it was largely due to his influence that the recognition was granted."[3] The Showers family now had two capable physician sons-in-law who would assist in the family efforts to improve and modernize the city of Bloomington and the university.

James Showers hired local architect John Nichols to design and build his newly married daughter and her husband a magnificent stone mansion on North Washington Street at the corner of Eighth Street, just south of the many other elegant Showers homes on that street. The elder Maud Showers ordered a large and spacious building to be constructed on nearby North Walnut Street to house the osteopathic office of her new son-in-law, Dr. Holland. It was essentially an upscale boarding house with a suite of professional rooms reserved on the ground floor for the doctor's practice and five bedrooms upstairs for boarders, but there was nothing cheap or tawdry about the building. It shared the block with luxurious private residences in an excellent neighborhood on the same street as James and William Showers themselves lived. "The new building will be commodious in all its proportions, and the workmanship and material will be the best that money can secure," reported the paper.[4] Maud also provided a house for the newlyweds in University Courts, the new and desirable neighborhood immediately north of Dunn Meadow, between Seventh and Tenth Streets.

But all these new houses paled before the luxurious mansion that William's son, W. Edward Showers, built for himself on the corner of Ninth and North Washington Streets.[5] With two-story columns topped by Corinthian capitals and a temple-like pediment facing the street, it cost an unbelievable $10,000 and was probably the most expensive private dwelling yet constructed in

James Showers commissioned architect John Nichols to build this stately home
for his daughter, young Maude, and her new husband, Dr. Burton D. Myers.

*From the collection of the Monroe County History Center, 202 East 6th
Street, Bloomington, IN, www.monroehistory.org, 1986.077.0235.*

Bloomington. (For comparison, a common worker's cottage could be built
for $1,000 and a two-story family house would cost about $3,000 or $4,000.)
The new house boasted elegant front porches on both the first and second
floors and numerous large windows.

The grand front room of W. Edward's house was separated from the parlor
behind it by towering French pocket doors; both rooms had elegant fireplaces
with beautifully carved mantels. As in Nellie's and Jennie's houses just up
the street, there were vast expanses of highly decorative oak floorboards and
ornate moldings. The dining room had wood-paneled walls and a wooden
coffered ceiling. Edward's bedroom had a walk-in closet with a safe built into
the wall, where he could safely keep money overnight.[6] All interior doors had
elaborate paneling, and the upstairs bathrooms had delicate pastel-colored

W. Edward Showers's mansion.

From the collection of the Monroe County History Center,
202 East 6th Street, Bloomington, IN,
www.monroehistory.org, 1992.161.0035.

Arts and Crafts–style tiles on the walls. Because of the continued inadequacy of the city's waterworks plant, the house possessed its own built-in water system. Rainwater from the roof was collected by downspouts and directed into a massive brick-lined cistern in the basement. Boilers then heated the water and pumped it up to the attic, where it could be stored temporarily in tanks beneath the sloping roof. When a family member (or a maid) turned on a hot-water spigot in the house below, hot water issued forth, fed by gravity. The original sinks and bathtubs were preserved by all subsequent owners of the house and are still in place today. It's unclear where the toilets originally

Maud was also president of the board at Bethany Park, the Chautauqua-like summer camp in nearby Morgan County that was sponsored by the Christian Church. Her presence on the board coincided with some of its most popular years of attendance. There were lectures each morning at 11 AM, featuring prominent speakers who were well-known throughout the Midwest speaking on topics of interest; there were also Bible lectures and musical entertainments each night. Maud probably had much to do with choosing the programs each year. The assembly ran for approximately three weeks each summer and attracted so many people from so many states that the Monon railroad offered a special rate for travelers bound to that destination.

flushed to, as the city had not yet built sewerage, but we can assume there was a sanitary vaulted cesspit. Showers family members would not have adopted any method that was unhygienic; they had invested too much time attempting to clean up the city.

Maud Showers was now at the height of her activities as a progressive reformer. She served as president of the Local Council of Women between 1903 and 1906 and was an indefatigable campaigner who seems never to have stopped to catch her breath. The Local Council of Women was an umbrella organization that represented the united membership of every local women's group. These included the Women's Christian Temperance Union, the YWCA, Sorosis, the Cemetery Association, the Unique Club, the Wednesday Club, and many others. The Council offered membership to any organization that was interested in joining, provided its representative was a woman. The Monon railroad was eager to join, and Mrs. E. M. Seward served as its representative.[7] The Council of Women ultimately offered seats on its committees to men who were interested in its causes; one of these was the ever-helpful Sanford Teter. For a time the Local Council of Women was allied with the National Council of Women as well as the International Council of Women, whose wide-ranging goals encompassed the beautification of communities as well as world peace. The president of the National Council was the progressive feminist, educator, and lecturer May Wright Sewell, whose Classical School for Girls had been attended by both Beryl Showers and Bertha Matthews. Sewall was viewed by some women as a champion of women's rights, but others regarded her with suspicion.[8] The minutes of the meetings of Bloomington's Local Council of Women certainly hint at some small-town uneasiness at the radical goals of the national and international groups. For instance, the International Council wrote to all local affiliates asking them to participate in mass peace demonstrations on May 15, 1902; this was discussed during the meeting in Bloomington but no action was taken. The National Council also sent the local affiliate a daring proposition that read:

> Whereas there is at present in the United States untaxed [church] property to the amount of fully $3,000,000; and whereas the greater part of this untaxed property is productive in the sense that it produces a revenue over and above its immediate necessities; whereas a fundamental principle of our Constitution is that there shall be no union of Church and State; and whereas, in exempting from taxation such an enormous quantity of church property, we are thereby uniting church [and state] and placing a heavy additional burden upon the taxpayer; therefore [be it] Resolved; that we, the National Council of Women in convention assembled, hereby request our National and State legislatures to pass such laws as will exempt from taxation only such properties as are used for purely public purposes, and are not sectarian in any degree.[9]

It's unlikely that this was greeted with any degree of enthusiasm by a majority of the Local Council of Women, whose meetings often began with a prayer. Many of the club ladies were pious churchgoers who had labored for years to send missionaries to foreign lands. Maud herself was a staunch member of the Christian Church and an occasional member of the Women's Christian Temperance Union, but it's very possible that she was the one who spearheaded these radical suggestions, since she was on friendly terms with Sewall. (The proposition by the National Council to tax church property was never voted on, although a committee was appointed to further investigate the idea.) The Local Council was quite progressive for a small city like Bloomington in the turn-of-the-century Midwest, but it was not radical. It sought to improve its community not through shock tactics but through goals that anyone could agree on: sanitation and hygiene; tree and flower planting; education; charity to the helpless; and the need for a public library. Under the influence of the

Local Council of Women, schoolchildren participated in annual flower-arranging contests and competed with each other to plant flowers in their yards. Because the city of Bloomington had not followed through on its promises to clean up the courthouse square around the public hitching rack, the ladies of the Local Council continued to lobby against the amount of garbage and manure that could still be seen on the streets. The ladies opposed the construction of a speaker's stand on the courthouse lawn, since they had invested so much effort planting flowers, trees, and shrubs there. One would think that these well-educated and progressive women would support a speaker's stand where democratic debate could take place, but their opposition was based on the belief that the stand would "prove to be only a rendezvous for loafers through the week."[10] But Maud had a far more pressing concern than loafers; she wanted to build a hospital for the community. Charitable health care for the indigent was part of the concept.

> The ladies of this splendid organization are constantly engaged in charitable work and their many experiences have caused them to see the dire need of a hospital. Only yesterday one of the members said a 16 year old boy, the son of a soldier whose father and mother were both dead applied at a number of homes for aid. The boy was sent to the Knightstown soldier's home and from there was adopted by a family who refused to longer care for the youth when they found he was afflicted. His trouble is a bad sore on his limb. The organization here finds many cases of sick persons who, to be cared for properly, should be treated in a hospital. It is the desire to bring the matter before the public asking the cooperation of any or all the organizations of Bloomington, as well as the churches, the city and citizens.[11]

In addition to pathetic hardship cases such as this boy, there were others who needed drastic medical intervention. Bloomington possessed some extremely dangerous industry. In addition to Showers, major employers included the Monon railroad (soon to be joined by the Illinois Central, which surveyors were then busy laying out) and the stone quarries. The machinery at the Showers company occasionally removed the joints of fingers or maimed hands, but the railroad and the stone industry crippled or killed an extremely large number of men each year. Men laboring in the quarries often were crushed when massive slabs of stone shifted, and it was not uncommon for workers to have their limbs caught and ripped off entirely by the rapidly revolving machinery, causing horrifying headlines in the newspapers. The Monon railroad killed or mutilated people on a weekly basis, year-round; troubled people seemed drawn to the tracks like moths to flame. Drunk and mentally ill people appeared to be constitutionally unable to resist the lure of the tracks and would frequently lie down with their heads resting on the rail, awaiting decapitation. The summer and fall of 1904 was a particularly gruesome one, and the number of men who were cut to pieces by the railroad was unusually high. Boys were particularly prone to injuries because of their games along the tracks:

> Herbert Trinkle, age 12 years, son of Oris Trinkle, a blacksmith at Linden, was run over and killed by a Monon freight train about 7 o'clock Saturday night. Young Trinkle, with two companions about the same age, were bantering each other to see who could cross the track the last time before an approaching engine could pass. The unfortunate lad miscalculated the speed of the engine on his last trip and was caught beneath the wheels and while badly grounded up [sic]. He lived almost two hours after the accident, but was unconscious. A particularly sad feature of the affair was the fact that the boy's father was passing near by at the time, it was dark and he did not know who the boys were. He found a lantern and was shocked almost to distraction when the dim rays of the lantern flashed upon the mutilated form revealed to him the features of his own son.[12]

Nine days after young Trinkle's death, a prominent farmer was run over while driving his team across the tracks, and the newspaper noted that his brother had died only a short while previously in the identical manner. Four days later, a German cook at the Monon yards had both legs crushed by a passing train. He was taken to a doctor's office, where his legs were amputated. Despite the care he received, he died the same night. Doctors' offices of the era in the smaller cities and towns of the Midwest were grim by modern standards; surgeries were often performed in ordinary examination rooms using chairs or tables that had built-in leather straps to restrain the patient. Part of the move to launch a medical school at Indiana University was the desire to bring medical care into the twentieth century. City schools had required vaccinations against contagious disease since the 1890s and there was an increasing awareness of germ theory. Maud and her associates knew the time was right for Bloomington to have its own hospital. They purchased the Hopewell farm on the southern edge of the city for $6,000 after running a series of fundraising events and soliciting subscriptions from individuals. The idea was to refit the existing brick two-story farmhouse on the property for hospital purposes. Maud Showers spoke before the city council and made an impressive case for the city's need for a hospital, and all but a single councilman agreed that the city would subsidize a small amount (one dollar a day) to fund the hos-

Bloomington Hospital's official history states that the Council of Women originated the idea after one of the members arrived at a meeting in 1905 and told the others that her husband, a physician, had worked fruitlessly the night before to save the life of an unknown boy who had been run over by the train. Deeply touched by the terrible accident, the women supposedly decided to create a hospital so no more lives like this would be lost. But none of the minutes from the group's meetings at that time reflects any version of this incident, and plans for a hospital were already underway in 1904. The anecdote about the dying boy was first told decades after the event by the daughter of one of the women on the Council, so it's quite possible that an actual accident like Herbert Trinkle's was misremembered and mythologized over the passage of time.

pital in exchange for the hospital maintaining a room for the sick poor of the community.

The Council of Women proceeded to purchase the property, running up a debt in order to do so, and organized additional ongoing fundraising events to pay for the cost of remodeling two rooms with beds for use as hospital wards. They also equipped an additional room on the top floor for surgeries. A modern reader might be appalled at the idea of jostling a sick person up a flight of narrow stairs to an ordinary bedroom that had been converted into a surgery, but it was undoubtedly more sanitary than many of the patients' homes were. Given the fact that the fastidious and hygienic Maud was in charge of converting the former Hopewell residence into a hospital, the physical structure was likely scrubbed, painted, washed, and equipped in such a way that no fault could be found by anyone who would need to spend the night there. Maud was most likely given assistance and advice by the two doctors who had married into the Showers clan, Dr. Holland and Dr. Myers. These two gentlemen had just collaborated in establishing Indiana University's new School of Medicine, so no one in the community could doubt the worth of their opinions.

The concept of a hospital was completely novel to Bloomingtonians. In the days before the hospital, anyone who had needed an appendectomy or a tumor excised had been treated at home in his or her bedroom by a doctor who would bring his black bag, don an apron, roll up his sleeves, and set to work using scalpel and saw, and (if the patient was lucky) primitive and dangerous anesthesia. A few backward citizens undoubtedly would have grumbled that they saw little need for a hospital. Consider that every inhabitant of 1906 Bloomington had been born at home and fully expected to die at home surrounded by family, as his or her ancestors had done. The idea of going somewhere other than one's own bedroom to seek medical treatment (or to die) was a novel concept for many. But those people were free to continue paying their doctors to make house calls; the hospital's mission was to provide not only services for those who could pay but also charitable health care for the poor, who otherwise had no option except to die.

Maud became the head of the new hospital board, which was under the direct supervision of the Local Council of Women. She immediately set to work soliciting material help from the community:

> Inasmuch as the hospital is now a certainty it is proposed to prepare plans for its maintenance. Since funds and supplies to this end will come as free offerings, it is urged that each housewife in preparing her winter's supply of jellies and preserves set aside one or more glasses of jelly and as many pint cans of preserves as she may be willing to donate—such contributions to constitute the fruit supply for the hospital. It is hoped that each woman of our city will feel personally interested to the extent of giving at least one cup of jelly or one pint of preserves.[13]

The hospital held its grand opening reception in early December of 1905. Donations of vegetables, meats, fruits, jellies, and other foodstuffs suitable for hospital purposes were requested. Even schoolchildren were invited to participate: "Children are asked to bring a potato, apple, cabbage, etc."[14] The pantry may have been well stocked, and scores of curious people may have toured the rehabilitated brick farmhouse, but there was not yet a single patient. Only a day or two after it opened, the hospital was thwarted in its first attempt to minister to the needy. An impoverished couple, John Crockett and his wife, had been traveling by two-horse wagon from Kentucky to Peru, Indiana, but their progress was checked when Mrs. Crockett went into labor. She gave birth in the wagon some distance outside town, without medical assistance or shelter. That night the temperature was sixteen degrees above zero, and the infant died within five minutes of its birth from exposure. When Crockett came into the city to obtain burial for his baby, officials found that he was destitute and his wife was still suffering and in need of medical assistance. Although the hospital offered to treat his wife, all expenses to be paid by the township, Crockett wanted none of their charity and absolutely refused to let her be moved to the hospital.[15] This was a grave disappointment for city officials as well as the hospital ladies. But less than a week later the hospital was able to welcome its first two patients: a woman named Miss Mitchell, and a respected Indiana University lecturer, Professor Eigenmann, who was operated on for appendicitis. Eigenmann's surgery was successful and Miss Mitchell had no complaints, which must have greatly relieved Maud and the other ladies on the hospital board. Patients began to trickle in, first by ones and twos and then in growing numbers.

By 1906, the end of the hospital's first year, the converted house that served as a hospital was already at full capacity with ten patients, and the two wards completely filled so that beds had been added in the hallways; applicants were even being turned away, although charity cases were kept on.[16] In order to enlarge and improve the spartan facilities, a series of fundraisers was held by the hospital board. One of these, held on the courthouse square, featured vaudeville, fortune-tellers, "a fish pond, an art gallery, moving pictures, stereopticon views in the court room, ice cream booths, candy booths, sandwiches and coffee booths. From five to seven o'clock a full supper will be served for the small sum of 20 cents. There will be ponies for the children to ride, and a free band concert. Autos will take passengers about the city for a small sum."[17] This event was attended by two thousand citizens and raised more than $200 toward the hospital debt (more than $6,000 in modern currency), but it may seem puzzling to us that anything as necessary to a modern city as a hospital had to be funded by bake sales and carnivals. It's an example of how individual women stepped forward and filled a need that their own local government refused to recognize. This group of citizen activists created a primitive hospital and then improved it again and again, paying off one debt only to borrow money again in order to make further improvements. The extended Showers family strongly supported the hospital for many decades to come, and Drs. Holland and Myers were untiring advocates who worked as ceaselessly as

The newspaper's illustration of the second and
much larger hospital building, late 1910s.

Maud did. When the Council of Women decided in 1919 to hold a major fundraiser and build a larger, modern hospital structure with thirty beds, proper heating and lighting, an elevator, and "sun parlors," William Showers ordered the entire building to be equipped completely by the Showers company. Most of the furniture for the rooms and the hospital offices were specially designed and finished in the Showers factory.[18] Maud's daughter, Beryl Holland, would serve in later years, as her mother had done, as president of the hospital board.

IMPROVING THE CITY

Much had been done by the Council of Women to improve sanitation and hygiene, but the city was still lagging in many respects. Despite constant reproaches by the ladies, the courthouse hitching rack was still in place and both the city and local businessmen had failed in their promises to keep the square clean. The courthouse itself dated to before the Civil War and was crumbling. Sanford Teter, along with other city councilmen and prominent businessmen, suggested a new courthouse. The idea gradually gained momentum; the newspaper issued a clarion call to "replace the building that has disfigured the public square for years."[19] When the county commissioners finally agreed to build a new courthouse for the sum of $115,000, church bells rang and factory whistles shrieked to announce the glad news. James Showers was promptly appointed to the committee set up to assist the county commissioners in selecting an architect, along with other prominent businessmen. His name is on the plaque that hangs inside the courthouse today.

In addition to building a new courthouse, the city finally received a second railroad after more than three decades of active lobbying. Surveyors arrived first and were followed by teams of Italian linesmen, who rapidly installed the tracks for the new rail line that would lead to Indianapolis instead of Greencastle. The Showers brothers and other prominent businessmen had wanted this line for years and had made many trips to Indianapolis to meet with railroad officials. Another advance was the new city sewer system, which would render the old privies obsolete, at least for anyone who lived in the central core district served by the new cast-iron pipes that were now installed. Those on the fringes were out of luck and had to continue using their outhouses. William Showers made a trip in 1905 to Milwaukee, St. Paul, and St. Louis to inspect the sewage systems in those cities. As a result of his help, and thanks to Maud's ceaseless activism regarding hygiene, the city of Bloomington finally resolved to invest in sewerage.

But in order to have sewers that flushed waste to the new treatment plant, a larger supply of water was needed. The original city waterworks that the Showers brothers had spent so much of their own money on was no longer capable of supplying enough water to the greatly increased population. (Thanks to the "boom," the city's population in 1890 was 4,800 and double that by 1910.) The original waterworks lake was completely inadequate for a larger city and could never be relied upon in the face of the frequent late-summer droughts. The university instructed its students not to take baths and not to wash more

The new courthouse, with its unsanitary hitch rack.

From the collection of the Monroe County History Center, 202 East 6th Street, Bloomington, IN, www.monroehistory.org, 1983.008.0001.

frequently than necessary, but the Showers Brothers Company and other manufactories needed large amounts of water to power their steam-driven machinery. The last time the city had experienced a killing drought was in 1899. The *Telephone* had then complained,

> The present dry spell is causing much inconvenience and annoyance in the city. Wells and cisterns are rapidly becoming exhausted, and it is with difficulty that water is secured for the necessities. Another week will exhaust the supply at most of the factories, and now it is almost impossible to get water with which to do washing. It is necessary to haul it in barrels, secured at springs adjoining the town at 15 cents a barrel or more.[20]

The Showers Brothers Company was in better financial shape than were smaller companies to endure the drought, but it was nevertheless expensive to hire a railroad tanker car to have water hauled from the Star Quarry spring on a regular basis. "It is estimated that one-fourth of people are either buying or borrowing water. It costs $5 a day to supply the Hotel Gentry," the *Telephone* reported (more than $127 in modern currency).[21] Besides the inconvenience in not having water with which to wash clothing, there was the significant danger of fires raging unchecked without water in the hydrants to fight them. The city needed a permanent solution to the chronic shortages, which the new sewerage would soon exacerbate.

The problem was that the reservoirs on the city's west side had been built on top of porous karst limestone, which could not hold water for very long. Water did not trickle through the dam, as many believed at the time, but percolated beneath it to emerge as a marsh on the lower side of the dam. Enough water was wasted each year at the waterworks to supply the needs of 20,000 people, the people were told at a special meeting called by the city in 1903 to address the issue. James Showers stated that it was no longer practical to rely upon the present location, which could not furnish the needs of the city any longer. "He said he did not believe fifty dams if built there would hold the water as it seems almost an impossibility to stop the leaks. Mr. Showers favors Griffy Creek or Bean Blossom and thinks the city should at once make tests for water there. By building a concrete dam at Griffy Creek he believes the city would have a water supply sufficient for a town of 20,000 population."[22] William Showers also supported the idea of a lake at Griffy. But due to infighting between the two political parties, no significant action was taken to address the water problem. Although the Showers brothers were quite right in calling for a municipal water source at Griffy, that lake would not be built for nearly another twenty years owing to the city's stubbornness and reluctance to invest any more money than necessary.

The city resolved to repair its leaky reservoir by digging down to solid rock and using concrete to seal in the lake. The city added a second dam and lake to the first, thus forming the landmark that locals called Twin Lakes, but the stopgap measure did not function as well as hoped. By late 1908 another terrible drought had emptied both reservoirs, leaving the city gasping for water. Even the large clock atop the new courthouse dome stopped working, for it was powered by water. The Showers brothers were right about Griffy, but that was small consolation to them. During the water shortage that year the factory had been operating minimally, if at all. It was behind on its orders to the tune of forty rail-cars of furniture and could not afford to stay closed any longer. William announced that the factory would start up again after the company had imported a sufficient amount of water by tanker car, and it set a force of men to dig up the old factory pond so it could be used again for a water supply when the rains came that autumn.[23] Water was the one subject that probably vexed the Showers family more than any other, and a reliable supply was the one thing that continually eluded their grasp.

GASOLINE WAGONS

A small newspaper item almost escapes the reader's eye: W. N. Showers was going to Indianapolis to buy a White Steam automobile, "which will be the finest car ever seen in Bloomington. It will have 40 horse power and will be a hill climber."[24] Two days later, the newspaper added that the car would cost $4,200 and would be royal purple in color; it could accommodate eight passengers. The vehicle would be shipped from the factory in the East and arrive the following week. When it arrived, William and his wife Hanna, son W. Edward, and son-in-law Sanford Teter took the train to Indianapolis to fetch the vehicle and then drove it home. The trip took four and a half hours on the unpaved pike roads. "The fad for the gasoline wagons did not take much until last season when several were brought to town and it now looks as if the fad will turn to a craze next season," reported the newspaper some months later.[25] Today the purchase of cars is a comparatively ordinary event, but then there were only a handful of automobiles in Bloomington. William, with his background as a manufacturing man, was keenly interested in technology and machinery, as was Sanford Teter. William chose the best automobile available on the market at that time, manufactured by the White Sewing Machine Company and the favored car of presidents Theodore Roosevelt and William Howard Taft. Steam cars at this time far outnumbered internal combustion cars; they were less noisy and produced no poisonous fumes. A small amount of fuel was burned in order to create steam, which was super-heated in a closed coil system. The steam drove the pistons, which propelled the automobile. The car had two seats in the front, a bench seat in the middle accommodating three more persons, and at the rear, set high above the others for good visibility, a seat that accommodated three more. The vehicle was so high off the ground and so long that it was almost the size of today's sports utility vehicles. There

Like all his family, William Showers was kindly and helpful.

From the collection of the Monroe County History Center,
202 East 6th Street, Bloomington, IN,
www.monroehistory.org, 1985.010.

were no fixed windows and in case of rain, rolled-up shades could be lowered on all sides. In order to start the vehicle, different tasks had to be performed at different points on all sides of the car: adding water (the White Steam could travel 150 miles on one gallon of water); pumping the fuel to the proper pressure; opening valves and lighting the pilot flame. The driver sat in front of a complex arrangement of various pedals and a foot-activated horn, and a steering wheel with an inner throttle control that moved independently; he needed to keep an eye on countless pressure gauges and valves that were continually changing, and attend at once to anything that went amiss. The White Steam was in effect "a train without tracks"[26] and was so complex a mechanism that most drivers today would probably choose to walk rather than attempt to drive it. William appears to have mastered the mechanics well enough in one day to drive it back to Bloomington. Sanford Teter was so enchanted by it that he ordered a White Steam for his own family the following May, followed by a succession of other vehicles. Sanford and Nellie were adventurous enough to drive a touring auto all the way to Virginia in 1908, taking photographs along the way. The leisurely round trip took about a month and they only experienced a single breakdown along the way.

William's purchase of a car is notable in two ways. First is his familiarity with and confidence while using this exceptionally complex piece of machinery; being a former "mechanic" (the operator of machinery) was undoubtedly useful. Second, the price: $4,200 in 1906 represents an astonishing $99,000 in modern values. Early automobiles were fragile and not designed to last for a decade or more, as modern cars are. An automobile of those days was an ephemeral pleasure, easily damaged and soon to be replaced. In 1906, a person in Bloomington could take the same sum expended upon William's car and build a quite acceptable two-story family house, or construct three or four humble workers' cottages. William may have begun his factory career living in a worker's cottage of his own, sharing the tiny space with his brother and their respective wives, but at this point he was able to spend a fortune on a single vehicle. "I enjoy the use of a good auto," Mr. Showers remarked to the *Telephone*, "and I feel I am entitled to some of the pleasures of life as I go along. It is about the only amusement I care for."[27]

James, in contrast, was interested in the new "gasoline wagons" but less so in personally piloting one of the early automobiles, although he experimented with it. He hired at least two African American chauffeurs to drive him around town. One managed to turn the car completely upside down after striking a

Sanford and Nellie Teter during their automobile excursion
to the East Coast and back. Teter is seen repairing a
broken spring using a piece of fitted lumber.

Courtesy Nancy Teter Smith.

curb, damaging it substantially, while the other received a ticket for speeding
through the corner of Kirkwood and College Avenues and nearly striking a
child. The fine was steep for a worker of that day: one dollar (about $20 in
today's values). The newspaper tutted that the smooth new brick pavements
around the square were encouraging speeding. But although James was not a
hands-on driver, he was nevertheless quite enthusiastic about the new technology.[28] By the summer of 1910 James had joined several of his family members
in helping organize an "auto social,"[29] in which all the local automobile owners
planned a car caravan with their friends and wives along a circle route that
wound its way through three counties. Charles Sears's new four-door Marmon
auto sounds like a sensible family sedan in comparison to the White Steam,

In 1915 W. Edward Showers helped form the Weidley Motor company in Indianapolis, assisting the inventor with a cash infusion and becoming the company's first president. "The Weidley motor has been enthusiastically received at the National Auto Shows and has proved its immense value in racing cars." The company supplied motors for the Chalmers and the Owen Magnetic car. The business's plant started out with fewer than ten men but within three years was employing 350 workers in a plant a block long. By 1919 it had a three-year contract to supply motors that was worth $20,000,000, as reported by Jacob Piatt Dunn in *Indiana and Indianans* (vol. 4, p. 1704).

seating five passengers. "No man in Bloomington gets more pleasure out of a car than Mr. Sears," noted the paper.[30] The following month, members of the extended Showers family motored north to attend the Indianapolis 500 auto race. "Nobody who was not present could imagine the size of a crowd of 85,000 people," Charles Sears told the newspaper upon his return. "The streets were so crowded that autos had to seek space on the sidewalks. The excitement was beyond description. Offers of $50 were made for rooms at hotels. Many lay down on the cement sidewalks in front of the Union Station, using the slightly elevated curbs for headrests. Old news papers were used by some for pillows."[31] Showers family members who attended the Indianapolis 500 that year were William and Hanna Showers, Sanford and Nellie Teter, Charles Sears and his wife, Will Sears and his wife, and Dr. J. E. P. Holland and his wife, Beryl.

Sanford and William soon replaced their expensive White Steams with Premier autos, but W. Edward beat them all for conspicuous consumption when he purchased the most expensive auto yet to be seen in Bloomington, for $5,000 ($113,600 in modern currency).[32] The man who had enjoyed the most lavish wedding and built the most extravagant mansion in the city was now driving the most expensive vehicle. (He later also bought the first twelve-cylinder automobile in Bloomington.[33]) But the private hobby of a wealthy family could still end up benefiting the community at large, as was seen by the formation of the new Automobile Club, whose mission was to improve the main roads in and out of Bloomington. James Showers and his nephew Charles Sears were in this club, with their friend Fred Matthews as the president. The group argued, "During the summer months hundreds of automobiles make trips between Indianapolis, French Lick and Louisville and practically all of them avoid Monroe county—going by way of Seymour and Columbus—because of the bad roads. These tourists mean considerable in a commercial way to the county, so the improvement of a road leading through the county is to be pushed first."[34] This was a sound observation, because there was indeed much money to be gained from tourism. Thanks to lobbying by these wealthy automobile lovers, the city would soon benefit from better roadways; surfaces would be covered with "asphaltum" instead of brick. And the quest to improve the roads and encourage tourism soon resulted in the city's winning the new Dixie Highway route.

Chapter

11

"THE WORLD'S LARGEST
FURNITURE FACTORY"

IN 1907 the Showers Brothers Company had built the largest veneering plant in Indiana at the north end of their existing building. This new addition had its own separate power plant and what the *Bloomington Telephone* described as "remarkable machinery of the latest design." The Coe Automatic Veneer dryer was

> an enormous machine, made of solid steel, and 120 feet long. Four miles of steam piping are required to heat it, and a 120 horse power boiler is required to supply it with power and heat. The cost of this machine alone was $15,000. It bakes veneers bone dry within fifteen minutes from the time they come dripping wet from the wringers. It is the only machine of its kind in the state. Another enormous machine is the rotary veneer cutting lathe, with its knife 100 inches long, which will turn an enormous saw log into one twentieth inch veneers quicker than it takes to describe it.[1]

The campus on which the factory was located was filling up, with the three Victorian buildings now firmly joined together by later additions to create a single large and irregularly shaped structure surrounded by outlying smaller buildings that housed the sawmill, power plants, and the company pond (kept in case of fires or municipal water shortage). The company was basking in a long spell of productivity and good income; the workforce was dedicated and

A rail car stands next to a foundation during the construction of Plant 1.

Accession 2010/013, collection of Indiana University Archives.

This view of the construction of Plant 1 shows the characteristic sawtooth roof.

Courtesy Nancy Teter Smith.

loyal and knew exactly what was expected. The company was also preparing to launch a new chapter of its history.

The company's board of directors voted in 1910 to massively enlarge their plant and hired Chicago engineer C. H. Ballew to design the new factory. The new building, which they soon dubbed Plant 1, would be large enough to vastly increase production and would allow them to employ a much larger workforce. The new building was constructed in part directly around the much smaller Victorian structure that already stood on the site, thus eliminating any need to vacate the premises or to interrupt production. The new factory contained 6.75 acres beneath one roof and offered seemingly endless room in which to spread out and expand, and the company's output actually showed an increase instead of a decrease during the construction. The new building was brick atop a timber frame structure. Side windows were still relatively small, but were much better than the Victorian iteration. The great improvement in lighting came from the sky itself, thanks to the sawtooth profile of the roofline which permitted endless rows of slanting, north-facing skylights that bathed the second floor in light. These skylights, the newspaper claimed, amounted to a full quarter of the entire roof area: 128,000 square feet. The wooden truss construction supposedly permitted the glass in the skylights to be kept in perfect alignment from year to year by accommodating any shrinkage of wooden elements by the tensioning of bolts. The owners were not unmindful of the danger of fire inherent in a factory that contained masses of wood, and they had maintained a private fire brigade and equipment at the factory for years. The new building was "fireproof from without, while the inside is coated with fire-proof paint."[2] Hot-water radiator coils snaked overhead, just beneath the skylights; these were intended to melt any falling snow from beneath the tin roof so as not to obstruct the skylights. Heating a room from the ceiling is inefficient, but it probably worked well to keep the roof and skylights clear.

The refurbished veneer mill enabled veneer to be shaved from water-soaked green logs and passed through a drier 122 feet long. Heated to 220 degrees Fahrenheit, the veneer was dried and ready in an impressive twenty-seven minutes flat, which meant that it could be worked into finished furniture on the same day that it was cut from the log. The veneer mill communicated directly with an entrance on the north end of the factory, while the sawmill fed its products into the east side of the factory. The raw product then passed through work stations where it was cut, dressed, assembled, and glued. At the south end of the huge new building the staining and varnishing was performed; the finished goods then passed down through elevators or slides to the first floor for packing and shipping.[3] The Monon and the Indianapolis Central railways passed on the west and east of the factory, respectively; the new factory had track facilities that allowed thirty cars to load at a time. The local press was awestruck at the sheer scale of the new building and claimed that the new plant was the largest of its kind in America (the company probably supplied this information). From this point onward, for at least the next decade, the Showers Brothers Company billed itself as "the world's largest." Because of the loss of the company records, it is impossible to state with certainty whether Showers Brothers was in fact the largest in terms of income, or whether it was largest in the quantity of pieces produced (although both were certainly quite substantial).[4] Very probably no other furniture company of that time was quite as large in physical square footage. An article written ten years later for the company newsletter compared the original Bucktown factory building against the vast Plant 1.

> Originally there was little chance to work at all when the mercury hovered around the zero mark, because the [old] factory could not be satisfactorily heated.... C. A. Sears and John Sears smile when you recall to them their method of carrying shavings out of the factory to the boiler room in what resembled a laundry basket. The factory covered an area of ground about the size of a town lot.... One man stacked all of the lumber in the early days. Today there are more men employed in the lumber yard than were employed in the entire plant then.[5]

Despite the sheer size of the factory, William Showers was still interested in the welfare of the workers. He intervened with local prison authorities on behalf of a paroled convict from Michigan City in northern Indiana who had come to Bloomington after serving his time and applied for a job. The plant employed him and found him to be a "steady and faithful" worker; his pay was increased from $1.25 per day to $1.75. The man married and his wife had a baby, but trouble was brewing. The warden of Michigan City prison received information that the man had been violating his parole, getting drunk constantly and bothering the community. Word was sent down to Bloomington, and he was arrested and thrown in jail.

> Mr. Showers took hold of the case and telegraphed Warden Reed, who telegraphed back instructions to the officer he had sent [to Bloomington], to see Mr. Showers. When the officer got at all the facts he at once bade the paroled man liberated from jail and expressed himself as being very indignant with the way the prison authorities had been fooled. When information is given which caused the return of a paroled man, the person giving the information gets $25, and it is said the men who sent in the false information were after the $25.[6]

William Showers stands during the construction of Plant 1 with the new factory whistle. William particularly loved whistles; he personally picked out the whistle for Plant 4 although he never lived to hear it.

Courtesy Nancy Teter Smith.

James Showers also helped men in trouble. In his memoirs he recalled,

> One time the son-in-law of a good friend of mine, was giving his wife and her family much concern, for he would drink to excess, every once in a while, and mistreat his wife, while drunk.
>
> Chancing to meet him on the street one day, I called him by name and said, "You are a good fellow, you mean to do right, you can do right[.] Won't you try to do right, from now on?" Nothing more was said between us at that time, only he promised he "would try."
>
> About a year later, his wife came to me and holding out her hand to me, said, "Mr. Showers, I want to thank you for the happiest year of my life[.]" "Why," I said, "I don't know what you mean!"—Then she told me that her husband quit drinking a year ago, that it prevented a possible separation between them, and that my intreaty to her husband and assurance of my faith in him had brought it all about.
>
> Just a few sincere words, can help lots of times. If I had given him a lecture instead, and criticized his drinking, who knows it might have driven him to be worse instead of better?

The Showers factory was turning out countless thousands of pieces of furniture for Sears, Roebuck & Co. during these years, and the economic depression of the 1890s was only a memory. In 1911 the company was immensely uplifted by an event that gave it additional national recognition.

> W. N. Showers, Sanford Teter and J. M. Smith were looking out of a factory window one day when they happened to see a group of serious-looking men carefully scanning the ground adjacent to the window which lighted the work-bench of one of their finishers. . . . "Have you lost something?" asked Mr. Smith. . . . "No"—came the answer— "but we have found something. The center of population is located right here." The speaker was Professor Wilbur A. Cogshall, head of the department of astronomy of Indiana University. His companions included his assistant and a number of other interested scientists who, basing their survey on the calculations of the U.S. Census Bureau, had discovered that the exact population-center of the country had chosen the Showers factory-yard as its home.[7]

Because Professor Cogshall had already located the population center some six miles east of Bloomington in Benton Township only a couple of months previously, it's very possible that influence was exerted in order to reposition the marker at a central and public location within the city proper. And what public spot would have been more appropriate than the front door of the largest industry in town? Showers Brothers was delighted to have the honor of having the center of population on its campus. The company had a circular limestone marker carved and placed a tall flagpole with a light above it.

James and William were both old men by this time, proud of their accomplishments and delighting in their families. James was mostly retired but still regularly attended board meetings at the Citizen's Loan and Trust Company. In 1908 his young grandson, the son of Dr. Myers and young Maude, died; the newspaper claimed he had a blood disease so rare that there had only been about seven previous cases ever reported. An expert in children's diseases had been summoned all the way from New York City's Bellevue Hospital but went away the next day, unable to cure him. The boy had been named after his grandfather, and the loss was hard for the family since the lad was bright and beloved by everyone.[8] In addition, James and William's eldest sister, Sarah Showers Sears, died in late September 1910 after having suffered from an unspecified illness for many years. (It is possible that she suffered from chronic ill-health and asthma, as her mother had before her.) "She was a good wife, a thoughtful, loving mother who during health was ever watchful of her children's welfare," noted the *Bloomington Telephone* on September 27, 1910.

William was younger than James, but he was feeling his age. He no longer worked long days beside his men, but he was nevertheless greeted with smiles by the workmen whenever he visited the factory. He had turned much of the daily business of the company over to his son, W. Edward, and spent his summers relaxing on his country estate several miles northwest of Bloomington, which he had named Weary Wood.[9] He built a comfortable house there with its own waterworks, and added a pond and golf links. William always enjoyed traveling and had traveled to the West with friends several years earlier; in 1912 he resolved to reward himself with another treat: a tropical vacation with his loved ones. "One of his heart's desires was being fulfilled this morning when President W. N. Showers, of the famous Showers Company, and his family, left at 9:15 this morning in a fine private Pullman car for a 3 weeks' tour through the south, also a trip by steamer to Cuba," announced the *Telephone*.

> The party is composed of the following members of the Showers family: Mr. and Mrs. W. N. Showers, Mr. and Mrs. Joseph Smith and daughter Miss Ethel, Mr. and Mrs. W. E. Showers and daughter Elizabeth Jane, Mr. and Mrs. Sanford Teter and daughter Mary Louise and son William Showers Teter[.] Miss May Sparks and Miss Della Stevens, two nurses who have been with the Showers family, accompanied the party. When a Telephone reporter called upon Mr. Showers in his car this morning and was asked who was to enjoy the trip he said, "Oh, just my little family."

The center of population was marked by a disk-shaped
slab of limestone, a flagstaff, and a light.

Accession 6043, collection of Indiana University Archives.

The Pullman car "Rover" is carrying the party and is an ideal one for luxury and comfort. It is fitted with a large observation apartment and a rear platform. Each of the families of the party has a private stateroom and berth. The car is artistically appointed and is heavily rugged. The culinary department is well supplied. An expert chef is in charge and a colored porter and waiter are employed. This morning a number of friends of the Showers family decorated the car with cut flowers.

A careful systematic route for sightseeing and pleasure is to be followed, the first stop being at Memphis for tomorrow, and Sunday the 18th in Vicksburg. They will arrive at New Orleans for the Mardi Gras the 19th and 20th, and also spend the 21st and 22nd sightseeing. The 23rd will be enjoyed in fishing at Pass Christian.[10] The route will then be through Mobile and Pensacola to Jacksonville, the 24th. Then for 522 miles the special travels over the Florida East Coast railroad through summer resorts to Palm

Beach, where they arrive the 25th, and at Miami the 26th. Here the party travel over the new Flagler ocean railway to Key West, 90 miles across a railway built above the edge of the ocean. At Key West a steamer will be taken to Havanna [*sic*], Cuba, where the tourists view the sights on Feb. 28th, 29th and March 1st and 2nd where on the 3rd the homeward journey will be commenced. The route will be up the East Coast to St. Augustine for the 4th and 5th of March. The special will then be attached to the Seminole Limited on the Illinois Central, and pass through Georgia, Tennessee, returning to Effingham, home March 8th.[11]

A hard-working man who had built up a furniture empire with his own hands could not ask for more: traveling in comfort on a private Pullman, following a grand circuit along the American Gulf Coast and extending the trip to an exotic tropical isle, all with his family by his side. Sanford brought his camera along and recorded scenes of colonial architecture surrounded by palm trees. This would be the last major excursion ever made by William, who was aging fast.

In late September 1912 Bloomington newspaper readers were surprised to learn that Maud had married for the third time in a quiet ceremony at the home of her daughter Beryl and her husband, Dr. J. E. P. Holland. The new groom, like Maud's second husband, was a local judge, James B. Wilson, and it is likely that they had met each other nearly twenty years earlier when Maud's previous husband had introduced her to the members of the local legal profession. Judge Wilson had also been a longtime supporter of Maud's campaign for a city hospital and had participated in the public demands for improved city hygiene. Only members of the immediate families were present, along with Maud's close friend Mrs. Flora K. Moore of Vincennes. The home was decorated with American Beauty roses, yellow dahlias, and palm fronds, and the forty-nine-year-old bride wore white Ottoman silk trimmed in point lace. This third marriage was the point at which Maud finally divested herself of her ties to the Showers company, selling her shares in the corporation and stepping down from the corporate board of directors in order to become a judge's wife.

The new Mrs. J. B. Wilson remained an active member of the hospital board and was intimately involved with the new campaign to obtain a Carnegie library for Bloomington. The community needed a better library than "the small library a few women have been conducting in a room of the court house, using such books as have been given by various people, largely for children."[12] A meeting was held to discuss the issue and consider setting up a library board. A committee was appointed, consisting of three members of the extended

Showers family: James Showers, Sanford Teter, and Noble Campbell (who had married Roxie Smith, or Smythe, William and James's niece). By agreement, three of the library board seats were required to be held by women and soon thereafter, Maud Showers Wilson became one of those board members. In 1913 the city began negotiations with the Carnegie Foundation regarding how much it was willing to give annually, and by 1918 the new library was built. Maud had successfully imposed her love of order, tidiness, and hygiene upon the community, and as an avid reader she had now succeeded in helping create another beneficial public institution.

A SECOND REBIRTH

In the spring of 1912 the company built a glass plant near its campus in order to have ready access to the materials it needed for its mirror-backed dressers and glass-fronted cabinets. This new small factory (twenty by sixty feet, with a fifty-foot ell) would be known as the Nurre Glass factory. It was named for J. M. Nurre, a glass professional who had relocated to Bloomington in order to start up the plant and who shared ownership of the new business with Showers Brothers. But the improvements didn't stop there. In early September of 1912, older readers who scanned the newspaper headlines might have thought they were reading the events of '84 again. "Spectacular Fire Causes $12,000 Loss,"

The new Carnegie Library was located on the lot where the Colored School had stood for several decades. The newer and larger segregated school was located ten blocks farther west, which was a significant inconvenience for the black children who had lived quite close to the old school. It was unfortunate that the Showers family's support of a public library had the result of seriously inconveniencing the black community they had been friendly with for many years.

declared the *Telephone.* "Fire thought to have started from the engine room of the saw mill at the big Showers furniture factory, completely destroyed that section of the plant last night . . . and caused the biggest fire Bloomington has had for many months. The loss is about $12,000 and insurance of $7,000 was carried in various companies." Flames were so high that when seen at a distance, observers mistakenly believed that the main factory building itself was on fire. The contents of the sawmill were so flammable that within minutes the building was doomed. The fire fighters were hindered in their efforts by low pressure in the water mains, which were not large enough to provide vigorous streams of water to drench the building. The sprinkler system recently installed in the main factory protected the rest of the buildings.

> The greatest excitement of the fire was caused when the valves on the big boiler opened to allow the steam to escape. The intense heat caused a high pressure of steam to arise in the boilers and there was great danger of them bursting. Fortunately the pressure did not become too great for the valves and the expected explosion did not occur. Several hundreds of people were witnessing the fire and a general rush for a place of safety was made when the first roar of steam came. The noise was heard many blocks away.
>
> W. N. Showers, Edward Showers and Charles Sears were on the grounds, directing their employees in fighting against the flames. About 75 men were stationed among the lumber piles to the north of the mill to see that a fire did not break out there, and others were on the roof of the main plant. A large two-story frame house near the veneering plant that is owned by the company as a residence for their night watchman, caught fire several times but no great damage resulted.
>
> Mr. Showers stated last night, that not an hour's time will be lost at the factory as a result of the fire. . . . Another larger mill had already been planned for and its construction will be pushed now as rapidly as possible.[13]

The sawmill was not the only structure on the sprawling site to be rebuilt. The veneer mill would be enlarged and the entire factory would receive a makeover that would double its size. The company announced only days later that by the first of May in the following year it would be operating an immense new factory building, to be built to the north of the existing plant. "The proposed new building is 200 feet wide, and 460 feet long," reported the *Telephone.* "The building of such a plant will mean much to Bloomington in the additional employment of from 225 to 250 men. This new plant will have 200,000 square feet of floor space."[14] Engineer and architect C. H. Ballew, who had designed the existing factory, arrived from Chicago that week to supervise the construction of the new plant, which would become known as Plant

2. Much of the furniture produced by the two factory buildings was destined for Sears, Roebuck & Co., which offered inexpensive furniture through its mail-order catalog. By May of 1914, Showers Brothers Company had already manufactured 31,728 jobs (presumably pieces of furniture) for Sears, which represented 63.38 percent of all the company's jobs to date in that year (55,551 total jobs completed).[15] It's quite obvious why Showers Brothers felt it needed a special manager—Maud's son, Erle Showers—just to deal with orders for Sears.

By the following April the new factory addition was officially opened. Seen from either up close or at a distance, from the courthouse dome or from the top of the nearby Maple Heights neighborhood, the sheer size of the Showers campus was incredible. Plant 1 had covered nearly seven acres of ground and Plant 2 was almost the same size. The grand reopening gala featured an all-day open house with guided tours of the new factory, "both the old and new part,"[16] and refreshments were served by many of the Showers women: William's wife, Hanna Lou; W. Edward's wife, Bertha; and Nellie Showers Teter, Jennie Showers Smith, Mrs. Charles A. Sears, and Mr. and Mrs. W. H. Sears. "No less than 8,000 people—over half the population of Bloomington—besides many from out of the city joined in the ceremonies of the Showers Bros. company yesterday and last night," reported the *Telephone* on April 22, 1913.

> It was a gala occasion—inspecting the great plant through the day; a merry minstrel [show] at night and then a dance. Everybody was happy, with hearts full of well wishes and extending congratulations; Wm. N. Showers, the president, being the central figure, and it was quite in place that his good wife should receive her full share of the honors, while the officers of the company, the superintendents and loyal working men came in for their full share of credit.
>
> At 8 o'clock there was great applause when President Showers opened the evening exercises by blowing the whistle that was used in the first factory in 1868, and then Mr. Showers touched an electric button which set in motion the motors that operate the machinery in the new factory No. 2—all combined a furniture plant twice as big as any similar factory in the world.

Company manager W. Edward Showers welcomed the audience and expressed appreciation of the goodwill between the company and the people. He invited all to enjoy the minstrel show, which lasted until nearly 10:30 that night. Seating for more than two thousand people was arranged, courtesy of the local Gentry circus, and tickets were handed out by William Showers himself with the assistance of Charles Sears. Joe Smith, William's son-in-law, was the doorman. "The music was good and the ready wit, much of which was directed at various employees of the factory, created much amusement," the *Telephone* summed up. This glowing evening must have seemed the zenith of accomplishment to William as he went home to his elegant home on North Walnut Street late that night. From a small manufactory housed in a rough shed to an immense new factory filled with new equipment, the Showers Brothers Company was now the king of the furniture trade.

This was an era of grand expansion for the company; economic vitality combined with personal affluence on the part of family members. William and James's trusted nephew and factory manager, Charles Sears, became the president of the city's new Country Club and enjoyed a country estate like his uncles did. Sanford Teter helped the members of the old Commercial Club, who had been promoting Bloomington since the 1890s, organize a new Chamber of Commerce that drew up an agenda to promote the city's growth. Teter became the first president of the new organization and lobbied successfully to have the route of the new Dixie Highway come through Bloomington. An avid car enthusiast, he understood that the future of the automobile was very bright indeed, and that tourism would follow on the heels of improved roads. He pledged that the Bloomington community would donate $5,000 to the construction of the new highway and oversaw the fundraising. He also wished to improve the route to Indianapolis, which in those days wound pointlessly through Ellettsville and Gosport before arriving in Martinsville and then Indianapolis, a sixty-five-mile trip that took several hours.[17] (Today it's a forty-mile trip that takes no more than an hour from downtown Bloomington.) He took on the obstructionist Mayor Harris, a Democrat who had been blocking all Republican efforts to build a new city reservoir on the north side of the county, and served as head of the Citizen's Water Committee that fought the mayor all the way to the state Public Service Commission. But Teter was halted abruptly by a terrible illness at the end of 1915.

"Sanford Teter seriously ill.—Prominent citizen has attack at 4 A M and condition is alarming," reported the *Telephone* on December 7. After retreating to bed with a terrible headache, Teter had become helpless and suffered a paralytic stroke. Two days later the paper reported, "Sanford Teter on the Edge of the Valley of the Shadow of Death.—It is with exceeding sorrow and regret that the community learns this afternoon that Sanford Teter, one of Bloomington's foremost citizens, remains in the same critical condition with but very slight chances of recovery—and his death may come at any time. In-

This comic photo apparently celebrates the coming of the Dixie Highway to Bloomington. The car is resting on the population stone in front of the factory and bears a round sign reading "Safety first," and the word "Dixie" on the hood. The man in the rear is the aging William Showers.

From the collection of the Monroe County History Center, 202 East 6th Street, Bloomington, IN, www.monroehistory.org, 1991.127.0001.

deed, the chances as *The Telephone* goes to press are very much against him." Dr. Emerson, a "famous specialist" from Indianapolis, arrived and performed emergency surgery to relieve a blood clot that was causing pressure on the brain. In pain and enormously weakened, Teter remained in bed for the next six months, suffering unimaginable agonies from kidney stones. In June 1916 he was placed on a bed in the back of W. Edward Showers's huge car, his doctor accompanying him, and driven to Long Hospital in Indianapolis for X-rays. His devoted wife, Nellie, his brother, Walter, and sister-in-law and assorted nurses traveled in a second car; the trip, going slowly on rough roads along the Gosport route, took more than four hours. Teter was so glad to be in a car again that he seemed to "be fresher when the journey ended than when it began."[18] The X-rays showed that the left kidney contained six large stones and a hundred small ones; the right kidney appeared healthy.[19] Teter underwent a three-hour surgery to remove the damaged kidney. After a month of recuperation in the hospital he was home again, his left side permanently disabled from the stroke. Doctors forbade him to engage in any vigorous exertion, and he was compelled to drop all of his commercial and political activities. The hardest part must have been giving up driving a car. If not for this forced retirement in his early forties, it is altogether possible that Sanford Teter might have solved Bloomington's ongoing water problems and run successfully for mayor or congressman. The loss to the city's development caused by his dropping out of politics cannot be underestimated. Making the best of a bad situation, Teter equipped the entire top floor of his family's new house on North College Avenue as a home gymnasium for remedial exercises.

Although overexpansion would later cripple the company, its enlargements during this decade were extremely profitable. Plant 1 was built in 1910; the Nurre Glass factory and Plant 2 were both built in 1912; the Dimension Mill (Plant 3) was built in 1915; John Nichols designed an elegant corporate office at Tenth and Morton Streets in 1916 (described as "the prettiest building in Bloomington"[20]), and a sample room and grocery was added that same year. The new administration building contained a unique feature: an auditorium on the top floor capable of seating nine hundred people, planned specifically to offer space for presentations, meetings, music and dances, silent films, and vaudeville.

Nurre Glass, like Showers Brothers, was a multigenerational family business. In addition to mirrors it manufactured plate-glass windows, car windshields, the very first experimental glass basketball backboards, and the popular rectangular glass tiles used to cover the walls of kitchens and bathrooms throughout Bloomington in the 1920s. The company led the way in manufacturing free-hanging wall mirrors (virtually all American mirrors were previously set into pieces of furniture). At its height, the Nurre Glass company had over 8,000 accounts nationally, including at large department stores like Gimbels, Bloomingdale's, and Wanamaker's.

Interior of the Showers administrative building. At the time of its opening it was called "the prettiest building in Bloomington."

From the collection of the Monroe County History Center,
202 East 6th Street, Bloomington, IN,
www.monroehistory.org, 1989.072.0006.

A description of the Showers factory at its height was published on March 12, 1919, in the *Indianapolis Star*:

> An idea as to the immensity of the organization is . . . the fact that more than 1,000 men are employed and the monthly pay roll aggregates $60,000. In the Showers Brothers factories there are seventeen acres of floor space. The average yearly consumption of lumber is 24,000,000 feet, the approximate value of which is $550,000.
>
> An outsider might be inclined to think that in a . . . series of factories spread out over an expanse of seventeen acres there would be not a little chance for confusion in the manufacture of any product. Such is not the case. . . . Business is handled on a north and south basis, so that there is not the least chance for confusion at any point. For instance, a large order for some type of furniture is received in the office. The filling of this order is begun at the north end of the plant where the log yard is located. Here $75,000 worth of logs are awaiting movement south, into the wheels of the various factories for ultimate production into furniture.
>
> A giant electric crane gives the logs their start from the log yard and they are carried to the mill on an electric trolley, where they are cut up into the required lengths and breadths. From the mill the lumber is placed in yards for seasoning and drying and later transferred to the largest battery of dry kilns in the world. These kilns have a capacity of 502,400 feet of lumber at one time. After the process of drying and seasoning in the kilns, the lumber . . . is taken to the dimensions plant and the veneer mill. In the dimensions plant the lumber is sawed into rough forms, approximately the shape and size required for the finished product.
>
> Unlike most furniture factories, Showers Brothers have their own veneer mill, where a great lathe peels the logs into sheets almost as thin as paper. It is in this mill that 25,000,000 feet of veneer a year is produced and in the same length of time 4,000,000 feet of material for drawer bottoms and back panels turned out. The dimensions mill and the veneer mill feed the two Showers plants proper, where the furniture is really made. Each of these two factories is complete in itself with designing rooms, gluing rooms, machine rooms, carving rooms, storage warehouses and loading platforms, the latter capable of reaching twenty-four cars at once. It is in these two factories that the actual product, which started in the log yards, at the northern extremity of the chain of factories, reaches materialization. Showers Brothers also have their own mirror factory with a capacity of 1,000,000 feet of plate glass annually.
>
> The buildings that house this great furniture industry are models of factory construction, with brick and concrete walls and metal and glass roofs. The many plants are operated and lighted by electricity and heated with steam. A ventilating system changes the air completely every four minutes. There are no dust pipes or belting overhead to obstruct the light.

Showers Brothers had been in business for almost fifty years by this time and the company was at the top of its game. If Hollywood had ever made a movie about the company, it undoubtedly would have ended at this very point with the fairy-tale conclusion "They all lived happily ever after." But real stories have a way of continuing beyond the "happily ever after" part.

This illustration, taken from company letterhead, shows the vast plant.
Unlike earlier exaggerated views, this one is fairly accurate
in depicting the scale of the campus.

Collection C270, collection of Indiana University Archives.

Chapter

12

THE *SHOP NOTES* YEARS

IN 1917 THE COMPANY STARTED a biweekly employee newsletter that would appear for the next decade. *Shop Notes* was a miscellany that combined official news from the company with jokes, advertisements, and notes of interest. *Shop Notes* contains news about employees' weddings, new babies, sick relatives, and bereavements; it mentions workers who have recently purchased new automobiles and the results of employees' hunting and fishing excursions. There are previews of upcoming vaudeville events and detailed examinations of the performance of the company baseball team, the Showers Specials. Many of the issues contain short items about the early history of the company. Editorials praise home ownership and thrift, holding up the example of the factory founders as a template for others to follow. *Shop Notes* records many instances of the company's benevolence toward its workers; it notes that in October 1916, Showers management made a gift to each of the thousand-odd employees of the factory: a passbook at the Showers Brothers Savings Bank with one dollar credited to each worker's name.[1] (Adjusted for inflation, this equals an outlay by the management of nearly $20,000 in today's values.) The country was preparing for war; workers were paradoxically advised to spend freely while practicing thrift. They were also advised to kill flies, plant gardens,

The Showers auditorium with the vaudeville show "The King of Timbuctoo," with the musicians sitting in the front row.

*From the collection of the Monroe County History Center,
202 East 6th Street, Bloomington, IN,
www.monroehistory.org, 1988.051.0002.*

give their children good educations, and clean up after themselves. *Shop Notes* is a curious little publication, filled with anecdotes, manufacturing facts, and profiles of the major figures at the factory. Because it honestly recorded the ups and downs of the company, *Shop Notes* is a valuable historical record of the factory at its height, a decade-long portrait of a large company and the concerns and interests of its staff and workers. In its pages we find a parody of the Lord's Prayer involving Superintendent Charles Sears:[2]

> Mr. Sears is my boss. I shall not want another.
> He maketh me make more warehouse [finished goods] all the time.
> He leadeth me into noisy machine rooms.
> He restoreth my knowledge.

He leadeth me into the inner office on the green carpet.

Yea, though I am short on warehouse, I will fear no evil.

His looks and his smiles they comfort me.

He prepareth some work for me, in view of my ignorance.

He annoys my head with questions. My brain boileth over.

Surely Sears and warehouse will follow me all the days of my life,

and I will dwell in the Bughouse forever.[3]

We also hear about the vacations of the factory leaders: "General Manager W. Edw. Showers returned Wednesday from a three weeks sojourn in Pass Christian, Miss., with a coat of tan which is the envy of all who see him. Mr. Showers was ordered south by his physician to recuperate from the effects of a year of unusually hard work, but we rejoice that he is with us again much improved in health."[4] And we read the gentle jokes of a bygone era: "What is the best way to drive a nail so I won't hit my finger?" The answer: "Hold the hammer with both hands."

Shop Notes reminded its readers constantly that to own one's own home was "the very foundation of the best earthly happiness. . . . Rent money is money lost—gone forever. It shows good business judgment to own your home."[5] Profiles were run of men who had built their own homes, featuring photos of the new dwellings. *Shop Notes* was committed to the notion that men who owned their own homes would tend their yards with pride, thus improving the appearance of the community, and would become "steady" workers and model citizens. "The home is the most powerful factor in the character building that makes for the loftiest and best citizenship," the newsletter claimed.[6] A workingman who did not own his own house was viewed as footloose and irresponsible. "Building a home might seem impossible but there are many who have done it in spite of big obstacles. Doing the thing that seems impossible is usually doing the thing that's worth while."[7]

We understand much about the mindset of the men at the Showers factory when we read editorials in the company newsletter. The *Shop Notes* writers appear to have been greatly influenced by the rags-to-riches stories of Horatio Alger, and their opinions reflect a moralistic Victorian ethos. Their editorials reminded the workers to stop and think about their mothers, sisters, or daughters before relating a dirty story; suggested to them what a pleasant place the factory would be if the workers would only stop throwing bits of wood and trash out the windows and into corners; and exhorted them to fall into step and attend the Monday night workforce meetings designed to improve efficiency. "Stop and think," one article began. "Do you realize that we enjoy the advantages of a bank, a store, a restaurant, and a nurse? And do you remember that we are working in the largest furniture manufacturing plant in the world[?] I wonder if you realize that the plants have 17 acres of floor space, and are using about 300 machines. Do you always remember that you are working for the largest and most progressive furniture factory in the world?"[8] The older members of the workforce knew quite well how lucky they were, but the younger ones may have been more complacent.

Shop Notes contains a large number of biographical profiles of longtime employees, both white and black. Their hard work was held up as a valuable example of the proper work ethic. Take for example the profile of "Cap" Anderson Johnson, described as "for thirty-three years an employee of the Company, and a leading colored citizen . . . a model that many townsmen might well emulate." The biography continued:

> The well kept lawns, the huge blankets of rambler roses now in bloom, along with other varieties of flowers are only a part of his efforts. The long, even rows of vegetables, the little strawberry patch, three or four kinds of berry bushes and fruit trees are the things that go to make the home, says "Cap."

> . . . "Cap" left the "Bluegrass" state of Kentucky in 1885 and came straight to Bloomington. . . . When asked what he possessed as a nest egg to start out in life with, he modestly stated that he had nothing but just himself, not even a wife. He was then twenty years of age. Shortly after coming to Bloomington he started working for the Company, where he still remains. Through the influence of W. N. Showers, "Cap" was soon shown the advantage of owning a home so that when old age came he would have the satisfaction of knowing that he could be independent. He borrowed $600 which was spent for a plot of ground and a house. Originally the ground consisted of three acres and this small-size farm has never been idle since the day the deed was turned over to "Cap." "Only once in all these years have I failed to raise enough potatoes to carry me throughout the year, and I estimate that during the time that I have lived in my own home, I have raised enough garden truck to practically pay for the place."

> . . . "Cap" usually busies himself by caring for a number of hot beds, where he raises enough early truck for his own use and also enough cabbage, tomato and sweet potato plants to furnish the entire neighborhood for their planting later. This season, he raised 5,000 sweet potato plants, 1,500 cabbage and 1,500 tomato plants, most of which were sold. Next spring he anticipates increasing this number for the demand this season was much greater than he could supply. Last year [1918, during the war] when . . . there was urgent plea being made for all patriotic citizens to do their bit by raising all the garden produce they could, "Cap" went bigger and better than ever. His wife canned

Lewis Chandler, Lester Burnett, and James Buka worked in the packing
department at Showers. They wore layers of protective clothing because of the splintery nature of their job.

*From the collection of the Monroe County History Center, 202 East 6th
Street, Bloomington, IN, www.monroehistory.org, 1994.084.0014.*

300 quarts of fruit alone and many other provisions which were used during the
winter. As a start his family has forty-five quarts of cherries canned for the coming
season, to say nothing of the numerous other articles that will be stored up for the
cold days.[9]

Exemplary workers like "Cap" Anderson Johnson, many of whom had large
families with many children, did not expect a life of ease when they went home
after ten hours of hard work, six days a week. They did not expect to be able to
put their feet up, smoke a cigarette, and relax. They dived headlong into physical labor once they reached home in order to make their gardens yield and keep
their homes mended and painted. "Cap" Anderson was not the only worker
who enjoyed an additional income through extracurricular activities outside
the factory walls. The aging president of the Showers corporation had once

lived in a similar manner and counted every penny, but he had not worried about humble needs like this for more than thirty years; the younger owners had never experienced this kind of life at all. The gap between the lives of the owners and the workers was increasing with every year that passed.

The factory remained a very dangerous place of employment, just as it was in its earliest decades. Care and attentiveness were needed when operating machinery. *Shop Notes* printed a list of injuries in each issue as a method of warning company workers what could happen if they were not careful. The August 11, 1917 issue listed the past two weeks' injuries: a splinter had lodged in someone's left eye; the ends of two fingers had been caught in the chain of the sawdust carrier; someone was struck on the cheek by a nail that had glanced upward from a hammer, almost causing blood poisoning; a splinter had lodged in a finger while sanding; a saw had slipped and caught a finger on the end, severely cutting it; a lumber stacker had slipped and fell, "mashing" a finger that became infected; another man suffered heat exhaustion and lost two days of work. Capital letters in an item from December 1, 1917, emphasized the lesson: "DID YOU EVER GET SCHUYLER FENDER TO SHOW YOU HIS HAND. ASK HIM SOME DAY TO TELL YOU WHAT HE WOULD GIVE FOR HIS FINGERS. LET HIM TELL YOU THE LESSON HE LEARNED BY SEVERAL HORRIBLE ACCIDENTS. TALK TO BILLY GRAY AND SEE WHAT HE HAS TO SAY ABOUT ACCIDENTS. GET THE HABIT, BOYS, 'BE CAREFUL.'" The lesson seems not to have been taken to heart in the least (it may not have been possible with such inherently dangerous machinery), and a sample of injuries from a later *Shop Notes* included "steel in eye," a broken finger, a "mashed left foot," two workers (both female) who had overheated and collapsed, several dislocations, a nail in a foot, and two men seriously scalded on their feet while rolling logs into the boiling hot veneer vat.[10]

The Showers Brothers Company was one of the first furniture factories in the nation to hire women, and introducing women to what had been tradition-ally an all-male workplace was undoubtedly a shock to older male workers. The company must have entered into the experiment with every expectation of profiting by following national trends. *Shop Notes* observed, early during the new venture,

> We have something over forty girls employed in the plant now. They are working in every department except the Packing Rooms and Lumber Yard [where the heaviest labor was conducted]. In all departments the girls are showing their willingness to do their part. In many ways the girl has proven superior to the average boy. She is more

This photo, taken inside the factory, shows employee Dale Hardy
(second from lower right) with fellow workers. In the back row
stand three young women workers in overalls and caps.

Courtesy Guy Hardy.

ready to be taught about the work, she absorbs all advice given her by her shop mates
and goes about her work with an evident desire to learn and advance into higher paid
positions. . . . Showers Brothers Company is employing women in order to get more
help, not cheaper help. The idea is to pay the same wages to women that we pay to
men, if they are able to handle the work of men. Women have long been anxious for a
chance to prove their powers and their skill. They have begged industry to pay them
wages large enough to justify their entrance into industry. They now have their opportunity in our plants and from all indications they have come to stay and make a
permanent place for themselves.[11]

Hiring women was not just an experiment in improving gender inequality; it was a warning note for the men: "Last week the boys in the factory were astonished to find a number of girls had been employed in Finish Department No. 2. Mr. Antle and Mr. Burkes [foremen] report that they are easily taught. In fact they are already doing better work and more of it than the average boy. It is very probable that a large number of girls will be employed in all parts of the factory soon."[12]

Some time afterward, the newsletter proclaimed: "One year's trial has convinced us that women have a rightful place in industry. Women have not only done their bit in our plants during the war, but they have continued to work and seem to enjoy the factory atmospheres as much as if they had been born to the work. . . . They are holding positions in almost every department and they have been giving satisfaction. A number have been operating machines."[13]

> We, in our wisdom said at first, "It will never do to allow men and women to work together; constant associations will break down the barriers of respect." There were those amongst us who were loud in their denunciation of the experiment, saying, "the courts will be full of divorce cases. Let's not do this thing." But we brought women into the shops and the result is this,—instead of the loud-talking, swearing, and questionable stories formerly indulged in by men, we have a more quiet, gentlemanly bunch of male employees, every courtesy and consideration being extended to the women. The tone and morale of the organization is steadily on the increase.—When will we cease to learn?[14]

Showers Brothers also hired "old" men during 1918, when many able-bodied young men quit their positions to join the armed forces. Shop Notes recorded,

> A few years ago it was very difficult for an old man to get work in a factory or mill. The times have changed a great deal since then. . . . A man past fifty was formerly considered past his days of usefulness in a job demanding strength and speed. This erroneous belief has been disproven since the entry of this country into the world war. The old man has been found to be a very efficient workman if properly placed. . . . It is surprising how much work he can do, and do well. . . . Our firm is anxious to employ as many men of this sort as possible.[15]

When the United States finally entered the World War, Showers factory workers were reminded that even if they weren't able to go "Over There" to fight "the Hun," they could nevertheless participate in the war effort. The management enthusiastically purchased war bonds and encouraged all the workers at the factory to do the same, and any man who left for the war was assured that his position would be waiting for him when he returned. The

Showers Brothers Company filled military contracts for the War Department and provided all items at cost, without any profit to the company. The company manufactured oak typewriter tables and medical and surgical chests for the Medical Supply Department, and made a large quantity of dressers and tables to be used in the government's housing program. The Ladies' Auxiliary of the company, which had several Showers women as members,[16] made twelve hospital bedshirts, eighteen sweaters, eighty-nine handkerchiefs, three trench caps, four pairs of wristlets, thirty-five pairs of socks, and (inscrutably) a baby cap, and produced individual contributions amounting to $75.25 to give to the Red Cross (which, when adjusted for inflation, is equivalent to slightly more than $1,000 in today's values).

The war disrupted business badly because rail freight had to yield the right-of-way to military trains that were bearing soldiers and materiel to the front. Boxcars filled with Showers furniture sat on sidings for days, sometimes weeks, before making their way to showrooms. Manufacturers were ordered by the government to reduce their output in order to save materials for the war effort. At a meeting of all furniture manufacturers in Cincinnati on September 16, 1918, the U.S. Chamber of Commerce ordered all factories to reduce the number of active patterns, make no new patterns, and eliminate all metal pulls, trimmings, drawer locks, drawer guides, metal dustproof bottoms, and metal wheel casters. Drawer liners in buffets were to be eliminated; beveled glass could no longer be used in mirrors and mirror consumption in general was to be reduced by at least 25 percent; and wooden dowels were to be substituted for metal screws wherever possible. Many pieces of furniture were to be reduced in length. Even the Showers company's method of crating was altered in order to save the number of screws and nails used on each crate. Wartime austerity was welcomed as a chance to improve overall factory thrift and the company's line was reduced from 300 patterns to approximately 100.[17] The newsletter reprinted a number of patriotic and nostalgic letters from the front written by ex-employees who had joined the army, and it printed many photos of them in uniform, standing in front of their tents in far-off Europe.

Despite the war, workers at the company enjoyed many benefits that other Bloomingtonians did not have. Between 1917 and 1920 they could purchase foodstuffs at the company store, where the prices were lower than at any of the other local shops. The children of workers chased each other around a modern playground installed by the management.[18] Any workers who were injured on the job were sent immediately to the company nurse, who was capable of administering first aid. A matron tended to the needs of female workers. A company welfare department looked after the families of employees who were experiencing long-term disabilities that prevented them from working. Showers Brothers usually collected and burned its own wood scraps but began making these scraps available to its workers at a very low cost to be used for winter fuel. The price of scrap wood from Showers was so cheap in comparison with the firewood available in the city that there was always an immense demand for it.

And yet, even though the *Shop Notes* decade represented the financial height of the company, it's also obvious that new problems were arising. The enormous workforce was no longer a small and committed band of brothers but a vast horde. Indifference at work was noted in the corporate minutes from January 18, 1916:

> The beginning of the year found us surrounded with many good and honest employ-
> ees. However they lacked the welding together into an efficient machine. We have
> probably devoted more energies and time to the perfecting of our organization than
> to any other one phase of our business. . . . During the last year we instituted weekly
> meetings among the men which have had a very desirable influence. We have tried to
> educate and work for the interest of every employee. . . . It is only fair to give credit
> to our Superintendent [Charles Sears] . . . as his constant efforts have been directed
> along the line of closer co-operation, better feeling and bigger men in all depts.[19]

Because of the continual emphasis on killing flies and keeping the factory clean, we can assume that the factory had become infested with flies and was habitually quite filthy (there are references to lingering stenches where the pots that contained horse-hoof glue were emptied, and to men spitting tobacco on the floors). An ongoing lack of attendance at the meetings of the packing and finishing rooms was noted with disfavor; it was observed that many workers were unfairly taking advantage of the Saturday half-day privilege by staying away for the entire day.[20] More troubling was the news that the easy availability of lumber was coming to an end; by 1919 the company newsletter was noting that logs from "the lumbering district" of Mississippi, Tennessee, and Arkansas were becoming hard to obtain. "The [price of logs] has been giving the purchasing department more concern than anything. There seems to be no limit as to where the price of lumber and logs will go. The next trip will be made into the state of Illinois where it is hoped a better supply can be had."[21]

The company recognized the fact that the employees wanted diversions and did its best to provide them. The company auditorium constantly hosted

The Showers factory campus, 1921.

From the collection of the Monroe County History Center,
202 East 6th Street, Bloomington, IN,
www.monroehistory.org, 1987.128.0002.

minstrel shows, dances, traveling vaudeville troupes, comedians, silent films, musicians, educational programs, and plays. In September 1919 another blacks-versus-whites baseball game was held, and an audience of five hundred cheered on the athletes (the Black Diamonds lost to the Showers Specials). Baseball proved so popular that the company set up a ballpark on its property at the top of Cherry Hill on the north side of Bloomington and built bleachers for the public. The Women's League was dedicated to dancing and parties and held tutorials in the latest dance steps. There was a boxing club, a football team, and a Boy Scout troop specifically for the sons of employees. A small number of employees regularly attended the regional fox hunt with their hounds and reported back to their interested coworkers. But annoying antisocial undercurrents were circulating; teenaged boys repeatedly vandalized the benches that had been placed in the public playground that the company had built, and bullying had been observed there. The management represented order, sense, morality; but an increasing number of young men on the workforce simply wanted a paycheck with no educational or uplifting lectures. Worst of all, employee morale was fading:

> There seems to be a feeling among some of the men at least that since the main office has been separated from the factory the usual and welcome visits [by management] have some what fallen off. As one old colored man in the packing room said: "Well since Mr. W. N. [William Showers] moved over in the new office we don't get to see very much of him any more. We all used to like to see him come through here ever so often but it seems like an age since he has paid us a visit."[22]

William's absence from the workingmen's area was attributed to the enormous increase in business during the past two years. If one assumes that William Showers read every issue of *Shop Notes,* this item was obviously a plea by workers for their boss to resume the frequent contact that was common in the old days. But the old president of the company was now largely preoccupied with his own failing health and only rarely stopped by the workplace to chat with his workers. His son, W. Edward, was also in poor health; he would spend much of the final twenty years of his life afflicted with illnesses that would take him away from the factory for longer and longer periods, including entire summers spent in Michigan and Wisconsin with his family. The workers no longer felt that they had a kindly and benevolent protector who would greet them each day and look after their interests, and *Shop Notes* constantly noted that quality supervisors were badly needed by the company.

Many of the editorials and articles in *Shop Notes* possess a hectoring tone that reminds one of a blustering sports coach who shames his players in hopes of extracting greater efforts from them. Even the new women workers came in for rebukes: "Comparatively few girls operate machines.... Why is it that many of our girls refuse such a fine opportunity [to learn a skilled trade]? Girls, don't say you can't do something without trying. Put your shoulder to the wheel and carry your burden. Study your job, learn the work, and make the industrial world realize its mistake in underestimating your ability."[23] And workers were chastised for not attending Monday night meetings with diligence: "We have tried most every conceivable way of conducting our social gatherings.... We have tried to give variety to the meetings by having someone speak on current events, combining the instructive side of the meeting with an entertainment

The Showers factory consumed more than 28,000,000 feet of lumber in 1920. The immense size of the factory made it difficult to find quality supervisors who could handle the scale of business.

Accession 7200, collection of Indiana University Archives.

and dancing afterwards. . . . Could any reasonable man ask for more? Why then can we not look forward to a bigger Monday night meeting?"[24] Working a ten-hour day using loud and dangerous machines and shifting heavy objects probably had much to do with the workers' reluctance to return to their place of employment two hours after leaving it when the evening whistle blew. The management of the Showers Brothers Company under W. Edward Showers appears to have lacked an understanding of the actual lives of its workers; the managers did not realize that constant exhortations to do things a certain way can be counterproductive rather than instructive. With the best intentions, they nagged their workers to adopt the same template of behaviors that had worked for the Showers brothers themselves: thrift, hard work, home ownership, savings, and investment. But their sermons fell on an increasingly deaf ears. After all, the twentieth century was already well advanced by this point, and the heyday of the rags-to-riches stories was past. Young people in particular had no interest in the prim ethics of their Victorian parents. They wanted to dance all night to Hoagy Carmichael's jazz combo, take their dates to vaudeville shows and the silent movies, and go joyriding in their new flivvers. It was certainly a lot more fun to spend money than to save it.

Chapter

13

ANOTHER BEGINNING

DEATH WAS SHADOWING William Showers. By 1919 the Showers family had suffered five losses in three years. James and William's aged brother-in-law and former partner, James Hendrix, and his wife Ellen (one of the four Showers sisters) had both passed away, as had their middle-aged daughter Laura; their brother-in-law Henry Hewson had also passed away. Most painful to William was the death of his wife Hanna in 1916. Six months before her death she had endured thirty X-rays in an attempt to discover whether she had abscessed teeth,[1] and the huge amount of radiation contained in those early, crude X-rays could not possibly have benefited a woman who was already ill. William was much quieter and sadder after her death. He began failing in the spring of 1919, afflicted by Bright's Disease, the now-outdated term for a number of different kidney disorders whose impact upon the body includes edema, high blood pressure, kidney stones, and difficult urination, which together result in general organ failure. At first he did not realize that he was in danger; he made an auto trip to Bedford early in April with his son and upon his return visited his niece Beryl Holland and asked for "some good books to read."[2] Never one to complain, he finally admitted to his son, W. Edward, that he was not feeling well. He was sent to bed and an Indianapolis specialist was sent for. Although he had been outwardly vigorous at seventy-three, supposedly looking no older than a man of fifty, his organs were shutting down. Surrounded by doctors and nurses, in his own bed at home rather than in the hospital, he drifted in and out of consciousness. He died, still unconscious, on Easter morning, 1919. His funeral was the largest ever seen in the city, according to the *Telephone*. All businesses and factories in town were closed during the hour of his funeral and hundreds of workers with their families and children attended the viewing, the service at the Methodist Church, and the interment at Rose Hill next to his wife Hanna Lou.

Shop Notes summed up what had made William an exceptional employer: "During the many [years] connected with the factory Mr. Showers has endeared himself to all. It was his custom each morning to give a personal greeting to each employee whom he might chance to meet, and in former years he knew each employee by name. Later the family grew in such numbers that he was not always able to do this but frequent were his trips through the plants and those he did not know by name he called 'Sonny' or 'Daughter.'"[3]

His newspaper obituary added, "Since the women have become a working force in the big plant, he was especially interested in their success and had matrons employed and all conveniences added for their welfare. W. N. Showers never regarded himself as above any one who worked for him as long as they had respect for themselves, and were honest in their efforts. . . . His greatest desire was loyalty in his employees, and his ability in securing such a spirit has been one of the mainsprings of his success."[4] *Shop Notes* wrote, "Mr. Showers will always be remembered as one of the foremost men in his community, as a thoroughgoing worker, systematic saver and a citizen proud and selfish of Bloomington's best interests."[5] The company newsletter printed a final anecdote:

> An incident . . . happening . . . a few short hours before he became unconscious, will . . . show why we revere his memory. A colored lady, old in years, who many times had been benefitted by Mr. W. N.'s generosity, learning of his illness, purchased with her hard-earned money a half dozen carnations, sending them with her card. They were received by this man, sick unto death. At once he dispatched a nurse to the far end of the city to this old and humble colored lady, bearing a message of thanks, and asking her to call and see him. Repeated acts of this kind have builded up in the hearts of his people a love that time and eternity can never efface.[6]

William's older and hardier brother James was bereft, having lost his best friend and his longtime partner. James had now outlived both parents, a stepmother, his first wife, his eldest daughter, his son, an appealing young grandson, a sister, and both of his two brothers. He was to live almost another twenty years.

William's character was held up after his death as a model for others to emulate. "Beyond question the best known man in the community. . . . Another principle of his business life was his absolute integrity and fair dealing. W. N. Showers did not know what it was to be dishonest; he would rather give than take. . . . He did not know the meaning of wealth as making a man better or more superior. . . . No man was more liberal."[7] His work in encouraging thrift and setting up the savings and loan to help his employees build their own homes bore fruit in many ways. Showers employee Thomas Alexander told *Shop Notes* that he bought the first two shares of stock available in the savings and loan company when it was first launched and made it a habit to deposit twenty-five cents each week. Over the past twenty-five years he had saved enough to build five houses, all of which were by that time completely clear of debt, and he owned a vacant lot upon which he planned to build a sixth house.[8] A photo of the little bungalow in which he lived, located at 519 E. Fourteenth Street, was featured in a separate issue of *Shop Notes*. Small and tidy, with a young tree planted in front next to the street, it was a perfect workman's cottage. A cottage like this could be built for a thousand dollars or less.

William's last business decision had been to substantially enlarge the company by building a new factory, Plant 4, on the south side of Bloomington. The roots of this idea dated back to 1914, when Showers Brothers first added "kitchen cabinets" to their line.[9] This phrase did not mean then what it does today: the built-in overhead and under-counter cabinets that are found in all modern kitchens. In William's day the term specifically meant the freestanding piece of furniture known generically as a Hoosier cabinet. Hoosier cabinets had been popularized by the Hoosier Manufacturing Company of New Castle, Indiana,[10] and were immensely successful. These cabinets were made of wood, with integral shelving and cabinetry above and below the small surface that served as a counter. Hoosier cabinets usually were furnished with a complete set of glass storage containers, or canisters, and measuring cups, and often featured a built-in flour bin with sifter. A Hoosier cabinet contained everything a thrifty housewife could need or use, packed efficiently into a single furniture item that was generally less than seven feet high. In an era of small bungalows and cottages, tiny kitchens were common and the Hoosier cabinet offered efficiency and compactness. The Hoosier Manufacturing Company had made a fortune with these cabinets, and William must have rationalized that there was plenty of room for competition. By 1916 the company reported that within one short year, Showers Brothers had developed the second-largest kitchen cabinet business in the nation.[11] The Showers company's first kitchen cabinets were originally built alongside other furniture in the Showers factory, but proved to be so popular that William decided that Plant 4 would specifically manufacture versions of this one item. Although William died before seeing the new factory finished, W. Edward oversaw the completion of the massive new structure, located at the southwest corner of Rogers and Grimes Streets, on what had been a large tract of open farmland on the fringes of the city.

Eight hundred feet long by 200 feet wide, the new plant contained 118,000 square feet of floor space and cost close to $400,000. The new factory was built of brick and steel with glass side walls that would admit natural light.[12] Two new rail switches were built to the new factory, which eventually employed four hundred men and manufactured up to three hundred Hoosier cabinets each day. The Corliss engine for the new factory's power plant had a flywheel fourteen feet in diameter, weighing 35,000 pounds, and capable of generating 575 horsepower.[13] Because so many new employee cars and delivery trucks would be using the southern end of Rogers Street, which was still unpaved, the city government pledged to improve the road and expressed gratitude that Showers Brothers had decided to build in Bloomington rather than elsewhere (which the company had considered). Bloomington's new Chamber of Commerce was instrumental in arranging the purchase of the new company land.

However, the Showers Brothers Company soon felt that it had invested a great deal in the new plant but had received little from the city in return. After the death of the ever-diplomatic and genial William Showers, a contentious relationship developed between the Republican-owned factory and the Democrat-controlled city government. *Shop Notes* reprinted a letter to the city council written by William before his death, in which he loyally wrote:

> Disregarding any superior advantages that might have been obtained by the expanding of our business in another locality, we have definitely decided to center our activities in Good Old Bloomington. For over fifty years my heart has been in this town and this community and it is one of my greatest pleasures to know that we are still going to aid in its continued success. After a lifetime spent in this community, I could not bring myself to do anything that might detract from the progress our city is making. . . . I am grateful beyond my power to express for the cooperation and loyalty so freely given to our new project.[14]

Studio portrait of W. Edward Showers.

From the collection of the Monroe County History Center,
202 East 6th Street, Bloomington, IN,
www.monroehistory.org, 1988.109.0314.

But Rogers Street remained unpaved more than a year after construction of Plant 4 and was so filled with potholes that in some places it was almost undrivable. The lack of streetlights made the road dark and dangerous for workmen leaving the factory after long shifts. The two new trucks that the company purchased to move materials between the two plants would soon be ready for the junk heap, *Shop Notes* warned. Faced with Democratic obstructionism in his home town, W. Edward Showers did not hesitate to look outside of Bloomington for the company's next expansion. Angered at the city administration's treatment of his company, he immediately began negotiating with Burlington, Iowa, regarding his plans to construct a huge new factory to service the western trade.

Shop Notes observed that the company had invested a vast sum on the Rogers Street factory, around which many of the new workers wanted to live, but that the city government had done nothing to encourage the building of new homes, leaving the matter completely in the company's hands. The situation was completely different in Burlington, where local businessmen had immediately formed an organization that had already let a contract for twenty-five houses to be constructed in anticipation of the new factory.[15] "What has become of the live-wire citizens [in Bloomington] who promised to lend their moral and financial support? There has been a dead silence for the last five months. . . . Several years ago an attempt was made to move the University and a great wail from enthusiastic citizens could be heard all over the state. What are those same neighbors doing to handle the situation now? Absolutely nothing. . . . Bloomington at the present time is so dormant that nothing short of an earthquake can wake her from the long nap she has been enjoying."[16] The *Telephone* found this editorial in *Shop Notes* so appropriate that it republished the text for those who had not had the opportunity to read it already.

Showers Brothers was by far the largest employer in town, responsible for the economic health of an entire community. When payday arrived on alternate Saturdays, shops downtown did noticeably better business. It was not only the biggest fish in the local pond, it was very possibly the biggest fish in the entire sea. *Shop Notes* commented, "It has long been a cherished idea of the executives of our company that the time would come when they would remove all doubt in the minds of the trade that our company is the largest manufacturing establishment of its kind in the world and second to none in progressiveness."[17] The term "largest" might have meant several different things: largest in gross sales and/or profit; largest in number of items produced; or largest in terms of the physical campus. The owner of the largest furniture factory in France, E. Schwander & Co., visited Showers Brothers to observe its facilities and acknowledged that his own plant "hardly begins to compare."[18] The colossal productivity of the company is illustrated by statistics from the company newsletter:

The Showers Brothers Company will use a quantity of lumber sufficiently large to build a board walk from New York to San Francisco and back again to the state of Indiana . . . 28,208,600 feet of lumber will be used for furniture in a single year. This is an increase of approximately 6,000,000 feet over that used during the preceding year. . . . We expect to use approximately 235,300 pounds of nails . . . 1,145,816 casters, 495,000 pounds of glue, and 27,000,000 feet of veneer, approximately one-half of which we will cut on our own lathes.[19]

The company could not understand why the city did not treat it with more respect when it was not only the biggest employer in town but also arguably the largest furniture manufactory in the nation.

Workmen inside the Showers factory.

From the collection of the Monroe County History Center, 202 East 6th Street, Bloomington, IN, www.monroehistory.org, 1989.072.0015.

THE 1920S

W. Edward Showers's new and massive plant in Burlington, Iowa, can be regarded in hindsight as a fatal investment. As with the four Bloomington plants, Plant 5 was erected swiftly and a huge number of men were hired. The building was vast, with five and a half acres of space beneath a single roof. We don't know how many men were employed by it, but if Plants 1, 2 and 3 were any guide, the better part of five hundred men could have worked there. Burlington was an industrial city whose other factories included Chittenden & Eastman, "the Northwestern Cabinet company, the Leopold Desk company, the Embalming Burial Case company, the Burlington Casket company, the Noelke-Lyons and Ford manufacturing companies, the Burlington Box company and the Burlington Cigar Box company."[20] Because of the sheer quantity of new hires for Plant 5, a number of the new workers were either the rejects of the other local factories or completely new to manufacturing. The factory was built

completely new, with all-new machinery, and had no built-in workers' culture to learn from and rely upon. There were no old-timers to guide the newcomers. The factory was slow to achieve the standard of quality that W. Edward and superintendent Charles Sears were hoping for,[21] but even worse, Plant 5 was constructed and finished just as the nation dived into a sharp recession.

Shop Notes recorded frank statistics from the pep talk that W. Edward gave to employees at a company meeting in March 1921. Nationally, 73 percent of furniture manufacturers had cut their wages since the beginning of the year and the industry was "face to face with the biggest struggle it had had in fifty years."[22] Showers Brothers had reduced the selling price of its furniture to remain competitive, and was experiencing an approximately 20 percent loss on the cost of labor. The company did not want to cut wages, so the only recourse was for the men to work harder. "Our company is paying higher wages than any other furniture manufacturing establishment in the country," W. Edward told the men. The workers were asked to "stop piddling" and get down to an honest day's work. "We cannot carry extra weight; it's a fair fight and competition is keen. The best organization will win. Where do we stand? . . . This meeting was not called to announce a cut in wages, but to present conditions confronting us and to ask every man to place his shoulder to the wheel in order that wages might be kept where they were." The workers do not seem to have immediately heeded the call to action, to judge from *Shop Notes,* but by the end of the year production costs had modestly improved and wages were not cut. By the following year the company newsletter reported excellent reception at the Chicago furniture show. Nevertheless the 1920s were plagued with recurring mini-recessions, and financial worries endured until the end of the decade. The company did not feel altogether confident during the 1920s. No one at the company knew that they would soon look back nostalgically upon these very years as a carefree and fortunate era.

Workmen in machine room.

From the collection of the
Monroe County History Center,
202 East 6th Street, Bloomington,
IN, www.monroehistory.org,
1989.072.0019.

In 1921 the company stopped printing lists of new employees in *Shop Notes* because it was no longer hiring. It also made a decision that would have grieved William and undoubtedly annoyed Maud Showers Wilson when she heard the news: the company resolved to fire all the women workers who were on the payroll, effective October 7, with the exception of clerical workers in the main office. The workforce was informed of the decision at a company meeting.

> In every instance the girls who are employed in the factory today were complimented for the manner in which they have filled their positions. In view of the many unemployed men in the city, some of whom did service overseas, it was unanimously decided [by all foremen and block leaders] to abandon the employment of women in the factory in order to help alleviate the slightly strained situation. . . . While the removal of some women will materially affect production and the company will sustain a loss[,] it was thought advisable to make the change. . . . There are 43 women working in the factory at the present time. They have filled their positions efficiently and loyally. From a dollar and cent argument it would be much easier to retain them in their present positions for it is doubtful if men can fill their places as efficiently. However, Mr. C. A. Sears, General Superintendent . . . made the following statement: "I know we are going to have a hard time for a while trying to break men into doing some of the work that is now being done by women workers, but I believe the company owes a certain debt to the community and to those men who are unemployed with families to care for. The company may lose money by making the change but I believe that with the help of all men in the factory, we can adjust ourselves in a manner that will be satisfactory. . . . If it were not for the strained condition of some of our families in the city of Bloomington, I would not consider changing back to the pre war way. . . . I am sorry that it appears to be necessary to make this change but I believe we are doing the right thing by changing back to the old way."[23]

Shop Notes published an editorial explaining the company's actions.

> At the present time there are ex-soldiers and men with families who have told thrilling stories why they should be given employment over women[,] some of whom have no further responsibility than to spend their earnings for fine clothing and good times generally. No doubt there may be several instances of women working in the factory who have used their earnings to help rear families. These instances are very few. For the most part the women who have been employed are in no way called upon to support dependents. . . . The company has been lauded generally for the sensible move they have decided upon in replacing women with men. They have expressed their appreciation liberally for the manner in which the women have performed their work and they feel that the time has come for them to get back to the normal way of operating.[24]

The "normal way of operating" was obviously for men to go out to work and for women to stay at home. *Shop Notes* expressed regret that with the letting go of the women, the neatly swept floors and general cleanliness of the plant would become a thing of the past, since men are less prone to clean up after themselves.[25] The women workers were indignant at their treatment and went to the daily newspaper to complain. But the company newsletter did not mention an important reason for the company's decision: President Harding had just called upon the nation's employers to hire as many unemployed ex-soldiers as possible in order to prevent entire families from starving. Giving jobs back to unemployed former workers who had families was one thing; but taking jobs away from qualified women who needed to support their own families only created more unemployed individuals. It's obvious that female workers were not valued equally with men. As Showers Brothers had followed national trends in hiring women during the war, it also followed national trends in firing them. The year 1921 marks the end of the brief era of women's opportunities at Showers. With William dead, Maud retired from the board of directors, and W. Edward increasingly absent from the helm because of bouts of ill-health, there was no one left to speak up for the women.

Late in 1921 the foremen of Plant 4 were fired when it was discovered that despite being well recommended, "their best interests could not be counted on."[26] *Shop Notes* frequently noted the scarcity of good administrators for the satellite plants. But the company was cheered when the recession lightened and the plants began to roar with activity once again. "One year ago there was a dead silence in our factories," said *Shop Notes*. "There was an expression of anxiety on the face of everyone. The winter was only half gone. Ten weeks of idleness was drawing to a close yet none of us could foresee what the new year held in store for us."[27] All doubts about the vitality of the company were removed the following month when a furniture journal reported that the Showers Queen Anne bedroom suite had just set a world record: 40,221 pieces of this suite had been shipped.

This success could not be repeated in 1923, thanks to another fluctuation of the on-again, off-again economy of the 1920s. The costs of labor and materials were constantly increasing, yet the company could not raise its sales prices since it was committed to the manufacture of medium-cost furniture. "Our only hope is a larger output brought about by more efficient methods," *Shop Notes* noted in a pessimistic mode.[28] Two weeks later the newsletter reported that W. Edward Showers had emphasized that Showers must continue to expand in order to continue existing. "While our firm appeared to do a very great business during the past year, only a small part of the earnings were distributed to stock holders. The firm will spend a great amount of money during the year for improvements, expansion and better working conditions."[29] Nurre Glass also worked hard to enlarge itself nationally and established satellite locations in Burlington, Chattanooga (later moving to Memphis), and in Kansas City.

The overhead costs of Showers Brothers operations are staggering to read even now. The company paid a whopping $1,877,158.47 on freight for the combined output of the Bloomington and Burlington plants in 1922.[30] The combined output of the plants, if loaded for rail freight, would have formed a single string of cars seventy-seven miles long.[31] And yet this vast production served less than 1 percent of all American homes, *Shop Notes* admitted.[32] But despite the company's enormous production capacity, difficult problems were emerging. The costs of lumber were skyrocketing and it was becoming difficult to obtain the massive quantities of wood needed to maintain production. With Monroe County and all surrounding counties largely bare after being extensively logged, the sawmill supervisor was combing southern Indiana by automobile, looking for leftover stands of timber to purchase for company use.[33] Superintendent Charles Sears told the workers that they were getting paid a better average wage for production than they could earn at any of the other furniture factories that manufactured the same class of furniture.[34] Another huge potential cost was nipped in the bud before any expense had been incurred: a large workers' subdivision that would have stood between North Walnut Street and Kinser Pike. Workers were commuting to Bloomington on unpaved roads from Unionville, Ellettsville, and even Spencer and Belmont, and so the company initially proposed to spend $80,000 platting the property and constructing four- and five-room cottages, attractive and different in appearance from each other.[35] Presumably because of the increased cost of wood, this new development was deemed unfeasible. In any event, it made little sense to plat a new workers' subdivision on the opposite side of town from the new factory location.

Despite increased costs of production, despite the growing lack of good administration, the company soldiered on the way it always had, confident that nothing could go wrong, simply because it was the leader in its field. No problem would present itself that the company could not eventually surmount, due to its enormous size. It justified its continual growth by claiming

Workman applying spray varnish.

*From the collection of the Monroe County
History Center, 202 East 6th Street, Bloomington,
IN, www.monroehistory.org, 1989.072.0020.*

that as labor and materials increased in price, the only way to survive was to increase production. W. Edward Showers emphasized at company meetings that "our firm must expand to exist."[36] W. Edward and the board of directors unquestioningly accepted the unsustainable proposition that continual growth would in fact be a blessing rather than a curse; but this attitude was a relic of the frontier mentality of the previous century. A nation so large, so rich in natural resources could not possibly run out of raw materials, the owners of the company believed; and yet the logged-out landscapes of southern Indiana proved the contrary.

As it produced more and more furniture, with workers toiling ever harder for fear of having their wages cut, the schism between workers and management continued to widen. Yet the company bristled at the prospect of labor unions infiltrating the workforce. The patronizing attitude of *Shop Notes* is really astonishing to modern sensibilities:

> The average worker, for obvious reasons, possesses a lesser degree of reasoning power than does his employer. Because of this fact he is easily prompted to feelings of suspicion and uncertainty with regard to the motives and acts of those upon whom he is forced to rely.... He is likewise peculiarly susceptible to the influence of those whose principal aim in life is the fomenting of discontent.[37]

At this time the nation was wracked by strikes and by struggles by organized labor to win better wages and shorter working days. We can't know whether W. Edward approved of the wording of this editorial, which belittled the reasoning power of the very men it was written for, but he undoubtedly agreed that labor unions were a bad thing for the Showers company. In a different editorial that year, the *Shop Notes* editorial writer ingeniously combined the unlikely topics of home ownership and unionization:

> Just drop into a town in which there is a floating population who for the most part are dependent on the boarding house. Listen to the general run of conversation. Usually the town is poorly managed, the club is wrong, there are no amusements, everything is done up in "hick" style, and to listen to a boarding house conversation would sometimes make one feel as though he were mingling with a gang of i.w.w.'s.[38]

The i.w.w. was the union known as the International Workers of the World, often known as the Wobblies. The union was at its height at this time, and factory owners around the nation quaked in their shoes at the thought of hated Wobblies infiltrating the ranks of their workers. Issues of *Shop Notes* dating from this era also disparage anarchists and socialists. Management was nervous enough about the menace to finally offer a new incentive that it hoped would make workers turn their backs on organized labor: at the end of 1923 a group insurance plan was offered to anyone who had already worked for the company for one year. "When there is prolonged sickness in the home, the good house wife will not have to worry about the bi-weekly pay check which in the past has ceased to make its regular appearance. In case of death, the widow will have the protection of a year's pay issued in monthly installments." The editorial in *Shop Notes* on December 22, 1923, added, "It is hoped that the turnover in labor will be greatly reduced."

The company was concerned not just about labor organizers but also about the increasingly inadequate city infrastructure. Although the city's industrial leaders and city government had stood united to enlarge Bloomington throughout the past three decades, those original leaders had by now faded from the scene and the men who had taken their place had different outlooks and had to deal with different circumstances. The job of "booming" the city now belonged to the Chamber of Commerce, which had evolved from the earlier Commercial Club. The first president of the new Chamber had been Sanford Teter, who launched the new organization with a progressive set of goals, but his serious illness soon thereafter had required him to withdraw from active participation. His successors were lesser men than he, to judge from complaints in the papers that Bloomington was falling behind and had become a sleepy, backward place. Because the war had curtailed house construction, there was a serious shortage of homes that had not yet been resolved. There were no more Showers men on the city council, which might explain why it took five years for the city to make good on its pledge to pave the two miles of Rogers Street between the two factory campuses.

In March of 1924 Bloomington was shocked to read in the newspaper that an armed, masked burglar had entered the home of the 82-year-old James Showers and demanded his valuable diamond ring, worth $1,000 (around $12,000 in today's values). As his wife watched in horror, James refused to give the ring to the burglar and then fought him man-to-man. The effort was brave on his part, but the masked intruder brutally pistol-whipped the old man and departed with the ring. James was so battered about the face that he was almost unable to see, the papers reported, but apart from bodily bruising he was otherwise unharmed. Both James and Belle went to stay temporarily with their daughter Maude Myers, who gave them medical care and comfort while they were recuperating from the terrible experience. Within two weeks James was once again out and about, but Belle had a harder time recovering. She had not been physically harmed during the robbery but had been shocked to the core by the sight of her husband being cruelly beaten. It epitomized the times: there was no more respect for the old ways. Each day's newspaper carried sensational headlines about bootleggers, killers, and criminals; it is no exaggeration to describe the front page of the *Telephone* at that time as closely resembling an issue of *True Crime*. Older readers may have felt that the comfort of knowing one's place in the world had vanished, for the world was changing, and not for the better.

Chapter

14

FINAL SUCCESSES

IN MAY OF 1924 the old draft horse Cap, who for fifteen years had patiently hauled lumber from the sawmill to the veneer mill at Showers Brothers, was retired owing to the fact that "he was still willing but had not the sand to make the grade any longer." He was driven out to enjoy retirement at the Showers farm ten miles north of town, but apparently disliked the abrupt change from a muddy lumberyard to a grassy field. The first day Cap found himself on pasture, he jumped the fence and walked back to town. When he came to the bridge over Griffy Creek on the North Pike, he stopped to make sure no traffic was coming before he crossed it. He continued southward toward town. "He kept to the side of the road all the way to avoid accidents. He reached his old place of business without a scratch, but several days later was returned to the farm. It seems Cap would rather be hitched up than live the life of ease."[1] The editor of *Shop Notes,* the company newsletter, apparently approved of the old horse's work ethic.

That same year, Nellie Showers Teter became the first woman elected to the Board of Trustees of Indiana University. Her nomination was made by Indianapolis alumnae of the American Association of University Women, to which she belonged. The mission of the AAUW was to raise the standards of

A view of the wheat crop stacked neatly at one of the two Showers farms.

Accession 0091, collection of Indiana University Archives.

colleges and universities and to award fellowships and scholarships to women students. "We need more Madame Curies," reads one of the organization's fliers from the 1920s;[2] and the group wanted someone on the university's board who would look out for women's interests. To Nellie's immense surprise, she won against the incumbent, Edwin Carr, who had served on the board for twenty-nine years. "Where there are so many women and girls interested, there should be at least one woman on the official board," the newspaper said approvingly.[3] Nellie would serve on the board for the next forty-one years, making it a point to support the needs of women undergraduates, particularly in housing. When the university moved ahead with plans for the first on-campus women's dormitory, located at the far eastern edge of campus, Nellie was concerned that it might be too far from the library for college women to walk in adverse weather. She carefully paced the distance between the two sites to see how long it took and what the terrain was like. In the opening ceremony for the new dormitory, she was handed the keys as a mark of respect for her efforts in getting it constructed.

As a trustee of the university, Nellie Showers Teter made it a point to address issues that affected women students.

Courtesy Nancy Teter Smith.

During the 1914 drought, the governor of Indiana had actually threatened to remove Indiana University from Bloomington unless the water shortage was resolved; this threat resulted in the construction of the biggest dam yet at Leonard Springs. The governor of the state traveled to Bloomington to view the new lake and was satisfied by the sight of waves lapping against the dam. He departed with the assumption that the water shortage had been addressed and abandoned his threats to relocate the university, but it's very likely that no one informed him that the city had no money to install pipeline to this new reservoir.

By 1924, the Showers Brothers Company was completely fed up with the city government's failure to respond to the water problem. A serious drought had occurred the previous year, and the company clearly remembered bad droughts occurring in 1881, 1893, 1899, 1908, 1913–14 and 1922. All these events had adversely affected the community, but the drought of '23 served as a tipping point: the situation was intolerable. Workmen returned home after long hours of sweaty toil but found insufficient water to bathe with; their wives could barely get the laundry done. Each day the city faced the ongoing danger of a terrible fire breaking out with no water in the mains to fight the flames. Imported spring water was available, certainly, but it was quite expensive and posed great hardships on the poorer families.

There were no Showers men remaining on the city council, and after decades of Republican control the city was now governed by Democrats. The two parties had still not yet evolved into their modern forms but as is the case today, they constantly quarreled. Since 1903 members of the Showers family had supported the idea of damming Griffy Creek north of town, forming a large lake that would supply all the water needs of the city for the foreseeable future, but the city had stubbornly refused to explore this idea. Recognizing that the city would not—and could not—guarantee water to its residents, the university had already constructed its own reservoir above the Griffy watershed. The lack of adequate water not only annoyed the public but seriously handicapped Bloomington's industry, for factories needed copious amounts of water to operate their machinery. The two Showers plants consumed more than 21 million gallons of water annually, only 5.6 million gallons of which came from the city's municipal supply.[4] Production throughout 1923 and 1924 was repeatedly slowed or stopped due to lack of water, which made it difficult to fill orders. The company paid high prices for railroad tanker cars filled with water and also hauled 500 gallons of spring water daily from the spring at the new country club southwest of town.[5] The company dammed a spring on property it owned along North Walnut Street and piped the water from the pond to its plant; it also laid pipe all the way to the Monon railroad pond west of town and tapped that as well. It carefully maintained the company pond on its campus and directed gutter downspouts into it, saving every drop that fell onto its rooftops. But the company chafed at having to bother with water when it wanted to focus its full attention on manufacturing.

The city government had ignored the company's pleas for an improved water supply for many decades by this point. After all, it paid one-seventh of the total taxes received by the city each year.[6] Something drastic needed to be done, and Showers Brothers played its trump card in 1924 by threatening publicly to relocate its immense factories if something were not done about the water situation. It very likely had no intention of doing so, for a move such as this would have been prohibitively expensive. Nevertheless, the news spread and invitations arrived from major cities including Indianapolis, Louisville, Columbus, and New York, along with Indiana towns such as Terre Haute, Martinsville, Logansport, and Spencer. Even the humble village of Monon in northwestern Indiana solicited Showers Brothers' presence.[7] "Of course there isn't a man hardly who is now working for the company, but what wants to remain in Bloomington indefinitely," observed *Shop Notes*. "We are all hopeful that the water question will be settled for all time to come."

The city at that time maintained a number of inadequate reservoirs west of the city, all of which had been built, mended, rebuilt, and mended again at enormous expense. All of them lay on top of porous karst limestone that allowed water to slowly seep away. James Showers and his business partners were indeed responsible for constructing the first lake on the west side of town because at that time, in the 1890s, the feat of laying pipe through the higher, rougher terrain northward toward Griffy Creek was too expensive to consider, and the habit of building to the west had stuck. On the west side of the city, the Leonard Springs reservoir had four separate dams built at different times; Twin Lakes was originally a single lake that had another dam added downstream to catch seepage from the first lake; and Weimer Lake was completely inadequate for the needs of a growing city. "We conclude that if all these springs were harnessed together, that during a dry season, such as we have just experienced, there would not be sufficient flowing water from all of them combined, to much more than half supply the present needs," the group in charge of investigating options had reported as far back as 1913.[8] The Democratic mayor had ignored this advice for more than a decade (possibly because the advisory group had included Republicans James Showers, Sanford Teter, and several of their friends). Mayor Harris steadfastly opposed laying any new pipes northward to Griffy Creek since the city had already invested a huge sum—probably more than a hundred thousand dollars by this point—on the western reservoirs. Despite repeated assurances from geologists that the Griffy valley was underlain by a structurally stable layer of excellent knobstone, Harris refused to consider the idea of a dam across the Griffy valley, because it would have plunged the city

The new reservoir at Griffy Lake.

From the collection of the
Monroe County History Center,
202 East 6th Street, Bloomington,
IN, www.monroehistory.org,
2002.041.0024B.

into debt. He must have felt it was better to remain debt-free and continue scrimping on water.

Showers Brothers then joined forces with the Citizens Loan and Trust, the Showers Brothers Savings Company, and the First National Bank (all of which were controlled or heavily influenced by the Showers family). In what amounted to a Republican water revolution, this group of banks and businessmen pledged to pay for the construction of Lake Griffy, forming an independent new water company whose ownership would revert back to the city within a few years. Following a mass meeting by hordes of citizens on the courthouse lawn calling for the city to accept the plan, the city council turned on the mayor and blessed the idea of the new lake, which would be the single most expensive work of civic infrastructure that the community had yet seen. Showers Brothers pledged $181,500 of the $728,000 needed (a quarter of the total), and individual members of the Showers family gave generous individual pledges as well.[9] The Showers company's pledge, adjusted for inflation, would equal approximately $2.25 million today. (James Showers, who was still recuperating from the burglar's pistol-whipping, pledged $5,000, about $62,000 in today's values.) Throughout the early months of 1925 *Shop Notes* proudly published photos of the lake slowly filling up behind the new concrete dam. As the mayor's supporters had predicted, the water from the new reservoir tasted and smelled horrible for the first few months, filled as it was with rotting vegetation and mud; the Showers factory was forced to continue to import pure spring water for the men to drink at work. But by the next year all was well again. The Showers family viewed the construction of the large new lake with relief, knowing that the factory would never shut down again due to lack of water.

Flushed with success, Showers Brothers pledged to invest a million dollars in upgrading its existing plants and building a refrigerator factory. Two to three hundred men were expected to be hired for the construction crew under the supervision of the Ferguson Company, which had erected Plants 4 and 5. On March 17, 1924, the *Bloomington Telephone* featured a front-page photo of

Reservoir - 1 mile in length
Capable of increase in
capacity 4 times

"It so chanced that the writer was in conversation with W. Edward Showers soon after he had decided to take over that Bloomfield factory and bend it to fit the Showers program. 'So, your new factory is to be at Bloomfield?' he was asked. 'Oh yes,' he said, 'we already had plants at Bloomington and Burlington and we couldn't think of locating a new plant anywhere except in a town beginning with a "B".'" This passage from Dillon's *Thoughts Concerning the 60th Anniversary of Showers Brothers Company* (p. 38) is most likely only a joke.

W. Edward Showers hailing the launch of a "Greater Bloomington." The company's new growth wasn't confined to Bloomington, however; later that same year Plant 6 was opened. Formerly known as the VanMeter Chair Company of Bloomfield, Indiana, it would be the last of the Showers factories. Prosperity at the factory meant prosperity for the community at large, and Bloomington experienced a tremendous burst of new growth during the late 1920s. The population swelled as new citizens moved to the city. Entire neighborhoods sprang into being in a very short length of time, their streets crowded with bungalows and foursquares. These new neighborhoods included much of Elm Heights, south of the Indiana University campus; the southern ends of Lincoln, Washington, and Walnut Streets; the greater McDoel area surrounding Showers Plant 4; the nearby Broadview area; the western end of Prospect Hill; the far north section of Indiana Avenue, along with the Cottage Grove and Cherry Hill areas; Vermilia Street and Southern Drive; and the area around Union Street on the far-eastern fringe of the city. The area around the original site of the first Showers factory was knocked down, rebuilt, and gentrified. Near the end of the decade the *Telephone* noted that five hundred new homes had been added to Bloomington during the past year.[10]

Bloomington's Plant 1 and Burlington's Plant 5 maintained a friendly rivalry over which could produce the biggest output of furniture. Showers Brothers retrofitted Plant 4 to manufacture wooden radio consoles, which at that time were large pieces of furniture that were disguised to give no indication of their true function. (An "Italian Renaissance" radio console was one early style.) Radio as a recreational diversion was sweeping the country and a leader in the industry, the Crosley company, would soon contract with Showers to manufacture consoles for them. In 1925 the Showers company enjoyed another excellent year in sales. The opening day of the winter Furniture Market in Chicago resulted in an astonishing 10,563 orders for the company, its best opening day ever.[11] In 1926 the company produced an impressive 25,000 radio cabinets.[12] In 1927 another record was set when W. Edward Showers took the largest order for a single suite of furniture ever received: one thousand suites of #5612 dining furniture, consisting of tables and matching chairs, for the company's longtime client, the Haverty Furniture Company of Atlanta, Georgia.[13] In that year the company manufactured and sold 538,750 pieces of furniture.[14] Bloomfield's Plant 6 instituted double shifts to turn out the six thousand chairs that were necessary to fill the order. Filled with confidence,

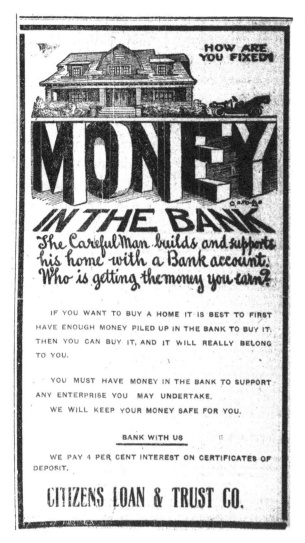

A newspaper advertisement for James Showers's Citizen's Loan Company emphasizes the important things in life: a house and an automobile.

the Showers Brothers Company continued to preach home construction, thrift and savings, and home ownership to its workers.

In 1927 the company commissioned a vanity-press book by Dale Dillon called *Thoughts Concerning the 60th Anniversary of Showers Brothers Company*. The book is filled with decorative woodcuts and is artistically printed. The story it relates is essentially a fairy tale for youngsters describing the hardships faced by the noble founders of the company. It made no mention of C. C.'s business reverses and ignored the fact that the brothers had had a female business partner for twenty-five years, but it successfully established a corporate mythology that included the notion that Showers, Hendrix & Kimbley had opened a "coffin factory" to meet the "red exigencies of civil war."[15]

And in 1929 Showers built a research laboratory on its campus to test new manufacturing methods. The lab "will be a miniature furniture factory, equipped with a complete array of the most modern pattern making and finishing equipment for the development of new designs, new woods, new finish treatments and improved construction methods," announced a trade magazine.[16] That same year the company's gross sales reached ten million dollars. According to Showers researcher Louis Orzack, "Thus Showers reached an apparent peak of dominance in furniture manufacturing in 1928 and 1929 when its gross sales reached $10,000,000 and it was listed by its president as one of the 100 or so factories which had produced $1,000,000 or more furniture per year, representing some 60 per cent of all production by the 3,200 manufacturers."[17] The last part of this statement regarding the 60 percent is difficult to believe, since *Shop Notes* had noted only six years earlier that Showers Brothers manufactured only 1 percent of all American furniture.[18] Did Orzack mean that Showers produced 60 percent of all the furniture in America, or that it was one of the one hundred companies whose combined output produced 60 percent of all American furniture? It's difficult to determine what he intended to convey, or how he arrived at this unreferenced statistic.

But dark undercurrents were increasing. Severe pilferage was noted in the workrooms, to such an extent that at times it interfered with completing jobs.[19] The night watchman at Plant 4 proved to be a slacker who fell asleep on the job the same night that a major fire started; the factory was saved from destruction only because a passing motorist noticed the fire and alerted authorities.[20] The company sawmill was closed because there was no longer enough lumber to cut.[21] And many of the less sophisticated workers assumed wrongly that investment in the company savings bank meant that they were helping the firm out, and refused to participate. *Shop Notes* dismissed this idea in two separate issues, reiterating that the company received no direct benefit from such investments.[22] This was evidently widely disbelieved, which shows the workers' growing distrust of their own managers. The management and the workforce had become dangerously sundered from each other.

Shop Notes ceased publication at the end of 1927, after a decade of chronicling factory life. It had complained in the late summer that workmen at the many plants were not sending in news items to be published, but it's more likely that a combination of factors led to discontinuing the newsletter, including the burden of editing, the cost of printing, and its distribution in three cities. The final issue of *Shop Notes* (December 22, 1927) commemorated the sixtieth anniversary of the company. "What has sixty years of furniture production meant to Bloomington?" it asked. "What has it meant to many of us? It behooves all of us to enter into the spirit of the 60th birthday. To a man such an age means the ebb of life, but to a business it means stability, sound principles and confidence to go forward."

Rows of finished furniture inside the warehouse were arranged along white stripes painted on the floors.

From the collection of the Monroe County History Center, 202 East 6th Street, Bloomington, IN, www.monroehistory.org, 1989.072.0013.

In the final days of 1927 the company held ongoing meetings in its auditorium for its hundreds of salesmen (there were now three hundred), going over the new publicity campaign. On New Year's Eve of 1927, the Showers Brothers Company hosted a banquet at the Bloomington Country Club for all its executives and leaders. Accompanied by speeches and songs, the news was announced that Showers Brothers now had a trademark: a mighty tree trunk and the date 1868, enclosed within a circle. A new national publicity campaign was announced, and the company launched it by taking out a full-page newspaper advertisement proclaiming a new day:

> Our 60th anniversary marks the dawn—a new era in furniture.—As the sun, old and reliable, begins each day with dawn—so does the Showers Brothers Company, on its sixtieth anniversary, announce a new era in the manufacturing and distributing of furniture.—For sixty years, since 1868, three generations of the Showers family have made furniture—made furniture for the Great American Home—for people like you and me.—During the year 1927 we manufactured and sold 538,750 pieces of furniture—and thus began the development of a truly nation-wide service in furnishing the Great American Home.—Today the yearly sales of Showers furniture through the country's leading retail stores amount to twenty millions of dollars. And this annual business, the product of six huge plants, grew from one single-story workshop established sixty years ago by the Reverend Charles Showers.—Reverend Charles Showers was a circuit rider going from community to community preaching the Gospel. He made his home in Bloomington, Indiana, the present site of four of the six Showers plants. In riding about the countryside, he found and supplied a demand for furniture. This original Showers furniture was made during the circuit rider's spare time at his home.—and so this little home shop, through sixty years of progress—three generations—grew to six of the world's largest and most efficiently equipped plants. Now, the Showers Company is preparing to announce to the public a greater program. ... This month marks the dawn of a new era in furnishing the Great American Home. Thousands of dealers will see the Showers Brothers furniture at the American Furniture Mart in Chicago. Ask your dealer to show you the beautiful Showers bedroom and dining room furniture and kitchen cabinets that he bought during this market, each piece marked with the above trade mark. If your dealer has not been supplied, write us—the Showers Brothers Company, Bloomington, Indiana. W. Edw. Showers, President.[23]

The real-life shopkeeper and hotel manager C. C. Showers had been transformed into a mythical preacher loping along on a horse, making furniture at home in his spare hours. And the date of the beginning of the company was not given as 1860, the year C. C. Showers set up shop, but 1868, the date that his sons probably became full partners in their father's company. By the time

The trademark of the Showers Brothers Company was introduced to celebrate the company's sixtieth year of business.

this advertisement was written, memories had become blurry. These pieces of misinformation would affect public perception of the company for decades to come.

A second full-page advertisement the following month extolled the efficiency of the Showers plants:

> To make furniture with no waste in the making—no plan or idea has been overlooked to achieve the acme of economical product. [Each of] the Six Big Showers Plants have been built on gently sloping hillsides so that all raw material enters the top floor of each factory building, eliminating the power expense of hoisting thousands of feet of lumber.—Each of the Six Big Plants is operated according to a specially devised "block" system. Units of furniture are retained in one "block" until all operations assigned to that particular department are completed—then those units travel to the next "block" by conveyors—really a track of ball-bearing rollers.—To make furniture with no waste in manufacturing—make it strong—make it beautiful—is the sum-up of the Showers policy. We choose to mark our Sixtieth Anniversary with the beginning of this new and greater plan—a nationwide service of furnishing the Great American Home—putting within the reach of modest incomes furniture that is beautiful—that is well-constructed—that is sold at a fair piece, each dollar of cost representing a dollar's worth of real value to the buyer.[24]

This policy was in the tradition of Showers Brothers: offering fair value to people of modest means. The company was thinking optimistically and appeared to be prosperous and orderly, but this burst of general optimism was marred by a hard blow just a few weeks later.

Chapter

15

EVERYTHING CHANGES

ON FEBRUARY 20, 1928, Sanford Teter died at his home after a paralytic stroke. He had battled kidney disease for thirteen years. "During his long illness his cheerful disposition and sense of humor never left him," his obituary noted. "He was one of the pioneers in the work which brought about a greater Bloomington.... There was no more popular man than Sanford Teter. He was as near an ideal citizen and business man as a community could have; he was a neighbor and friend who could always be counted on in times of stress."[1] The family was deeply grieved; Teter's continual good spirits, intelligence, and helpfulness had been much loved and relied upon. After he had recovered from his two surgeries twelve years previously, his doctors ordered him to avoid active community life. He had effectively been exiled to the sidelines, unable to participate in civic or business affairs. "A brave man is not afraid to die," observed the *Telephone* in a tribute to Teter. "But, though the facing of ... imminent death requires great courage, it requires greater courage on the part of a strong man to sit by the window for twelve years watching the rest of the world go by without being able to join in the activity."[2]

The tribute printed in the paper after his death hailed his contributions to the public good, saying "no man did more for Bloomington during the days of his active career. He served as a member of the city council ... and became president of the Chamber of Commerce at a time when the agitation was just started for good automobile roads. At that time there were very few automobiles in general use, but Mr. Teter was one of the far-seeing men who could visualize what the future would bring in the way of auto development and travel. He insisted that good roads would do as much to develop Bloomington as any one thing." The paper added that one of the greatest afflictions of his illness was that he could no longer handle a motor car. Sanford Teter had been a diplomatic and generous man, and both the company and the community felt his loss keenly. Showers Brothers halted operations for the remainder of the week as a mark of respect. His devoted wife Nellie never married again.

Nellie's brother, W. Edward Showers, was seriously ill as well and vacated his huge mansion for a smaller home on North Walnut Street. Both he and his cousin Charles Sears, who was also unwell, often missed weeks of work at a time because of ongoing health problems, and this soon resulted in a drastic shakeup at the Showers Brothers Company. Three weeks after Teter's death, W. Edward announced he was stepping down from the presidency and would become chairman of the board of directors (a nominal honor requiring little work other than showing up for board meetings), while the head of the Nurre Glass company, J. M. Nurre, would assume the leadership of both companies. Charles Sears was optimistic that he could continue to handle his workload and was named First Vice President and Production Manager over all plants. Lane Siebenthal took over for Teter as secretary and treasurer of the board of directors.

That autumn, Charles Sears suffered a sudden stroke while sitting down to breakfast. An hour later he was dead, at the age of 63. "Mr. Sears had in fact been in ill health for more than three years," explained the newspaper,

> but in the meantime had been on duty at the factory most of the time. His trouble was with terrible headaches that were so severe that he was compelled often to be out of the factory. He had the attention of a number of specialists, and finally about six months ago underwent a serious operation for sinus. He was in the St. Vincent's Hospital for several weeks and improved slowly, though his impaired sight did not return as was expected. After returning home several high class specialists gave him a rigid examination, but could find nothing radically wrong, and they recommended that he go to Arizona to spend the winter.[3]

Sears had shipped his beloved automobile out to Tucson and had rented a pretty cottage for his wife and himself to pass the winter in. He had undergone a successful tonsillectomy the week before he died.

Charles Sears, studio portrait.
From the collection of the Monroe County History Center,
202 East 6th Street, Bloomington, IN,
www.monroehistory.org, 1988.109.0322.

"Charles Sears had been connected with the Showers factory since he was nine years old, starting as a water carrier boy," noted the *Telephone*, "and he has been a part of the organization for 56 years. He was not only a relative but a special friend of James D. and Wm. Showers, and the three worked side by side when he was a mere lad. Step by step Sears was promoted as the factory grew from a work shop to be the largest institution of the kind in the world. He was part of its success from his water carrier days, all the way along, reaching the position of vice president and general manager. For years he was at the head of the department of labor and superintendent of the manufacturing department. It is an apt saying but true with Mr. Sears that he knew the business from A to Z. In the last few years he has been taking more or less of a vacation during the winter, but on the whole has spent almost all of more than a half century working every day. He and W. E. Showers, chairman of the board of directors and largest stockholders in the Showers plant, have always been very close friends, and worked harmoniously together. One of the last requests that the late W. N. Showers made was, 'Charley, I want you to stand by Ed, and Ed I want you to stand by Charley.'"[4]

Everything was changing. In 1929 the company discontinued the Showers Brothers Savings Bank and turned its accounts over to the Citizen's Loan and Trust. "It will be the policy of the company to manufacture furniture and divorce itself from any other outside interest," it announced.[5] In October the New York Stock Market crashed, but Bloomington initially took little notice. The news failed to make the front page of the *Telephone* and was not even mentioned until a week later, when an article was published in which John D. Rockefeller assured the nation the "the fundamental conditions in the country are sound." A small front-page item on the same day said that the stock markets had staged a comeback, enabling the New York Stock Exchange to "catch up on the tremendous amount of business that has been transacted recently."[6] The following day stocks surged by five to twelve points, according to the *Telephone*. The following month Showers Brothers Company confidently predicted that the next year, 1930, would be their biggest ever.[7] Obviously, it was not evident to midwesterners during the final months of 1929 that their entire world had changed, and not for the better. The stock market crash might have been front-page news to bankers in New York, but for ordinary people in Bloomington, life continued as usual for another few months. But disturbing incidents began to make headlines: a banker in Indianapolis leaped from his eleventh-floor office,[8] and the president of the First National Bank in New Harmony, Indiana, killed himself with a gun.[9]

It's painful to dwell on the decline of a once-great factory, and equally painful to describe the decline of a once-confident and proud little city. The Great Depression made a terrible impact on Bloomington that lingered for decades to come, long after the rest of the nation had returned to normalcy.[10] Its boom days over for good, the city of Bloomington had a stricken aspect. Housing was short because construction had nearly stopped. Gripped by a great economic downturn, the nation had no spare money with which to buy furniture. Incoming orders for the factory diminished alarmingly and gross sales declined from approximately ten million dollars in 1929 to about two million in 1932.[11] The payroll shrank from $1,571,278 in 1929 to $438,732 in 1932. The number of workers declined from 1,298 in 1929 to 799 in 1932, and hourly wages were cut from forty-eight cents an hour to as low as twenty-two cents, less than half.[12] By the next decade Bloomington had become "one of the most seriously depressed areas in the state. This situation . . . was responsible for a sizeable out-migration of persons seeking employment elsewhere in the state."[13] Management changed once more during the early 1930s when the aging W. Edward Showers, despite his chronic ill-health, came back from retirement and resumed control of the company, undoing the corporate merger of Showers Brothers and the Nurre Glass factory. But he could not stop the tide from turning, and he died of heart disease in February of 1935.

Cataclysmic events can provide opportunities as well as difficulties. Guy Burnett had begun work at Showers Brothers as the traffic manager, responsible for ordering the necessary materials required for manufacturing and then shipping out the finished materials. Due to the management changes he quickly made his way up the hierarchy at the factory. He became assistant to the president in 1930, vice president in 1932 (when W. Edward Showers temporarily returned to try to pull the company out of the doldrums), vice president and manager in 1934 and president and general manager in 1935 after W. Edward's death. It was Burnett's painful duty to keep the firm in the black no matter what it required. The Showers Brothers Savings Bank that had helped so many workers buy their own houses and afford Christmas presents had been liquidated and the company welfare department, with its pensions and cheap firewood, was terminated. The group insurance and health insurance plans were also discontinued. However, the big field behind Plant 4 that once had been used to grow hay for the company horses was subdivided into workers' vegetable patches, and seeds and plants were given to workers who intended to garden there.[14] There was no longer any help to be had when a man came in with a tale of hardship at home, because everyone was in the same boat, including the company itself. "I guess things changed after the management changed. Ed died and Nurre came in for a while and then Burnett took over. That's when the changes came in," an anonymous Showers employee told Louis Orzack when he was researching his 1953 thesis about the Showers company.[15]

Walkouts began at Showers Brothers in 1935, the year of W. Edward's death, for the workmen were no longer willing to accept lower wages as they had temporarily done in the old days under James Showers. The few orders the company received often languished for want of a workforce, and without steady income the company was unable to invest in renovations and upkeep. The plants were showing signs of aging and wear. "That place is just sub-standard," an anonymous informant told Orzack. "At Showers the workers are older men, there are no younger men there. There's no future. . . . The workers there had the education minimum, the lowest common labor."[16] Orzack noted in 1953 that "the Showers worker of today typically is a man of advanced years. Reportedly, there are men in their seventies employed there" and added that the only teenagers who worked there were rural lads who lacked high school educations and were restricted to seasonal work rather than fulltime jobs.[17] He recorded a Showers personnel officer admitting that "a lot of people working there couldn't probably get a job anywhere else because of their age and physical condition."[18]

The problem was that all the young workers had been wooed away by the new RCA factory. In 1940 RCA had purchased the former Plant 4 on South Rogers Street from the Showers corporation. RCA gave it a facelift, installed a new radio assembly line and advertised for young men and women. RCA would not hire anyone older than thirty-five and preferred workers in their teens and twenties.[19] More than half of the new workforce was made up of women. The working people of Bloomington were unspeakably grateful that RCA was willing to hire hundreds of people at good wages—better than at Showers. By 1950 RCA was working a peak of three thousand workers and manufacturing television sets; Showers was employing a fraction of that at approximately five hundred people in 1952.[20] But there were still many workers who could not find employment at either factory.

> Two thousand men and women in the community now need real jobs and are anxious to obtain such jobs. Several hundreds of these people have been working on WPA projects but this type of employment is steadily decreasing. Only by the new RCA factory and industrial expansion can these 2,000 men and women have a chance to get jobs in Bloomington. Otherwise they must go through a period of hardship, with public relief staving off want and hunger, and finally they must leave Bloomington and go to other cities in search of jobs.[21]

The Showers company in its final years must have seemed a sad ghost of its former self to those who remembered the vibrant years of the 1910s and early '20s. Workers no longer liked or trusted their management and even went so far as to charge that Showers Brothers Company kept a false set of books in order to "prove" that the company was not making a profit.[22] The oral histories preserved at the Monroe History Center tell a painful tale of decline and demoralization. Former Showers foreman John Oscar Pardue claimed years later that when RCA opened its own factory, half of the workers at Showers left to go work there. "A lot of our qualified men, smarter, educated and all . . . sure, they went to RCA." It was because "RCA paid . . . maybe a nickel or dime more—and that's what they went for."[23] Former Showers employee Frank Godsey estimated the number of workers who left Showers to work elsewhere as less than half of the workforce, but he agreed that "skilled people" were the ones who left, those who were interested in electronics or could repair wooden cabinets. He believed that Showers Brothers had experienced a gradual dumbing-down of the workforce, and agreed with Pardue that Showers "worked an awful lot of people that really wasn't mentally capable of working anyplace else."[24] Pardue recalled "there was not very much education people at all" working there. "The vice president in there . . . he was well educated. . . . He was just too smart for the people that worked there. He didn't understand our ways. And I made the remark, if he was that well educated he didn't belong at Showers Brothers, for the people there were really not educated."[25]

In addition to a minimally qualified workforce, the factory building was hopelessly obsolete by this point. The building was unpleasant to work in, with mechanical equipment that inadvertently heated the air to uncomfortable temperatures, making the workers describe it as "a sweatshop."[26] Workers habitually spat tobacco juice on the floors and the toilets were not kept clean.[27] But the biggest problem was that in terms of efficiency the factory was lagging further and further behind the more modern competition elsewhere in the nation. A plant that had originally been arranged and set up according to the standards of 1910 and 1913 did not necessarily function well thirty or forty years later.

"Between 1920 and 1930 there was not too much changes in the plant," Pardue remembered. "They never bought a bunch of new machinery or nothing. . . . That's one thing that hurt Showers . . . they was never much to buy new equipment. They just kept working their old or fixing it and battling and fixing it and just kept operating old machinery."[28] Godsey agreed; he had traveled once with company managers to North Carolina and Virginia to inspect the latest manufacturing equipment. "About the first plant that we went into[,] I seen that we [at Showers] weren't even in it as far as manufacturing was concerned because everything was conveyerized and their manufacturing techniques were right up-to-date. So I seen right there that we couldn't compete with them. . . . Some of our equipment was 50 years old or better." He noted that Plant 1 was still using equipment in the 1950s that had been installed when the building was new, back in 1910.[29]

The aging Showers family was failing throughout this era. Belle Allen Showers, James's wife, had died near the end of 1926, only thirty-seven days before their sixtieth wedding anniversary. She had been involved in many of the good causes supported by the Showers family, including the cemetery association and the hospital. In 1935 W. Edward died, as noted earlier. In 1936 the newspapers briefly marked the passing of Maud Showers Wilson. Maud had been in poor health for the previous five years and had entered the Methodist Hospital in Indianapolis for observation and treatment. There she was stricken with heart trouble and asthma and died. "Mrs. Wilson was the last surviving incorporator of the Local Council of Women that founded the Bloomington Hospital about 30 years ago," the paper noted, referring to Maud as eighty years old instead of seventy-three.

> Mrs. Wilson had served as president of the board of hospital trustees since its founding with the exception of one year. She still held the post at the time of her death. Realizing the community's need for a library, Mrs. Wilson was responsible for building the city library and had served as president of the library board until one year ago. She was the first member of the Board of Children's Guardians and Monroe County's first probation officer. For 45 years, Mrs. Wilson had served as a member of the board of directors of Bethany Park and until recently had served on the Board of the First Christian Church. She was affiliated with the Women's Club, Century Club, Wednesday Club and was a life member of the Christian Church Missionary Society that she helped organize. Mrs. Wilson was an early leader in the equal-suffrage fight in Indiana.[30]

This was all true, but the article omitted everything that had made Maud special: that she was an intelligent woman, a good public speaker, a savvy political lobbyist, and an indefatigable campaigner for her host of good causes. It made no mention of a two-month trip she had made to the Holy Land, or her travels to California and to the East Coast. It ignored the fact that throughout her life,

Maud in her stately old age.
Courtesy Jim Holland.

the farmer's daughter who had married at sixteen had made it her goal to utilize opportunities to help others who were less fortunate. Maud did more than anyone else in Bloomington, except for the two Showers brothers themselves, to make the city into a much better place than it originally was.

James Showers died in early April of 1937 at the impressive age of ninety-seven years after suffering a bout of pleurisy. He could remember Conestoga wagons in the years when Indiana was still considered "the West" and he could recall Indians paddling canoes on the Mississippi and slaves in the southern

James Showers in his later days.
Courtesy the Helm family.

cotton fields. He had not participated in company life for more than thirty years but had remained active with the Citizen's Loan and Trust until the year before his death. "Local business came to a near halt as citizens paid homage to the . . . leader who has had the interest of the community at heart from the day he first looked upon its rutted, unpaved streets . . . at the age of 14," declared the *Telephone.*[31] James had spent a lot of time and thought on his memoirs in his last years and appears to have written some of the entries as early as 1927, when they were used as reference for the Showers Brothers Company's commemorative sixtieth anniversary book by Dale Dillon. Yet other entries were written only a year or two before his death. The pages were written in a large, open script with occasional strike-outs and additions; some of them referred to himself in the third person while others used "I." Some of the passages appear to have been edited by a secretary into typewritten form, probably around the time the commemorative book by Dillon was written. One of the entries fondly listed all of the models of automobiles he had ever owned. The memoirs reflect a man with little formal schooling who nevertheless was kind and well-inclined toward others—even Democrats.

With the death of W. Edward, the third Showers generation to head the business, the business smarts of the family seemed to be exhausted. With no more Showers men to take over the helm, the ownership of the company rested in the hands of Showers women, who lacked business experience. Although these women were indeed estimable and talented, they were faced with a bigger economic problem than they had the capacity to handle. Indeed, it's probable that nobody at that time, male or female, skilled or unskilled, could have made the factory profitable again. The women's understandable reluctance to expend large amounts of money during tight times had unfortunate results: "They wouldn't modernize or spend any money on the plants," recalled Frank Godsey. His wife, Lucille, who had worked as an executive secretary for the Showers management, added, "I will tell you what Mr. Burnett said to me—he was leaving, retiring—and he said to me. . . . 'Miss Murphy, don't ever get in a family business owned by women.'"[32]

Pardue noted that the price of Showers furniture was undercut by southern furniture mills, which manufactured similar furnishings for significantly less. In 1929 the average Showers wage was $1,211, which was more than the state average of $1,088 per year, but in Georgia the average furniture worker earned only $791, which obviously made the southern products far cheaper to manufacture.[33] Former company president Guy Burnett agreed: "Our rates here were the result of organizing us for that union. And our labor rates were higher than they were paying in the South. . . . It was purty tough." A harsh blow came when hometown furniture dealers in Bloomington chose to stock cheaper southern furniture rather than the locally manufactured Showers lines. Production became slower and slower and overhead costs could not be lowered.

Years later, Guy Burnett sounded bitter when asked about the unions. "That's what they all want," he recalled, "more money and more holidays. Don't want [to] work too much."[34] Beginning in the 1930s, labor unrest disrupted the company every year or so. Workers struck at the Nurre Glass factory in 1934; in 1935 a federal mediator came to Bloomington to help settle a strike by 1,100 Showers workers. In 1937 a massive walkout by 1,500 workers shut the factory down. In 1940 the plant was idled again after a strike; workers at that time demanded five-cent raises with a minimum of forty cents per hour regardless of the class of work, stoppage of work five minutes before lunch and before the end of the day in order to clean up, and paid vacations for all.[35] In 1942, 700 workers walked out. In 1943, 850 workers walked out despite the fact that the company was now engaged in the war effort, manufacturing desks for the government. In 1946 it happened again, with 600 workers. In July 1949 the factory opened again after several weeks of total closure due to lack of orders, with 600 men out of work. By August of that year, the working force of the Showers plants was only about 450.[36]

The multiple factory locations of the Showers Brothers Company had once been an asset but proved a disaster during an economic depression. "We had too damn many plants," remembered Guy Burnett. "When you got too many plants, you can't get business enough to keep 'em going, why, your operating costs go up."[37] Plant 4 on South Rogers Street was sold to RCA in 1940; the Bloomfield and Burlington plants were also sold off. The company was in the position of a prizefighter going down beneath a barrage of heavy blows to the head: BAM, the heavy cost of its subsidiary plants; BAM, labor walkouts that slowed production; BAM, the rising cost of materials that had to be shipped in from increasingly greater distances; BAM, cheaper alternatives available in the South. The Showers company simply could not prevail. Although it had been able to repay the $7,000,000 loan issued to it by the First National Bank of Chicago, it could not recapture its once-dominant position in furniture manufacturing without plenty of orders, good profit ratios, aggressive leadership, better workers, and an updated plant. The writing was on the wall.

It's useful at this point to examine the earnings of the company over the last decades of its existence. (See table 15-1.) Bear in mind that the actual *profits* (according to Moody and other market analysts) would very likely have been much different, but these were the earnings that were published in newspapers of the time and in company reports.

Guy Burnett retired in 1952 and was replaced as company president by Robert Dillon. A ray of hope came when the president of Indiana University, Herman B. Wells, joined the board of directors at Showers Brothers in 1953.

TABLE 15.1

Year	Earnings	Notes
1925	$1,587,812.20	Excellent earnings
1926	$1,567,966.07	Ditto
1927	$1,876,860.75	Ditto
1928	$1,867,908.77	Ditto
1929	$2,371,546.33	The company's best year ever; the stock market crashes in October
1930	$1,396,083.35	Despite the Crash, earnings are still over a million
1931	$1,117,307.67	Ditto
1932	$697,540.53	Hard times are catching up with the company
1933	$631,398.03	This represents the worst year of the Great Depression nationally
1934	$761,838.97	A slight recovery
1935	$1,071,877.74	The company is back over a million dollars of profit; Guy Burnett becomes president of the company in February; the first strike by workers at the Showers factory
1936	$1,176,171.69	Another good year
1937	$993,925.86	A massive strike
1938	$488,877.92	The U.S. economy experiences a sharp industrial decline this year
1939[1]	$758,971.79	A small recovery
1940		No data available
1941[2]	$331,485.17	This is half what the company made during the worst year of the Depression; the worst year to date, but worse will soon come
1942[3]	$140,582.27	Another strike; terrible earnings
1943	$207,802.20	Another strike; earnings improve slightly
1944	$85,462.18	Another strike; the worst earnings on record to this point
1945	$111,553.72	A slight recovery
1946	$293,484.26	Another strike, but a better year overall
1947	$538,257.04	The company earns half a million for the first time in eight years
1948	$399,304.18	Downturn
1949	$99,953.28	Things grow even worse
1950	$151,764.04	A slight but temporary recovery
1951	$59,729.71	A terrible year
1952	-$373,415.08	Loss, not gain; the company is hemorrhaging money. The 1954 annual report assesses the loss at even higher: -$438,602
1953[4]	-$208,122.00	More loss; the country experiences a significant recession
1954	-$293,990.00	More loss in the company's final year

Notes:

1. All data up to this year was printed in the *Bloomington World*, Mar. 15, 1940, Indiana University Archives.

2. Information for this year from a newspaper clipping found with other Showers clippings at the Indiana University Archives.

3. All figures from this year to 1952 are from the Showers Brothers Company Annual Report for 1952, which summed up numbers from the past decade, Indiana University Archives.

4. Figures for 1953 and 1954 were cited in the Showers Brothers Company Annual Report for 1954, Indiana University Archives.

Showers stacked bureau, 1950s.

From the collection of the Monroe County History Center,
202 East 6th Street, Bloomington, IN,
www.monroehistory.org, 1989.072.0008.

Nellie Showers Teter had met him during her work as a trustee of the University and had been extremely impressed. Wells was visionary, effective, and a splendid communicator, and was arguably the best president that Indiana University ever had during its long history. Hand-written notes thanking him for joining the board were sent to Wells by Nellie and her daughter, Mary Louise Hare. Nellie wrote, "I can't begin to tell you how happy we all are that you will be a director on our Showers Board."[38] Mary Louise gushed, "I have a much more secure feeling about Showers Bros. now that we will have your advice on the board . . . thank you, from the bottom of my heart."

Wells joined the board during the last three years of the company's existence, when it was hemorrhaging, and he appears to have assessed the company as a losing proposition. He therefore directed his efforts toward trying to sell off the damaged company. He wrote to a potential buyer, Mr. Charles Saltzman at Henry Sears & Co., frankly acknowledging that "sales were off" and that the major stockholders were "three old ladies" who were in the mood to sell.[39] Saltzman may have expressed interest, but the Monroe Circuit Court had exclusive probate jurisdiction over the trust created by the will of William N. Showers, deceased, and declined to approve a sale of stock to Saltzman.[40] Wells was busy with university responsibilities and missed many of the later meetings of the Showers Brothers' board of directors. Largely without his input, the company continued to spiral downward. The annual report of 1954 observed that gross furniture sales in general across the nation were down, but certainly not to the 29.6 percent decline experienced by Showers.[41] Dillon struggled against the inevitable but nothing availed. Not even his managing to lower the "complaint ratio" (the percentage of shipped orders that generated complaints from purchasers) from 8 percent to 0.9 percent could stem the tide. A letter of his dated February 3, 1954 (preserved in the Herman B. Wells materials at the Indiana University Archive), written during the depths of the economic recession, attempted to analyze why profits were down. It was the overall bad economy: attendance at the Furniture Mart had been 10–40 percent off; Nurre's glass sales were off 50 percent from the previous year; carpet manufacturers had reduced their prices by 6–15 percent nationally and mattress producers had cut their prices by up to 8 percent; two leading southern furniture producers, Vaughn-Bassett Furniture Company and Hooker Furniture, were both experiencing disappointing sales, and many furniture retailers had expressed concern over unemployment. Dillon wrote,

> All of this adds up to one very simple conclusion. It means that 1954 will be a good year for those of us who work hard and make it so. Our salesmen were directed at the opening of the Market . . . that they must go to work; work harder; plan more; think up interesting new approaches; and put in longer hours than they ever have before. We plan closer control over our men. Those that don't produce will be replaced. They must work, or the SHOWERS line will be given to someone that will get out and sell it. . . . I believe that with the line we have and the organization we have to sell it, we should materially improve our sales as the spring season gets under way.[42]

Bedroom suite, 1950s.

From the collection of the Monroe County History Center,
202 East 6th Street, Bloomington, IN,
www.monroehistory.org, 1989.072.0008.

But the 1954 furniture catalog was filled with uninspiring designs. Although the 1950s is remembered as the heyday of timeless Mid-Century Modern designs that are avidly collected today by connoisseurs, Showers Brothers played no part in this sleek, stylish design movement. Their furniture styles instead seemed expressly created for small-town midwesterners. One can practically hear the nails being hammered into the coffin of the business.

The final company president was one of the many helpful Showers sons-in-law, Robert Dillon, who had married W. Edward's daughter, Betsy Showers. Dillon stepped in when Guy Burnett quit, but even a Showers in-law could not stop the company's steady decline. There was probably a sense of relief mixed with sorrow when Dillon announced that the sale of the company to Storkline Furniture Corporation of Chicago in May 1955. The Bloomington newspapers hailed it as a win–win situation, particularly since the workers would be retained and the plant kept open. The directors finally voted to dissolve the corporation in June 1955;[43] a letter from Dillon to the shareholders afterward noted that the "liquidation of your company . . . is moving along in an

At the time of its sale to Storkline, the largest remaining share-holder of the Showers Brothers Company was the William N. Showers Trust, with 62,105 shares. The trust had been set up by William to continue through the lives of his children. Bertha Showers, the widow of W. Edward, owned 17,327 shares and her daughter, Elizabeth Jane Dillon, owned 15,474. Nellie Teter had 4,700 and her daughter, Mary Louise Hare, owned 1,400. Members of the board of directors comprised most of the remaining larger shareholders.

orderly fashion." Dividends were paid to shareholders based on a distribution of $1.50 per share. It was the bitter end.

Storkline was also a family business, specializing in furnishings for infants and children: cribs, high chairs, and prams. On May 31, 1955, the day before control of Showers Brothers passed to Storkline, the *Bloomington Herald-Telephone* carried ads from dozens of its usual advertisers (paint, insurance, metal salvaging, gas stations, drugstores, quarries, and the workers' union) all reading "Welcome Storkline." Storkline in return ran an enormous ad, almost full-page, thanking the community for such a warm welcome.[44] The feeling reflected in the newspaper was one of optimism and satisfaction that things would continue as they had done for so many decades. Privately, there were doubts among those who understood the seriousness of the problems facing the factory. Guy Burnett made a mental note to himself at the time that Storkline would probably have only two years of operations before it closed.[45] He was not far wrong in his assessment. Three years after the purchase of the Showers plant, a strike by workers shut down the factory. Soon there-after Storkline announced it was closing the plant for good. The equipment and the buildings were auctioned, and Indiana University purchased the va-cant campus along with the executive building with its beautiful wood-lined offices. The long story of the family-owned factory had ended.

Chapter 16

LEGACY

EVERYONE DIES IN THE END, but a large number of the Showers men suffered untimely deaths. The patriarch of the family, Rev. C. C. Showers, died after being struck by a locomotive; his son Hull died in his mid-twenties from a tonsillitis infection that became toxic, and his grandson W. Edward died of heart disease after a debilitating illness of more than a decade. James's son, Charley Showers, died in his twenties from tuberculosis; James's little grandson died of a rare disease while still a child. Sanford Teter, technically an in-law rather than a Showers, died at fifty-three after a dozen years of invalidism. After Erle Showers's death in 1940 from heart disease, there were no Showers men left and the family surname disappeared.

In her master's thesis on the physical structure of Showers Brothers Plant 1, Eryn Brennan argues that architect C. H. Ballew's 1910 building represented a transitional form between Victorian and modern architecture, and that this form ultimately doomed the company by not easily accommodating modern assembly lines. The sawtooth roof with its north-facing skylights was a progressive feature, but the use of brick and timber-frame for the building's shell was retrogressive. She observes that Albert Kahn was designing large factory buildings around that same time using reinforced concrete.

The benefits of reinforced concrete, including its fire resistant properties and impressive structural stability, were well known by the early 1900s. . . . Thus Ballew's decision to employ timber and brick rather than reinforced concrete for the design of his factory reflected a traditional approach to industrial design in 1910. Timber-frame construction necessitated a load-bearing exterior wall, which in turn limited the fenestration of the east and west facades of the building. . . . Hence Ballew's use of traditional building methods significantly reduced the amount of light able to penetrate the interior of the first floor. . . . The first floor of the factory was likely gloomy and ill-lit.

A reinforced concrete frame would have also contributed to significantly larger interior spans than those achieved at Ballew's Plant One. Kahn's reinforced concrete factories . . . constructed in 1905 and 1907 . . . possessed interior spans of thirty to sixty feet. In contrast, the timber-frame at the Showers Plant allowed maximum interior spans of only twenty feet. . . . The use of a reinforced concrete frame . . . would have nearly doubled the twenty foot span and allowed for greater flexibility in the arrangement of the machines inside the factory. This begs the question as to why Ballew choose to employ traditional brick and timber building materials. [1]

The notion that a reinforced concrete structure would have been better than the existing one is debatable. Reinforced concrete would have allowed greater interior spans, certainly; but furniture manufacture does not follow the same progression as an automobile assembly line. A series of completely different tasks must be performed at successive stages and in different places. In one building, veneer was shaved from raw logs that had been boiled. At the sawmill, planks were cut from other logs, planed, and cut to proper lengths. Both veneer and cut planks were unloaded at ground level on the north end of Plant 1 (at the second floor, due to the gently sloping terrain), and the work progressed through several work zones toward the south. The company described its system in a full-page advertisement in the *Bloomington Daily Telephone* on January 21, 1928: "Each of the Six Big Plants is operated according to a specially devised 'block' system. Units of furniture are retained in one 'block' until all operations assigned to that particular department are completed—then those units travel to the next 'block' by conveyors—really a track of ball-bearing rollers." Along the way, pieces were shaped by a variety of specialty machines that added dados, spindles, and other decorative details, and these pieces were then assembled into their proper configuration at the various "blocks." Surfaces were smoothed where necessary, veneer was attached, and finish was applied. The sanding and finishing areas were traditionally kept separate from each other, since any wood dust in the air would contaminate newly varnished surfaces. At the end of the process, finished pieces were lowered to the first floor at the south end of the plant, where they were either warehoused or crated and loaded onto rail cars. Although the configuration of Plant 1 might not seem optimum by modern standards, the layout of the 1910 building allowed the workmen of the era to put on their biggest burst of production ever. Brennan believes that the production line was less than efficient, but Showers Brothers Company itself was extremely proud of what it called its "straight-line" production process.[2] The system was obviously capable of turning out impressive quantities of finished furniture each day.

The decision to build with brick and timber-frame meant that Plant 1 could be erected by local day laborers who were familiar with that building method, rather than importing skilled laborers from the North to work with reinforced concrete. William Showers was such a booster of his local community that he would not have wanted to spurn local workers in favor of outsiders. Even though Plant 1 witnessed many years of decline, the brick and timber-frame building nevertheless helped create the greatest period of productivity the company ever knew. Although the structure and its machinery certainly aged, the building remained serviceable and would have been updated and eventually replaced like all the factories before it, but for the changing economic circumstances of the Great Depression and the war years. After all, brick walls are easy to knock down and easy to build onto, unlike reinforced concrete walls. Brennan's verdict that Plant 1 represented old-fashioned architecture instead of cutting-edge modernity is certainly true, but the choice of timber-frame and brick was probably not a fatal error. The building still stands to this day in its new capacity as Bloomington's City Hall, still sturdy, completely refurbished and weathertight, and will very likely stand for another century (if not longer).

There are many indications that the company's decline was already in place before the Crash of 1929 and Great Depression that followed. The company had spent enormous amounts of money during the 1910s and '20s and had counted on future orders to replenish its capital; it had enlarged too far and was significantly overextended. Brennan points out that one of the 1930s-era vice presidents was H. K. Ferguson, the head of the Cleveland construction firm that had built the South Rogers and Burlington plants as well as the Showers research building; she observes drily that "over-expansion of the Showers Company was lucrative for at least one Vice-President."[3] A series of separate factories requires a series of excellent overseers to manage and govern them,

A fire in the late 1960s completely destroyed Plant 2 on the Showers campus, leaving Plant 1 and a handful of the smaller structures.

Accession 66-1111, collection of Indiana University Archives.

and the company lacked this by the 1920s, judging from the constant comments in *Shop Notes*. It's quite likely that the workers in the various plants located in Bloomington, Burlington, and Bloomfield had no sense of being part of a shared community as they would have done if sharing a single campus. The immense workforce took advantage of lax (and patronizing) supervision by taking more and more opportunities to slack off.[4]

Lastly and most importantly, as Louis Orzack identified, were the damaging economic factors that were already emerging during the 1920s. These included price cutting due to increased competition; the price reductions demanded by large chains; the demand for new patterns each year to meet the expectations of the annual furniture show in Chicago; the increased use of metal and plastic in furniture manufacture; and even the tendency to smaller houses that needed less furniture. The local lumber supply was depleted and new factories were emerging in the South.[5] Because the Showers company early on had logged all the available hardwood forests in Indiana and nearby states, the cost of importing materials became steadily greater. Even as early as the 1910s, lumber was being sent by rail up from the Mississippi Delta for veneering purposes.[6] Furniture production was moving to the southeast states, where pine was abundant and workers were not unionized. Furniture could be made in Georgia and the Carolinas for a fraction of the cost that the northern factories had to pay. Although the Showers Brothers Company had made its fortune manufacturing inexpensive, affordable furniture, it could not cut costs any more without injuring its own profitability. After the start of the Great Depression, these factors slowly destroyed the Showers Brothers Company. Beginning in the late 1930s, a new generation of workers refused to perform such demanding and physical labor for half the wages of the previous decade and launched a series of strikes. The fathers and grandfathers of these strikers had worked gladly for James and William because of the special rapport between management and employees at that time, but James and William's kindnesses to their employees were only a memory by the late 1930s, and the old welfare considerations were a thing of the past. One can't blame the workers for demanding a living wage.

The later Showers administrators were unable to deal with these complex challenges. With each passing generation the overall company vision became more diluted and the administration grew more isolated from its workforce and more harassed by outside changes in the American economy. Given the formidable obstacles that beset the company in its last decade, it's quite possible that even James and William themselves could not have pulled the company back from the brink.

DOES SIZE MATTER?

In 1966 two fires occurred at the former Showers campus. The first fire in February destroyed the northern portion of Plant 1, which had extended all the way to Tenth Street. The second and larger fire that summer destroyed all of Plant 2. The remaining portion of Plant 1, now used by the City of Bloomington as its city hall, represents slightly less than half of the original campus's square footage. Although it's large, anyone who looks at the building today probably feels that the Showers Brothers Company was engaging in exaggeration when it claimed to be the largest furniture factory in the nation. Fewer and fewer people today remember just how immense the factory buildings really were.

During the period between 1910 and 1930, the Showers Brothers Company was the largest employer in the city of Bloomington, with more than 2,100 employees at its various locations.[7] If you assume that most of its workmen were married, and that most of the married men had children, then the company paychecks could easily have supported up to ten thousand people, a majority of the population of Bloomington at that time. The question persists: Was Showers Brothers truly the largest furniture company in the nation, as it often claimed? And was it the largest in the world, as was also occasionally asserted? I have been unable to find any primary document that uses the phrase "largest in the world," so that may have been hyperbole on the part of W. Edward Showers. Author and cabinetmaker Nancy Hiller, while researching an Arts and Crafts sideboard she had recently reproduced, learned that there was an English factory contemporaneous with Showers Brothers that claimed to be the largest furniture factory in the world: Harris Lebus. Intrigued, she traveled to England to do research that later resulted in an article for *American Bungalow* magazine.[8] She found that the histories of the two companies had many similarities: both were founded by cabinetmaker patriarchs who made significant relocations in the mid-1800s (Louis Lebus emigrated from Germany to England) to found prosperous furniture manufactories. Both companies were family owned until the final years; both companies were known for their benevolent treatment of their massive workforces; and both companies billed themselves as "the world's largest." They both served their country's war efforts during the First and Second World Wars; both suffered decades of economic decline in the mid-twentieth century and finally closed down after being sold into other hands. The chief difference between the two companies was that of style: Harris Lebus had better designs and was renowned for its clean and elegant Arts and Crafts patterns in the early 1900s, the same era in which Showers Brothers was mass-producing inexpensive and ornate Victorian furniture. Harris Lebus employed a thousand workers in the 1890s at a time when Showers had several hundred. The single campus of Harris Lebus was forty-three acres, which is also larger than any individual Showers campus. (The total acreage of Plant 4 was larger than Harris Lebus, but since forty acres of that was farmland it seems inaccurate to include it.)

But to compare Showers to Harris Lebus is fruitless, since their output was so different. Both manufacturers were specialists in their respective niches and both were undoubtedly the largest manufacturers of furniture in their respective countries. Because the company records have been lost, and because newspaper reports of the Showers Brothers output are intermittent and not always accurate, it's difficult to know exactly what the factory's output or income was from year to year. It seems fairly probable that at the time Plants 1 and 2 were built (1910 and 1913) and continuing into the mid-1920s, the factory was indeed the largest in the nation in terms of sheer mass and physical size. William and his son, W. Edward, both made that claim, and both men were well-placed to know what the industry statistics were. In fact, *Shop Notes* recorded several times during the 1920s that Showers had apparently set world and national records for sales of moderately priced furniture.

The company expanded between 1881 and 1929. Its continual enlargements were based upon the assumption that business would always continue to improve, and so growth became seen as inevitable, even necessary. A small group of economists today posit that growth is inherently unsustainable (this concept is known as steady-state economics), but that idea would have seemed ridiculous in 1920. But then and now, we agree that "the bigger they are, the harder they fall"; and the sheer size of the Showers plants became a detriment rather than an asset during the 1930s, as Americans stopped buying furniture. For two brief decades the Showers Brothers Company produced a mind-boggling quantity of affordable furniture after denuding several states of their hardwood forests, but then its production slid to a slow and painful stop. It's unsettling to consider that any of the modern factories of our own day that busily turn out immense quantities of new cars, televisions, and cell phones could just as easily be derailed by a sustained period of economic adversities and end up vacant, inhabited only by rats and pigeons.

TREATMENT OF WORKERS

An issue of *Shop Notes* claimed that it was company custom in 1872 (when the company employed only a handful of men) to "hand out to each man a live turkey, a gallon of oysters, and sometimes cranberries for the trimmings on Christmas eve.... When Uncle 'Billy' Showers ... handed out the turkeys and things to his men they say he got as much enjoyment from the giving as any who received."[9]

The Showers brothers enjoyed friendly relationships with their workers and were on a first-name basis with all of them until the early years of the twentieth century, when the workforce began to grow too large to keep track of. The brothers were dedicated churchgoing men and deemed it their duty to treat others with respect and with a high standard of ethics. They knew that their workmen worked hard and long hours using dangerous machinery, and they appreciated what a dedicated workman was capable of doing. In the 1920s retirement did not yet exist as an entitlement, and workers toiled for five and a half to six days each week. As long as a man had mouths to feed at home and bills to pay, he had to continue working until the day he staggered and fell. The Showers brothers did not work their men to death; they extended welfare provisions to their workers and had a form of pension for the oldest workers who had been with the company the longest time, regardless of race. Lifetime employees both black and white were hailed in the pages of *Shop Notes* for their longevity and faithfulness to the company. The Showers company offered lifetime employment to anyone who had worked there a long time and needed to keep working. When men chose this option, their work tasks were simplified and downsized to accommodate the frailty of old age.

William and James were frequently lauded for their kindly and interested treatment of their workers. "Both J. D. and W. N. [Showers] . . . knew every man in the factory personally and there was a friendship between the Showers brothers and their men which extended into the homes. If one of the men became ill, if there was sickness or tragedy in a family, both help and real sympathy were extended."[10] This kindness knew no limits based on race:

> One of the colored men who . . . worked in the institution when it was located at the corner of Ninth and Grant streets was Jesse Hampton. For a number of years Jesse Hampton was one of the best and most faithful workmen of the factory, then he fell ill and died. J. D. Showers was one of the first people to call at the Hampton home to extend his sympathy in time of great trouble, and when he found that nine small children had been left without a father he promised his help in a very practical manner. He told the stricken wife that until the children were grown up she could look to him for the necessary assistance to keep the large family from want. As the years passed he never forgot this promise and when one of the children, Maude Hampton, died he came forward and quietly paid for the funeral.[11]

WOMEN

The stereotypical view of women's history in America usually dismisses the 1800s as a long dark period characterized by repression and lack of the vote, followed by the dawning of new opportunities in the twentieth century. This view implies that women of the 1800s were essentially powerless, prone to fainting fits, confined to the home, and unable to actively engage in their communities. But this was not the case in Bloomington, where many women appear to have led active and productive lives. In 1887, in a small Indiana community, an intelligent twenty-three-year-old widow and single mother with pronounced leadership ability inherited a one-third interest in a thriving furniture factory and became a full partner with her brothers-in-law. Following her company's incorporation, Maud Showers became a board director and major stockholder. Maud was not the only local woman in this position of power; Mrs. Sarah Matthews, the wife of quarry owner Peter Matthews, inherited his share in the family business after he was killed by an explosion and continued running the family business in his place. Another widow of means, Mrs. Martha Buskirk, owned several choice downtown properties that furnished her with good rents. In addition to Maud, other Showers women participated at the company in later years as board directors and chief stockholders. During the First World War the company was a trendsetter in hiring women. Rather than keeping them segregated from any contact with the woodworking machines, Showers management invited women to do the same work men did. *Shop Notes* indicates that women were paid the same wage as men if they proved that they were capable of performing the same tasks.

The history of the company in the late 1800s and early 1900s in fact exhibits a pattern completely contrary to the conventional view of women's history in America. The company experienced several decades of managerial involvement by strong and capable women during the late 1800s, followed by a brief era of equality in which women workers were paid the same as men. These early opportunities were followed by the 1921 firing of all women working at manual jobs, followed by decades of waning economic influence. During these years of decline, the males in charge chafed under female ownership of the company and referred to them dismissively as "three old ladies," viewing them as impediments to progress. The promising early feminist revolution sputtered out in Bloomington—and around the nation—as the century continued unfolding. Maud Showers was a farmer's daughter who through a stroke of luck was able to use her opportunities to improve the lives of her fellow citizens through an intricate network of women's clubs. By lobbying the statehouse and the city council on multiple occasions, she became politically savvy and knew how to be a diplomat. She was an eloquent speaker and tireless activist. A city hospital for Bloomington would certainly have been organized eventually, but Maud made it happen sooner rather than later, planning events and fundraisers, counting the proceeds, collaring city councilmen, cajoling local businessmen. She was certainly far more empowered and more productive than most Bloomington housewives were during the mid-twentieth century. If Maud had time-traveled to the 1960s to read Betty Friedan's groundbreaking book *The Feminine Mystique,* she would have been puzzled by "the problem that has no name," having never experienced the life of a wife and mother as being unfulfilling herself. If Bloomington's example of women's lives in the 1800s is equally applicable elsewhere in the nation, the concept of the dissatisfied housewife is a twentieth-century phenomenon that bears no relation to women's experiences in the 1800s.

Virtually all the Showers women played a prominent role in the community in the late 1800s. Instead of staying in the home, concerned only with dinner menus and housekeeping, they actively ventured forth to reshape and improve their community through philanthropic projects that included enlarging the cemetery, cleaning the public streets, beautifying the public spaces, caring for the poor, and improving sanitation and hygiene throughout the city. They traveled at times to distant cities to meet and network with like-minded women, and they legislated at state levels to achieve their goals. Sincerely religious as well as philanthropic, they volunteered on multiple church committees. The Rev. C. C.'s wife Elizabeth did the same thing back in the 1860s and '70s with her Bible classes and with visiting homes, ministering to jailed men, and working with missionaries. Her daughters-in-law—James's wife Belle, William's wife Hanna Lou, and Hull's wife Maud—were all long-term members of multiple philanthropic women's clubs. They were followed in turn by the third generation, their daughters Jennie, Nellie, and Beryl. Nellie broke the gender barrier by becoming the first female trustee of Indiana University, and Beryl was one of the founders of a philanthropic women's organization that is still active today in Indiana, the Tri-Kappas (Kappa Kappa Kappa). The large amount of time that the many Showers women spent outside their homes working on their diverse projects and traveling to other cities is evidence that their goals were shared and supported by the Showers men. Men who have strong and capable women in their households are very likely to encourage women's participation in the workplace, and this was the case at the Showers company for many decades. Although the company let its women down badly during W. Edward's tenure as president, the early Showers Brothers Company must be hailed as a great supporter and encourager of women's opportunities in management, labor, and volunteerism.

THE CITY OF BLOOMINGTON

"The Showers family did . . . a great deal for Bloomington," one local citizen remarked in the 1970s. "They've never been given credit, I don't think, for the unselfish things that they did and I think that's a history all to itself that should be followed up."[12]

For several generations, the city of Bloomington reaped countless benefits from the presence of the Showers Brothers Company. The prosperous factory employed up to two thousand workers at its heyday, boosted the local tax rolls, and increased the economic vitality of the community. Employee turnover was low for many years because Showers Brothers was a good place to work and did not oppress its workers.[13] Showers family members launched new savings and loans companies that allowed hundreds of workers to purchase their own homes. They invested time and energy in the first electric company and the telephone company. Because the geographical area is prone to droughts, they sank a great deal of their own money into getting a water company launched and operating, despite innumerable difficulties. Showers family members served on the city council, the school board, the fair board, and the Chamber of Commerce, and were associated with countless clubs, real estate organizations, stone quarries, local businesses, secret societies, church committees, fraternities, and business groups. They helped pave the roads of the city and county, helped bring in a second railway connection, and gave the city of Bloomington the land now known as Showers-Miller Park. The former Showers factory building has been rehabilitated after decades of neglect and now functions as Bloomington's City Hall. For three seasons of the year, Showers Plaza in front of City Hall is home to the community Farmers' Market.

Showers family members invested in real estate and were keenly interested in what we would now call affordable housing for workingmen. All the core

Bloomington today should reflect that the boom times it enjoyed between the 1880s and 1920s were driven in large part by investments by the Showers Brothers Company and the family that owned it. With the decline of Showers Brothers came a decline in the overall economic health of Bloomington, and it became a shabby place for half a century. Only after substantial investments by Cook Inc. in the 1980s did downtown Bloomington start to bloom and thrive once more.

neighborhoods of the city were influenced by the Showers family, who platted and developed the neighborhoods to the north, west, and south of the factory, and built many houses for investment and rental purposes on the east side. Showers workers colonized the new working-class neighborhoods of Maple Heights, Fairview, and Prospect Hill, as well as the more distantly located South Park and McDoel areas; the more affluent administrators and officers of the company lived in Elm Heights, University Courts, and the North Washington district. Eryn Brennan comments that just as the physical work at Plant 1 was separated into skilled and unskilled, white and black, upstairs and downstairs, Bloomington's neighborhoods were similarly stratified, with wealthy owners living high on a hill overlooking their factory, their workers dwelling in small cramped houses in the distance. But every city has wealthier and poorer districts; even in countries that claim to be communist, political leaders never live next door to the ordinary workers. There's nothing intrinsically wrong with the concept of an inexpensive "starter home," and in fact the possibility of buying a cottage is extremely empowering for one who has never owned property before. The Showers family viewed home ownership as a positive thing because workers who owned homes were more committed to their jobs and would become good citizens. By making home ownership possible for any working man, the Showers family boosted its town, lengthened the streets, increased the population, and generated ever more schools and churches. The Showers family didn't create these new workers' neighborhoods because they wished to segregate themselves from their own workers but because they wanted to benefit their community, which for so many decades had suffered from a lack of housing, particularly for families of humble means. Today these core neighborhoods are experiencing a surge of vitality equal to that in the time they were first built, as new homeowners move in and lovingly restore these old houses. The convenience—and the low carbon footprint—of living within walking distance of downtown in a modestly

Plant 1 of the Showers factory has been completely rehabilitated and retrofitted, and now serves as City Hall for the City of Bloomington.

Photo by Carrol Krause.

sized dwelling is often pointed out by the residents of these areas today. James and William Showers had a simple dream: to "boom the town" by filling it with hard-working men who were model citizens, all of them sharing the American Dream together.

SUMMARY

It's sad that the Showers family has been so largely forgotten by the Bloomington public. Part of this is undoubtedly due to the fact that the company folded more than half a century ago, after two decades of distressing economic decline and labor unrest. The few people still alive today who remember the Showers factory retain memories only of the fading years, not the glory days. The collective failure to remember the Showers family's achievements is also partly owing to the fact that the family name is extinct and descendents of the extended family are dispersed across the nation. The passage of time and the family's distaste for self-promotion have resulted in its accomplishments being largely forgotten by later generations. When the company is remembered at all, it's in half-truths, as in the many newspaper articles from the 1960s and '70s that simply repeated that Showers Brothers had its origin making coffins and had once grandiosely called itself "the biggest furniture company in the world."

But the entire infrastructure of the modern city was either set in place, or modified and improved, by the Showers family: the electric and telephone service, the paved streets, the sewerage, the courthouse, the second railroad line, the Methodist Church building, the schools, the public hospital, the cemetery, the Carnegie Library, many of the core neighborhoods, and countless houses. Their most important achievement was the decades-long campaign to secure an abundant source of water, without which today's city could not have developed. As the largest employer in town, the Showers Brothers Company had an immense impact upon the civic tax base as well as on the economic vitality of the community. The company encouraged its workers to insure themselves, practice thrift, purchase homes, become better citizens, and educate their children. The family's efforts to "boom the town" were ceaseless. The modern municipality of Bloomington runs like a self-winding clock and no one today stops to consider who set it in motion; but the Showers family was largely responsible for starting it and making it run.

A paragraph from the funeral service for William Showers sums it up well:

> No one can estimate how much this city owes to the fact that three brothers began a small manufacturing business in its midst years ago, and kept at their work through discouragement as well as success until it became a great industry. No one knows how many homes have had comfort, how many children have had an education, how many lives have been given a chance because this commercial leader built up a great manufacturing industry here.

This book concludes with the same image that began it: the quilt that was sewn as a fundraiser in 1884 by the Showers women, covered with Tumbling Block squares bearing the names of male and female citizens who lent their help in time of need. This quilt is not merely a bedspread that was handed down by four generations in a single family. It was cherished and preserved because it symbolizes the importance of the Showers family and their accomplishments during ninety years of industry and hard work. The quilt is a metaphor for the city of Bloomington, because both the quilt and the city required the physical and financial contributions of many men and women working together to create something useful and beautiful that has lasted many long years. We no longer know the details of the story behind the quilt, just as we no longer remember the story behind Bloomington's infrastructure; but finally we understand the Showers family's role in making it all happen.

Notes

1. THE REVEREND AND HIS FAMILY

1. *Republican Progress,* Jan. 25, 1882.

2. Elizabeth Showers, spiritual daybook, undated opening entry.

3. Ibid.

4. *Bloomington Telephone,* Mar. 29, 1907. Researchers should be aware that the *Telephone* appeared in different editions under the banners *Bloomington Telephone, Weekly Telephone, Semi-Weekly Telephone, Daily Telephone,* and *Bloomington Daily Telephone;* some of these editions were published simultaneously. For simplicity's sake, I have chosen to refer to the paper as the *Telephone* throughout most of the book.

5. James Showers, memoirs, non-paginated.

6. *Indianapolis Sun,* July 11, 1937.

7. Dillon, *Thoughts Regarding the 60th Anniversary,* p. 9.

8. James Showers, memoirs.

9. Ibid. James was either mistaken about its being Griffy Creek, north of Bloomington, or he was mistaken about his age, for he was already a teenager when his family relocated to Bloomington.

10. James Showers, memoirs.

11. *Hearth and Home,* Oct. 16, 1869.

2. SHOWERS & HENDRIX

1. *Bloomington Republican,* Nov. 9, 1861. Isolated copy, in the collections of the Monroe County Public Library and the Monroe County History Center. The date at the bottom of the advertisement indicates when it first appeared in print, not the date of that particular issue of the newspaper.

2. *Shop Notes,* July 12, 1919.

3. *Bloomington Republican,* June 24 and Nov. 18, 1869, collection of the Indiana State Library, Indianapolis.

4. As before, the date indicates when the advertisement was first set in type, which provides information about when the company entered into this branch of business.

5. County commissioner records, collection of the Monroe County History Center. The commissioners paid Showers & Hendrix amounts ranging between $3 and $8 for individual coffins.

6. *Bloomington Progress,* Nov. 10, 1869. (The *Bloomington Progress* appears to have been renamed the *Republican Progress* later on.)

7. The firm purchased an out-lot in 1865 near the corner of what is now Ninth and Grant Streets for factory purposes.

8. *Shop Notes,* Aug. 25, 1917. The newsletter reproduces a daguerreotype of the four men gathered in the photographer's studio and adds that "Showers, Hendrix & Kimbley were located on North College Avenue in the building known as the old Fee Block, now occupied by Breeden & Co." Breeden was on the western end of the north side of the courthouse square. Showers & Hendrix moved several times.

9. James Showers, memoirs.

10. Ibid.

11. Ibid.

12. Elizabeth Showers, spiritual daybook.

13. Ibid.

14. Ibid.

15. This letter, dated Nov. 18, 1980, was written by Mrs. William C. Curry and contains recollections of her grandmother Jennie Showers. Collection of the Showers file at the Indiana Room, Monroe County Public Library.

16. *Daily Telephone*, Dec. 16, 1920.

17. James Showers, memoirs.

3. LEGAL TROUBLES

1. Dillon, *Thoughts Regarding the 60th Anniversary*, p. 17.

2. Ibid., p. 9.

3. See Deedbook Z, transaction #495, collection of the Monroe County History Center.

4. In the 1980s, researcher John Bendix conducted careful research into the history of the Showers company. His detailed notes can be found in the collection of the Monroe County History Center. The information about this bankruptcy was recorded in his notes and dated Nov. 30, 1869. Although Bendix's research is in every other way impeccable, this is not the correct date for the publication of the weekly newspaper, which would have appeared on Dec. 1. However, this information is not present in the Dec. 1 issue and it appears that a typo was responsible. Based on the overall high quality of Bendix's work I have no doubt that this entry indeed appeared at some point in the *Bloomington Progress*.

5. Stockwell v. Showers & Hendrix, 1870, collection of the Monroe County History Center.

6. Charles Showers & James M. Hendrix v. John Leonard, 1870, collection of the Monroe County History Center.

7. Elizabeth Showers, spiritual daybook.

8. B. F. Bowen, *History of Lawrence and Monroe Counties, Indiana*, p. 609.

9. Blanchard, *Counties of Morgan, Monroe, and Brown*, p. 594.

10. *Bloomington Courier*, May 18, 1876.

11. James Showers, memoirs.

12. Edwin Fulwider, *For My Grandchildren* pp. 61–64.

13. This handbill employs the same sort of promises made by Showers & Hendrix when they sold the overpriced hair mattress and the bureau made of green lumber, for the text greatly overstates the amenities available in Bloomington. The soils of Monroe County are rather poor and not "easy of cultivation," as the handbill promises; coal and iron ore are certainly not present in an inexhaustible supply; and the county is not at all well-watered with springs or streams.

14. Orzack, "Employment and Social Structure," frontispiece.

4. THE BROTHERS ENTER BUSINESS

1. *Shop Notes*, Dec. 23, 1922.

2. *Bloomington Courier*, Dec. 29, 1905.

3. *Bloomington Progress*, Oct. 9, 1870.

4. James Showers, memoirs.

5. Ibid.

6. Ibid.

7. Ibid.

8. *Shop Notes*, Dec. 23, 1922. This account is likely true because it was contained in a profile of the elderly James Showers, who presumably furnished the figures.

9. *Bloomington Courier*, Dec. 29, 1905.

10. *Bloomington Progress*, Jan. 12, 1870.

11. Some of these boys included the Showers nephews Charles and Will Sears, along with Schuyler Fender, "Coonie" Steinberg, and "Weed" Shaw (*Shop Notes*, Apr. 23, 1921). All these men would become lifetime employees of the Showers Brothers Company.

12. City record, July 7, 1876, pp. 44, 47; archives of the City of Bloomington.

13. Elizabeth Showers, spiritual daybook.

5. THE BOOMING '80S

1. If true, this would indicate that Elizabeth had enough personal income of her own to invest in, or make loans to, her sons' business. Many states in the first half of the 1800s did not allow women to retain their own property after marriage.

2. Blanchard, *Counties of Morgan, Monroe, and Brown*, p. 594, claims that Hull purchased a one-third interest in his brother's business when he turned eighteen. His mother died just before

this time; thus, Hull's purchase might be an indication that she left him money in her will.

3. *Republican Progress*, Jan. 12, 1881.

4. *Shop Notes*, July 12, 1919.

5. Brennan, "From Tree to the Trade," p. 15.

6. *Shop Notes*, Apr. 23, 1921.

7. *Bloomington Courier*, June 7, 1879.

8. *Bloomington Progress*, Apr. 12, 1882.

9. Ibid., Nov. 29, 1882.

10. Ibid., Aug. 24, 1881.

11. Ibid., Mar. 8, 1882.

12. *Shop Notes*, Mar. 9, 1918.

13. *Republican Progress*, May 3, 1882.

14. John Bendix, notes.

15. *Republican Progress*, June 4, 1884.

16. Ibid., Jan. 25, 1882.

17. Ibid., Oct. 12, 1881.

18. *Weekly Telephone*, Feb. 18, 1882.

19. Ibid., Mar. 18, 1882.

20. Ibid., Mar. 4, 1882.

21. Dillon, *Thoughts Regarding the 60th Anniversary*, p. 11.

6. DEATH AND FIRE

1. *Republican Progress*, Jan. 25, 1882.

2. Ibid., Feb. 22, 1882.

3. Ibid., Aug. 15, 1893.

4. Ibid., Aug. 30, 1882.

5. Ibid., Aug. 13, 1884.

6. *Bloomington Telephone*, Aug. 16, 1884.

7. Mrs. Martha Buskirk was a widow of means who owned several valuable properties on the courthouse square and nearby. There were a very small number of independent women like her in Bloomington in those days who owned shares in business interests or invested wisely to produce income.

8. *Daily Telephone*, Apr. 21, 1919. In later years William Showers served as a director of the First National Bank. It helps to have friends who are businessmen and bankers.

7. PROSPERITY AND LOSS

1. *Republican Progress*, Dec. 24, 1884.

2. Ibid., Jan. 21, 1885.

3. The court papers are in the collection of the Monroe County History Center.

4. *Republican Progress*, Feb. 24, 1886.

5. Ibid., July 7, 1886.

6. Ibid., Dec. 29, 1886.

7. Ibid., May 19, 1886.

8. Ibid., undated clipping, probably May 1886.

9. *Bloomington Telephone*, May 7, 1886.

10. *Republican Progress*, May 12, 1886.

11. *Saturday Courier*, June 5, 1886.

12. *Semi-Weekly Telephone*, Dec. 21, 1886.

13. By 1894 Maud had increased her share to between $50 and $100,000, according to an item in the *Republican Progress*, Oct. 10, 1894.

14. A valuable contact would have been made at this time, if not earlier, with May Wright Sewell, the educator, lecturer, and suffragist who lived in Indianapolis. Maud would later send her daughter, Beryl, to Sewell's school.

15. *Bloomington Telephone*, Nov. 11, 15, 1887. The first account says that Susan B. Anthony stayed at Maud's home while visiting Bloomington; the second says that she stayed with Mrs. E. M. Seward, while Maud hosted Mrs. Helen Gougar and Mrs. May Wright Sewell.

16. *Republican Progress*, Apr. 11, 1888.

17. *Saturday Courier*, May 12, 1888.

8. BOOM AND BUST

1. *Republican Progress*, Apr. 15, 1885.

2. Ibid., July 6, 1892.

3. *Bloomington Telephone*, July 29, 1910.

4. *Republican Progress*, Jan. 20, 1892.

5. Ibid., Apr. 5, 1893.

6. *Bloomington World*, Apr. 26, 1904.

7. *Republican Progress*, Oct. 7, 1890.

8. Stratford & Jones, *Bloomington, Indiana*, introduction.

9. Ibid.

10. *Bloomington Telephone*, June 2, 1893.

11. *Indianapolis Sun*, July 11, 1937. This quotation is apparently a lost piece of James Showers's memoirs, for it no longer exists in the manuscript.

12. James Showers, memoirs.

13. *Republican Progress*, July 18, 1894.

14. James Showers, memoirs.

9. MOVING TOWARD MODERNITY

1. *Republican Progress*, July 26, 1893.

2. *Bloomington Courier*, Feb. 28, 1896.

3. *Republican Progress*, June 1, 1897.

4. Boonhower, *Fighting for Equality*, p. 47.

5. Undated clipping, collection of Nancy Teter Smith.

6. *Bloomington Telephone,* Mar. 31, 1896.

7. *Bloomington Courier,* July 18, 1902.

8. Ibid., June 23, 1903.

9. Ibid., Apr. 24, 1903.

10. Ibid.

11. Ibid.

12. Ibid., Dec. 27, 1904.

13. John Bendix, notes.

14. Ibid.

15. *Bloomington Courier,* Dec. 29, 1905.

10. HOUSES AND A HOSPITAL

1. *Bloomington Telephone,* Sept. 25, 1903.

2. *Evening World,* Mar. 3, 1904.

3. *Bloomington Courier,* July 18, 1905.

4. Ibid., June 28, 1904.

5. At the time this book was written, W. Edward's house was a bed-and-breakfast called the Showers Inn.

6. Nocturnal burglars were common and always made news headlines. On Aug. 19, 1904, the *Evening World* recorded that burglars hit a series of homes in the course of a single night, including the Teter residence on North Washington Street, where the large family dog chased away the intruder.

7. *Bloomington Telephone,* Mar. 10, 1899.

8. This is according to Sewell's biographer Ray E. Boomhower, in *Fighting for Equality;* see pp. 84, 86.

9. Papers of the Local Council of Women, Lilly Library, Indiana University.

10. *Bloomington Courier,* July 22, 1904. This writer remembers the late 1970s in Bloomington, when the benches around the courthouse lawn were occupied for much of each day by men whose chief entertainment was attending court cases and afterwards uttering critical comments about the judges' performances.

11. *Bloomington World,* Sept. 6, 1904.

12. Ibid., Oct. 18, 1904.

13. *Bloomington Courier,* June 2, 1905.

14. Ibid., Dec. 1, 1905.

15. Ibid., Dec. 5, 1905.

16. *Evening World,* Sept. 19, 1906.

17. *Bloomington Weekly Courier,* July 10, 1906.

18. *Shop Notes,* Nov. 15, 1919. The Showers Brothers Company footed the bill for furnishings that included mattresses, cribs, cots, sheets, blankets, an obstetric bed, towels, pillows, and rugs, as well as eighteen dressers, nine chifforobes, thirty bedside tables with plate glass tops, two kitchen tables, two dozen rocking chairs, two dozen straight chairs, a rolltop office desk and office chairs, and even an oak wastebasket and a desk lamp.

19. *Bloomington Courier,* Feb. 13, 1906.

20. *Bloomington Telephone,* Aug. 29, 1899.

21. Ibid., Sept. 29, 1899.

22. *Bloomington Courier,* Nov. 29, 1903.

23. This pond was fed by gutter downspouts from part of the factory building. On and off, depending on the pond's condition, local children splashed in it during hot summers. It was undoubtedly polluted and no fish lived in it.

24. *Bloomington Weekly Courier,* July 18, 1906.

25. *Bloomington Telephone,* Jan. 15, 1907.

26. This information is contained in an instructional video on the 1907 White Steam owned, restored, and driven by entertainer and car collector Jay Leno; available at http://www.jaylenosgarage.com/at-the-garage/steam-cars/1907-white-steam-car-30-hp/; last modified Apr. 19, 2010.

27. *Bloomington Telephone,* Apr. 14, 1911.

28. Mrs. P. D. Evans of West Fifth Street became the first African American to own an automobile when she purchased J. D. Showers's old Glide automobile (*Telephone,* Aug. 20, 1917).

29. In addition to James Showers, the organizers included W. Edward Showers, Sanford Teter, Charles Sears, and his niece's husband, Noble Campbell (*Bloomington Telephone,* June 17, 1910).

30. *Bloomington Telephone,* May 16, 1911.

31. Ibid., June 2, 1911.

32. Ibid., May 9, 1911.

33. *Daily Telephone,* May 29, 1916. This car had a Weidley engine (see sidebar).

34. *Bloomington Telephone,* June 8, 1911.

11. "THE WORLD'S LARGEST FURNITURE FACTORY"

1. *Bloomington Telephone,* Apr. 16, 1907.

2. *Bloomington Weekly Courier,* July 19, 1910.

3. Brennan, *From Tree to the Trade*, p. 32.

4. The article in the *Bloomington Weekly Courier*, July 19, 1910, stated that the company's annual output amounted to a million and a half dollars' worth of product.

5. *Shop Notes*, Apr. 23, 1921.

6. *Bloomington Telephone*, Feb. 23, 1909.

7. Dillon, *Thoughts Regarding the 60th Anniversary*, p. 31.

8. *Daily Telephone*, Mar. 17, 1908.

9. William's estate lay along Maple Grove Road, and James's estate was just northeast of it on Bottom Road, adjoining in part. Even in retirement they must have enjoyed being near each other.

10. This famous resort was known for its beautiful beachside homes, luxurious hotels, and yachting. It was nearly completely destroyed by Hurricane Katrina.

11. *Bloomington Telephone*, Feb. 20, 1912.

12. Ibid., May 24, 1912.

13. Ibid., Sept. 3, 1912.

14. Ibid., Sept. 6, 1912.

15. John Bendix, notes.

16. *Bloomington Telephone*, Apr. 18, 1913.

17. Ibid., Feb. 21, 1928.

18. *Daily Telephone*, June 20, 1916.

19. Ibid., June 23, 1916.

20. Ibid., August 31, 1916.

12. THE *SHOP NOTES* YEARS

1. *Shop Notes*, Oct. 4, 1919.

2. Charles Sears was William and James's nephew who had begun at the factory as a water boy and worked his way steadily to a position of enormous importance.

3. *Shop Notes*, July 14, 1917.

4. Ibid., Apr. 7, 1917.

5. Ibid., May 17, 1919.

6. Ibid.

7. Ibid., Apr. 5, 1919.

8. Ibid., Apr. 21, 1917.

9. Ibid., June 28, 1919.

10. Ibid., Aug. 24, 1918.

11. Ibid., Oct. 6, 1917.

12. Ibid., Sept. 22, 1917.

13. Ibid., June 14, 1919.

14. Ibid., Dec. 29, 1917.

15. Ibid., August 10, 1918.

16. Mrs. Anna Hewson was chair (she was William and James's youngest sister); Nellie Showers Teter (William's daughter) was vice chair; and Mrs. Charles Sears was the treasurer. *Shop Notes*, Oct. 19, 1918.

17. Ibid., Oct. 19, 1918.

18. This was removed in the mid-1920s due to the increased need for parking, but the playground equipment was donated and moved to St. Charles School. *Shop Notes*, Jan. 13, 1923.

19. John Bendix, notes.

20. *Shop Notes*, June 26, 1920.

21. Ibid., June 14, 1919.

22. Ibid., Aug. 11, 1917.

23. Ibid., Aug. 24, 1918. The same editorial noted that only a very few of the 175 "girls" on the workforce had in fact become machine operators.

24. Ibid., Sept. 7, 1918.

13. ANOTHER BEGINNING

1. *Daily Telephone*, July 13, 1915.

2. Ibid., Apr. 21, 1919.

3. *Shop Notes*, May 3, 1919.

4. *Daily Telephone*, Apr. 21, 1919.

5. *Shop Notes*, Mar. 6, 1920.

6. Ibid., May 3, 1919.

7. *Daily Telephone*, Apr. 21, 1919.

8. *Shop Notes*, Mar. 6, 1920.

9. John Bendix, notes.

10. Hiller, *The Hoosier Cabinet in Kitchen History*, p. 4.

11. John Bendix, notes.

12. *Daily Telephone*, Mar. 28, 1919.

13. *Shop Notes*, May 3, 1919.

14. Ibid., Sept. 20, 1919.

15. Ibid., Nov. 15, 1919.

16. Ibid., Sept. 20, 1919.

17. Ibid., Apr. 5, 1919.

18. Ibid., Dec. 23, 1919.

19. Ibid., Sept. 18, 1920.

20. *The Burlington Hawkeye*, Apr. 22, 1923.

21. *Shop Notes*, July 30, 1921.

22. Ibid., Mar. 12, 1921.

23. Ibid., Sept. 24, 1921.

24. Ibid., Oct. 8, 1921.

25. Ibid.

26. Ibid., Oct. 22, 1921.

27. Ibid., Dec. 25, 1921.

28. Ibid., Jan. 13, 1923.

29. Ibid., Jan. 27, 1923.

30. Ibid., Jan. 13, 1923.

31. Ibid.

32. Ibid., Jan. 27, 1923.

33. Ibid., Apr. 7, 1923.

34. Ibid., May 19, 1923.

35. Ibid., Apr. 21, 1923.

36. Ibid., Jan. 27, 1923.

37. Ibid., May 19, 1923.

38. Ibid., Jan. 27, 1923.

14. FINAL SUCCESSES

1. *Shop Notes,* May 17, 1924.

2. Information on the American Association of United Women can be found in Nellie Showers Teter's file, collection of the Indiana University Archives.

3. *Bloomington Daily Telephone,* June 11, 1924.

4. *Shop Notes,* July 28, 1923.

5. Ibid., Nov. 4, 1922. It was a good thing that Showers men happened to be charter members of the new country club.

6. Ibid., July 28, 1923.

7. Ibid., Mar. 22, 1924.

8. *Daily Telephone,* Nov. 26, 1913.

9. Ibid., Mar. 7, 1925. See also the *Bloomington Telephone,* Mar. 17, 18, and 19, 1924.

10. *Bloomington Daily Telephone,* Feb. 14, 1928.

11. *Shop Notes,* Jan. 10, 1925.

12. Ibid., Apr. 16, 1927.

13. *Shop Notes,* March 19, 1927.

14. *Bloomington Daily Telephone,* Dec. 31, 1927.

15. Dillon, *Thoughts Regarding the 60th Anniversary,* p. 8.

16. *Furniture Manufacturer,* May, 1928.

17. Orzack, "Employment and Social Structure," p. 92.

18. *Shop Notes,* Jan. 27, 1923.

19. Ibid., May 28, 1927.

20. Ibid., Jan. 9, 1926.

21. Ibid., Mar. 6, 1926.

22. Ibid., Feb. 9, 1924, and Dec. 23, 1925.

23. *Bloomington Daily Telephone,* Dec. 31, 1927.

24. Ibid., Jan. 21, 1928.

15. EVERYTHING CHANGES

1. *Bloomington Daily Telephone,* Feb. 21, 1928.

2. Ibid., Feb. 28, 1928.

3. Ibid., Oct. 22, 1928.

4. Ibid.

5. Ibid., Feb. 13, 1929.

6. Ibid., Oct. 30, 1929.

7. Ibid., Nov. 20, 1929.

8. Ibid., Dec. 5, 1929.

9. Ibid., Dec. 28, 1929.

10. Louis Orzack noted in his research that Bloomington was harder hit than most cities during the Depression. The aftereffects were still apparent in Bloomington decades later. When this writer first came to Bloomington in 1976 it was shabby and poor, its drab downtown square ringed with cheap dollar stores and neon-lit pizza parlors. Not until Cook Group invested in the city in the 1980s and began restoring the buildings did new life begin to return to the community.

11. Orzack, "Employment and Social Structure," p. 127.

12. Ibid., p. 126.

13. Ibid., quoting in turn the Indiana Employment Service, *Labor Market Developments Report for Bloomington, Indiana Labor Market Area,* June 1943, p. 22.

14. Orzack, "Employment and Social Structure," p. 130.

15. Ibid., p. 112.

16. Ibid., p. 131.

17. Ibid., p. 137.

18. Ibid., p. 138.

19. Ibid., p. 155.

20. Ibid., p. 137.

21. *Bloomington Daily Telephone,* Mar. 22, 1940.

22. Ibid., March 15, 1940.

23. Oral history of John Oscar Pardue, Aug. 26, 1980, Monroe County History Center.

24. Oral history of Frank and Lucille Godsey, Aug. 27, 1980, Monroe County History Center.

25. Oral history of John Oscar Pardue.

26. Oral history of Frank and Lucille Godsey.

27. Orzack, "Employment and Social Structure," p. 139.

28. Oral history of John Oscar Pardue.

29. Oral history of Frank and Lucille Godsey.

30. *Bloomington Evening World,* Aug. 24, 1936.

31. *Bloomington Daily Telephone,* Apr. 7, 1939.

32. Oral history of Frank and Lucille Godsey.

33. Orzack, "Employment and Social Structure," pp. 116–17.

34. Oral history of Guy Burnett, Apr. 15, 1977, Monroe County History Center.

35. *Bloomington Daily Telephone,* March 13, 1940.

36. File C75.8, Showers Bros. Co. file, in the collection of Indiana University Archives. All these dates are carefully noted in clippings collected together in the file.

37. Oral history of Guy Burnett.

38. File C75.8, Showers Bros. Co. file, in the collection of Indiana University Archives.

39. Ibid., letter dated Jan. 11, 1955.

40. The terms of William's will set up a trust that would continue throughout the lives of all of his children. Nellie Showers Teter was still alive, although Jennie and W. Edward were dead.

41. File C75.8, Showers Bros. Co. file, in the collection of Indiana University Archives.

42. Ibid.

43. Ibid.

44. *Bloomington Herald-Telephone,* May 31– June 2, 1955.

45. Oral history of Guy Burnett.

16. LEGACY

1. Brennan, "From Tree to the Trade," pp. 34–36.

2. Dillon, in *Thoughts Regarding the 60th Anniversary,* uses the term "straight-line" twice: pp. 10, 38.

3. Brennan, "From Tree to the Trade," p. 60.

4. Oral history of Frank and Lucille Godsey. The Godseys recalled that loafers took advantage of the fifteen-minute breaks, extending them to half an hour.

5. Orzack, "Employment and Social Structure," p. 115.

6. *Shop Notes,* Mar. 24, 1917.

7. Orzack, "Employment and Social Structure," p. 96.

8. Hiller, "Harris Lebus—Arts and Crafts Style for Trade," *American Bungalow,* Summer, 2010.

9. *Shop Notes,* Dec. 23, 1925, p. 6.

10. *Bloomington Daily Telephone,* Apr. 5, 1939.

11. Ibid.

12. Oral history of Robert Cooper, July 1975, Monroe County Public Library.

13. Ibid.

Bibliography

Bendix, John. Notes. 1980s. Monroe County History Center, 202 E. 6th Street, Bloomington, Ind.

B. F. Bowen & Co. *History of Lawrence and Monroe Counties, Indiana.* Indianapolis: B. F. Bowen & Co., 1914.

Blanchard, Charles. *Counties of Morgan, Monroe, and Brown: Historical and Biographical.* Chicago: F. A. Battey & Co., 1884.

Boonhower, Ray E. *Fighting for Equality: A Life of May Wright Sewell.* Indianapolis: Indiana Historical Society Press, 2007.

Brennan, Eryn. "From Tree to the Trade." Master's thesis, University of Virginia, 2006.

Dillon, Dale. *Thoughts Regarding the 60th Anniversary of Showers Brothers Company.* Indianapolis: The Hollenbach Press, 1928.

Dunn, Jacob Piatt. *Indiana and Indianans.* Vol. 4. Chicago and New York: The American Historical Society, 1919.

Fulwider, Edwin. *For My Grandchildren.* Lakeview: The Keepsake Press, 1977. From the collection of the Monroe County History Center, 202 E. 6th Street, Bloomington, Ind.

Hiller, Nancy. "Harris Lebus—Arts and Crafts Style for Trade." *American Bungalow* 66, May 20, 2010.

———. *The Hoosier Cabinet in Kitchen History.* Bloomington: Indiana University Press, 2009.

Laderman, Gary. *The Sacred Remains: American Attitudes towards Death.* New Haven, Conn.: Yale University Press, 1996.

Leffler, Robert. Papers. 1980s. Monroe County History Center, 202 E. 6th Street, Bloomington, Ind.

Orzack, Louis. "Employment and Social Structure: A Study of Social Change in Indiana." Master's thesis, Indiana University, 1953.

Showers, Elizabeth. Spiritual daybook. Transcript of her unpublished manuscript. Monroe County History Center, 202 E. 6th Street, Bloomington, Ind.

Showers, James. Memoirs. Transcript of his unpublished manuscript. Monroe County History Center, 202 E. 6th Street, Bloomington, Ind.

Stratford & Jones, Artists. *Bloomington, Indiana.* Indianapolis: Wm. B. Burford, 1891. Collection of Indiana University Archives.

Index

CARROL KRAUSE is an avid reader, writer, traveler, and gardener; she weaves, spins, knits, and quilts. She is keenly interested in history (local and world, ancient and recent) and has served on Bloomington's Historic Preservation Commission. She has a BA in English and journalism from Indiana University, and for the last nine years has written a weekly column for the Bloomington *Herald-Times* on unique homes and the stories behind them. She has kept a daily journal since she was fourteen years old.

*The Showers Brothers Company administration building
at 601 North Morton Street has been the home of
Indiana University Press
since 1960.*

DIRECTOR: *Janet Rabinowitch*
EDITOR: *Linda Oblack*
PROJECT EDITOR: *Nancy Lightfoot*
PRODUCTION DIRECTOR: *Bernadette Zoss*
COVER AND INTERIOR DESIGNER: *Pamela Rude*
PRINTER: *Sheridan Books Inc.*

Printed and bound by CPI Group (UK) Ltd, Croydon, CR0 4YY

13/04/2025